ISRAEL, GOD'S

ISRAEL, GOD'S SERVANT

God's Key to the Redemption of the World

David W. Torrance

George Taylor

**HANDSEL
PRESS**

EDINBURGH   LONDON • COLORADO SPRINGS • HYDERABAD

Copyright © 2007

First published 2007 by Paternoster

Paternoster is an imprint of Authentic Media
9 Holdom Avenue, Bletchley, Milton Keynes, Bucks, MK1 1QR, UK
1820 Jet Stream Drive, Colorado Springs, CO 80921, USA

OM Authentic Media
Medchal Road, Jeedimetla Village, Secunderabad 500 055, A.P., India
www.authenticmedia.co.uk

Authentic Media is a division of IBS-STL U.K., limited by guarantee, with
its Registered Office at Kingstown Broadway, Carlisle, Cumbria CA3 0HA.
Registered in England & Wales No. 1216232. Registered charity 270162

British Library Cataloguing in Publication Data
A catalogue record for this book is available from the
British Library

ISBN-13: 978-1-84227-554-2
ISBN-10: 1-84227-554-2

Cover Design by J.G. Tordai / Panos Pictures
Edited and Typeset in 10pt Palatino by the Handsel Press, Edinburgh
Print Management by Adare Carwin
Printed and bound in Great Britain by J.H. Haynes & Co., Sparkford

Contents

Preface

This book brings together a number of addresses previously presented to conferences, public meetings and study groups. Originally and inevitably they contained a certain amount of duplication which has been removed as far as possible before being published together in one volume. In addition to the addresses we have added further material.

We wish to acknowledge and thank The Revd Jock Stein for his kindness and very considerable help in the removal of much duplication and in the ordering, structuring and preparation of this book. Without his guidance and generous help this book would not have been produced in its present form. We also wish to acknowledge the help of Mr Stephen Bird. Finally, we would like to thank Dr Robin Parry and the Paternoster Press for their encouragement and for kindly agreeing to publish this book.

David Torrance
George Taylor
April 2007

Introduction

'For God so loved the world that he gave his one and only Son, that whoever believes in him shall not perish but have eternal life. For God did not send his Son into the world to condemn the world, but to save the world through him'[1]

1

Jesus' words in John's Gospel make clear God's love for the world. In Christ God bound the world to himself in an everlasting bond of love. Everyone, whether Jew or Gentile, Israeli or Palestinian or those belonging to other nations are loved equally by God. In Christ all are redeemed. All of every nation are his beloved children and he is their loving Father. Not all will reap the fruits of his salvation in Christ nor enjoy his love. God has given to us all the freedom to receive or to reject him and his salvation. If we reject him, he still loves us and sorrows over us, 'not wanting anyone to perish, but everyone to come to repentance'.[2]

The prophet Isaiah[3] said, 'In all their distress he too was distressed'. Because we live in a sinful world, God's people suffer. Everyone suffers to a greater or less degree. The Jewish People have suffered incredibly through the centuries, persecuted at the hands of people, many of whom claimed to be Christian. They suffered terribly in the pogroms of Russia and Eastern Europe and in the Holocaust. They continue to suffer through the rise of anti-Semitism in many countries. Israel, since the creation of the State in 1948, has endured the hostility of all her neighbours, wars, rocket attacks, suicide bombings, all of which have left many dead. She endures considerable hostility from the member countries of the United Nations.

Palestinians also have suffered. Many innocent Palestinians have been caught up in violence which is not of their making. Others have chosen a violent way of life. Other peoples and nations are suffering, as in Iraq, Afghanistan, Sudan, East Africa, the Congo, the Philippines, China and elsewhere. No matter who people are and to which country

---

[1]   John 3:16-17.
[2]   2 Peter 3:9.
[3]   Isaiah 63:9.

they belong, our Lord suffers along with the people of the world. These words in Isaiah were spoken in the first place to the people of Israel, but they are also addressed to all people, for in Christ all are the beloved children of the Heavenly Father.

These words are spoken to those who love the Lord. They are also spoken to those who do not love him and have rejected him and his salvation. They are spoken to those who in their rejection of the Lord burn with anger against their fellow men and women. They are spoken to those who have been taught to hate the Jewish People and seek to destroy them. They are spoken to the suicide bomber. Despite their sin and violence against his people, God still loves them, although he hates their sin. He grieves over their unbelief.

When we consider the present position in the Middle East and the murderous relationships between Israel and the Palestinians, we require as Christians to keep all this continually before us. God loves the Jewish People and God loves the Palestinians, even those caught up as suicide bombers. He grieves over their sin, their rejection of himself and his salvation, he grieves over their violence towards their fellow men and women, but he loves them and wants all to repent, to receive his salvation and enjoy his love.

The Middle East is in turmoil. Violence and bloodshed abound, but God is present and actively at work in the Middle East today. The writers of this book believe that Israel continues to be God's servant and, together with the Church, is God's instrument, God's key, for the redemption of the world, although Israel and the Church have, under God, different roles to play. We believe that God has restored the Jewish People to their ancient Land of Promise, something anticipated and prophesied in scripture, in order to work out world redemption.

God's restoration of the Jewish People to the Promised Land and the creation of the State of Israel has thrown the nations into turmoil. As a result of his action the Middle East, indeed the whole world is in a state of turmoil, because what affects this tiny State of Israel in a remarkable way affects the entire world. This turmoil does not deter God from continuing his redemptive action for the world, even though the restoration of Israel has given rise to violence and conflict, which God in his love also grieves over. The trouble and violence is because Israel as a nation has not yet come to faith in Christ, although many individuals have in a wonderful way. The Palestinians as a people have not come to Christ and that is true of the majority in any nation. Hence there is turmoil, which will not cease until Israel and the nations acknowledge Christ and worship him as Lord.

Despite their continuing unbelief as a nation (and as a nation they have never fully believed or obeyed him) God continues to use the Jewish people and the tiny State of Israel, as his servant to witness to himself before the nations. Today as never before, through the restoration of the State of Israel, God is in love confronting, challenging the nations of the world – although the world does not see it nor acknowledge it. Neither the present turmoil nor the growing violence in the world will thwart God working out his redemptive purpose of love for the world.

Because it is God the Father of Israel's Messiah who restored Israel to the Promised Land, the present turmoil in the Middle East and the world will only be overcome by the world turning to Christ. What we are witnessing today is an immense spiritual struggle not just between Judaism and Islam, not just between Israel and the other Islamic States and not just between Israel and the other nations, which are hostile to Israel. We are witnessing a struggle between Christ and all the evil powers of this world.

In this light there is no political solution to the problems of the Middle East. There can only be a spiritual solution. Even so, Israel, the Palestinians and the nations live in this world. God came into this world in Christ to redeem the world. Hence, although the ultimate solution must be a spiritual one, we are called by God to practical action. We are called to wrestle with many issues. We require to understand why they have arisen, and seek as best we may a political solution, although ever keeping before us that the real solution is spiritual and can only be realised through prayer.

This book therefore begins by trying to understand the background to the present problems in the Middle East.

2

We should observe Israel, understand Israel, pray for Israel, for its safety and redemption, if we are serious about understanding God's purpose to rescue the world. Many Christians lament the inability of the political parties to find a way forward in the present crisis, yet they are unable to see beyond the political situation and consider what God may, or may not, be doing.

Professor David Flusser, of the Hebrew University in Jerusalem, in his Introduction to Elmer A. Josephson's book, *Israel God's Key*, wrote:

'The Jewish problem' is not at the periphery of Christianity, though there were always many Christians who almost never thought about the Jews, and were sure that they are good Christians. In reality, the Jewish problem is one of the central Christian problems: a wrong position toward the Jews means a distorted approach to God and his Word and a misunderstanding of the very claim of the Christian message. This I say, not because I myself am a believing Jew, but because I have learned and have taught the New Testament and early Christianity many years at the Hebrew University in Jerusalem.[4]

The present crisis in the Middle East, the conflict between local warring parties threatens to erupt into a regional war, possibly using biological, chemical and even nuclear weapons, with horrifying consequences for the whole world. Yasser Arafat was surely right when he said, 'Whatever happens in the Middle East, shakes and moves the entire world.'[5]

Despite all that is reported in the public media, many people do not have a great knowledge of the history of the Middle East and the complex background to the present crisis. This is covered in Part 1, which explains how politics and religion are woven together in the Middle East. It also explains why it is no longer credible for the West to dismiss the problems of the Middle East, or the wider problems of terrorism, as 'not a religious issue', or 'just the work of extremists'.

When Jesus said, 'salvation is from the Jews',[6] he was declaring both the importance and the uniqueness of the Jewish people as the divine instrument through whom God reveals himself to the world and redeems the world. In spite of this, or perhaps because of it, the Jews have continued to attract opposition, and Part 2 examines anti-Semitism.

The calling of the Jewish people to fulfil his purpose of love and salvation for humankind and for all creation, did not come to an end, as many in the Church would have us believe, with the coming of Christ and the creation of the Christian Church. Having made with Abraham an everlasting covenant whereby he would bless him and his descendants and make them a blessing to all the world, God did not cancel that covenant. He did not bring to an end his calling of Israel to universal mission. This is explained in Part 3 of the book.

---

[4]   Elmer A. Josephson, *Israel God's Key*. Bible Light Publications, Kansas, USA, page 5.
[5]   Conversation with the reporter Hala Jahen, quoted in the Sunday Telegraph, 10 February, 2002.
[6]   John 4:22.

Israel as a whole, in her continued failure to recognise Jesus as Messiah, does not recognise God's call to her nor yet understand her own mission to the world. Yet, she is still God's servant for the redemption of the world. She still witnesses to God because God is acting in her and through her, and through her God is challenging the nations. In her unbelief, however, Israel cannot witness to the Gospel in the positive way that God wishes.

Sadly, the Christian Church, for the most part, only partially understands Israel's calling and mission. There is a veil over the minds and hearts of most of the Jewish People so that they still neither see nor hear the things of Christ. There is also a veil over the minds and hearts of many within the Christian Church so that they fail to understand what Scripture says about God's on-going purpose for his covenant People. They fail to recognise what God is doing through them, in challenging the nations to faith in God.

Jesus rebuked the Pharisees and Sadducees for being unable to 'interpret the signs of the times'.[7] They could not see what God was doing in their midst. Surely, that rebuke can be addressed to his Church today. So why is there such blindness?

1 It is because, what God does and says is hidden and can only be truly discerned through faith and obedience to God's Word. Isaiah said, 'Truly you are a God who hides himself'.[8] We must seek God and search for him with all our heart and soul if we would find him and know that we are found by him. That is why, for example, Jesus spoke in parables. But he has assured us that if we do so seek, we will find.[9]

2 It is because in so far as God hides himself so also his servant Israel is hidden to all except those who have eyes to see and ears to hear. In Isaiah 49 there is a veiled reference to Israel as God's hidden servant. We also see a reference to it in the parable of the Sheep and the Goats in Matthew.[10] Those who were made to stand on the King's right, were astonished and asked, 'Lord, when did we see you hungry and feed you, or thirsty and give you something to drink? When did we see you a stranger and invite you in, or needing clothes and clothe you? When did we see you sick or in prison and go to visit you?' Likewise, those who were made to stand on the King's left were astonished that

---

[7] Matthew 16:1-3.
[8] Isaiah 45:15.
[9] Luke 11:10.
[10] Matthew 25:31-46.

they had seen the Lord in need and done nothing of these things. Jesus said, 'The King will reply, I tell you the truth whatever you did (or did not) for one of the least of these brothers of mine, you did (or did not do) for me'. Jesus is saying that he, in a mysterious way, is related to the hungry, the thirsty, the stranger, the naked, the sick and the prisoner anywhere in the world. Yet, in the first instance, these words apply to Israel, because God has drawn them into a marriage covenant with himself. We are being judged by our attitude to Israel, because our attitude to the Jews reflects our attitude to God.

3 Sadly, it is because in her sin the Church is proud. In her pride she has frequently, from early times, claimed that the Church has replaced Israel as the chosen people of God. Professor David Flusser of Jerusalem stresses this point in his Introduction to *Israel God's Key*, quoted earlier. The church has all too often claimed that God has finished with Israel because of her rejection of Christ. As pointed out in the chapters, 'The Mystery of Israel' and 'Is the Church the New Israel?', this is a failure to understand the grace of God and the nature of Christ's atonement.

4 It is because the Church and its members have frequently been anti-Semitic. The sad record of the Church is discussed in Part 2.

5 It is because many in the Churches yield to the secular pressures of the world, and seek to interpret events in the Middle East today in a purely secular way. They regard the present conflict between Jews and Arabs as solely political and tend to be deeply prejudiced in their judgements. They feel that God is not in the situation, apart from his demands for justice and peace. They fail to recognise that at heart the conflict is spiritual. They cannot relate Scripture to the events that are happening today. Frequently their opinions are motivated by concealed anti-Semitic sentiments, although they do not see that and would wish to deny it.

When the mainstream churches of the West mention, or seek to support, the churches in the Middle East, why do they only communicate with the Arab churches? Why almost invariably do they never mention or seek to communicate with the growing number of Messianic congregations in Israel? Most in the mainstream churches have no knowledge of, and no concern for, the Messianic congregations who today, although fewer in number than the Arab churches, are very much in need of support and encouragement. Missionary churches, which have worked in China or India or Africa, have always rejoiced when the indigenous peoples have come to faith in Christ. Why do the mainstream churches not rejoice more over the coming to faith in Christ of so many Jews? Why do the mainstream churches of the West, almost without exception do little or nothing to take the Gospel to the Jews in Israel or throughout the world? God commanded the Church to take the Gospel 'To the Jew First', as discussed in the last chapter.

The answer in part is because Messianic believers are too biblical for the mainstream churches of the West! Messianic believers cannot understand or cope with Gentile liberal theology. Their interpretation of Scripture and their theology would contradict the traditionally held views of many in the Gentile churches. Messianic Believers come from all strands of Judaism. Of those who come to faith in Jesus as Messiah, the majority come through the influence of a believing friend or through their own reading of Scripture. Some, remarkably, because they have received a vision of Jesus as Son of God and Saviour.

Some have previously been Orthodox, Reformed, agnostic or atheist. Interestingly, when they come to faith in Jesus as their Messiah they almost all accept and believe the Bible. They believe the promises of the Bible – and yet they should not be confused with, or identified with, Protestant fundamentalists. This is a mistake which many make. Members of the mainstream churches need to listen to Messianic Believers and learn from them. If they do so and learn to accept what God is doing through the Jews today, many in the Church will require to revise their interpretation of the Bible and rethink their theology.

The presence and growth of Messianic congregations in Israel is recorded in Appendix 6. These congregations are very young – 45 years ago there were none. Together with ethnic Christian congregations and house groups, there are now over 100. The Messianic congregations are mostly linked together as a loose association of independent congregations. In various parts of the world, the mainstream churches have not only communicated with but also formed unions with Congregational Churches. Their failure to seek to do so with Messianic Congregations must be attributed to an underlying and unrecognised tendency toward anti-Semitism, which is also seen in how the Churches approach the question of 'the land'.

Israel has said that Scotland is the only country in Europe which has not persecuted the Jews.[11] The command to take the Gospel 'to

---

[11] When T.F. Torrance was Moderator of the Church of Scotland General Assembly, the President of Israel invited him to visit Israel in 1978 and welcomed him as the representative of the only country in Europe that had not persecuted the Jews.

the Jew first' and then to the Gentile was cherished for many years by the Church of Scotland and from 1840 to 1960 the Church had two overseas missions, namely, 'Mission to the Jews' and 'Foreign Missions', which covered wherever the Church was working throughout the rest of the world. Today, the Church of Scotland along with most other mainstream churches has lost the vision of taking the Gospel 'to the Jew first'. Largely in consequence, and to no small degree, the whole work of overseas mission has shrunk considerably. The churches have found the work harder and it has become more difficult to catch the imagination and enthusiasm of the wider membership of the churches.

It belongs to God's strategy for world mission that the Gospel should be taken to the Jew first and then to the Gentile. This is not because Jews are more important or more loved by God than Gentiles. It is not because in itself mission to the Jews is more important than mission to the Gentiles. It is because, when the Jews come to faith in Christ, as Paul anticipated that they will do, in large numbers, mission to the whole of humankind will develop and prosper in a new and marvellous way.

This book is written in the hope that it might help people to understand 'the Jewish problem', to appreciate something of what God is seeking to do in his world today, and to help Christians engage more effectively in prayer for and mission to the world.

PART ONE

Chapter One

UNDERSTANDING THE MIDDLE EAST CONFLICT

The Historical Context

The land, which we call Israel, together with what we might call Palestine, has never been an independent country since the days of the Romans. The country was ruled by foreign powers. For the last four hundred years, until 1917, and together with present-day Syria, Lebanon and Jordan, it was a province of the Ottoman Empire ruled from Damascus.

In regard to population, until more recent times, the population was comparatively small. According to the Oxford historian, Martin Gilbert,[1] in 1880 there were approximately 470,000 Arabs and 24,000 Jews. This rose by 1914 to approximately 500,000 Arabs and 90,000 Jews. Since the mid 1800s Jews had been the overall majority in Jerusalem.

After the 1914-18 World War Britain took over control of the whole territory, including what we now call Jordan. What today we call Israel/Palestine was then Western Palestine. Britain renamed the larger part (Eastern Palestine) Transjordan, which was later renamed Jordan.

In 1917, when the Ottoman Empire collapsed many thousands of Turks left Palestine, vacating their homes and shops. Arabs took over their property.

In the first half of the 20th century, Jews fleeing persecution in Europe began to emigrate to Western Palestine; the immigrants did not attack or confiscate Arab villages – at this stage there was plenty of room for all. What the Jews did do was to buy desert and malarial marshland from absentee landlords living in Syria and Lebanon (and there is great complaint in Jewish writings of the period about the inflated prices paid).[2] Against all odds they transformed the land and cultivated it.

---

[1] Quoted in the Sunday Telegraph, February 10, 2002.
[2] Martin Gilbert, *A History of Israel*, pages 28, 46.

The British High Commissioner's report in 1925 includes a description of the Jezreel Valley:

> When I first saw it in 1920 it was a desolation. Four or five small squalid Arab villages, long distances apart from one another could be seen on the summit of low hills here and there. For the rest, the country was uninhabited. There was not a house, not a tree . . . a great part of the soil was in the ownership of absentee Syrian landlords . . . the country was infected with malaria . . .

According to an Anglo-American Committee of Enquiry,[3] there were 674 registered Muslim and Christian immigrants between 1920 and 1922. Between 1923 and 1945 there were 1,238 Muslim and 714 Christian registered immigrants. Between 1920 and 1945 there were 367,845 Jewish registered immigrants. Undoubtedly there were also Arab immigrants who were not registered, and of these there is no accurate assessment. Martin Gilbert suggests there were 50,000 Arab immigrants between 1919 and 1939.[4] The figures from different sources do not tally.

The population lived in a few towns and in scattered villages. Large areas were either thinly populated or uncultivated and barren. As Jewish numbers increased and Jews began to develop and cultivate the land, Arab immigration also increased.[5] Arab population increase has also far outstripped Jewish increase. (Factors like these perhaps lie behind Israeli cynicism about Arab claims 'to have always occupied the land', but to be fair, many land holdings never had documentation, and again, many documents did not survive later conflict.)

However, very understandably the local Arab population became fearful of the new immigrants, especially as they had an ideal of forming their own state in the land. This fear led to Arab attacks on

---

3   Anglo-American Committee of Inquiry, *A Survey of Palestine* Vol. 1 (page 185). Quoted by Joan Peters in *From Time Immemorial*, Michael Joseph, London 1985 (page 431). With its 150 pages of appendices, this is one of the most authoritative books on the subject.

4   Martin Gilbert, *The Arab-Israel Conflict* p18.

5   Malcolm MacDonald, no friend of the Zionists, said in 1939, when the Arab population of Western Palestine was over a million, 'The Arabs cannot say that the Jews are driving them out of their country. If not a single Jew had come to Palestine after 1918, I believe that the Arab population of [Western] Palestine today would still have been about the 600,000 figure at which it had been stable under the Turkish rule.' Quoted in Joan Peters, *From Time Immemorial: The Origins of the Arab-Jewish Conflict over Palestine*, Michael Joseph, London, p.242. However this figure is much greater than Martin Gilbert's figure of 470,000 for 1880.

Jewish communities and many Jews were killed. The Jews formed a defence organisation called the Haganah; at first it was purely defensive, but as the conflict grew it became more aggressive and some Arab villages were attacked. This conflict started in the 1920s, and grew into full-scale civil war.

One of the worst atrocities against Jewish communities was the massacre of the whole Jewish community in Hebron. The worst atrocity against an Arab village took place much later in Deir Yassin near Jerusalem.[6]

During the 1939-45 War, the British brought in large numbers of Arabs, approximately 40,000 from Egypt alone, in order to help the war effort. Many, or most, of these were settled in the Gaza strip. After the War, British soldiers who were policing Palestine witnessed the Jewish immigration and tried to stop it – preventing boats landing, and sending others back. Many of these soldiers who are still alive today sympathise with the Arab population because they felt that Palestine was being taken over by the Jewish immigrants. What many did not realise was that during the early decades of the 20th century there was also an influx of Arabs who sought advantage from the new prosperity brought by Jewish immigration; these new Arabs would be counted as 'Palestinians' if they lost their homes in the coming conflicts.

After much agonising among the nations of the world, the United Nations in 1947 decided that Western Palestine (now just called Palestine) should be partitioned into a Jewish sector and an Arab sector. The Arab nations rejected this because it would mean 'recognising the existence of a Jewish State on Arab soil'. Taking into account the number of Jews, the Jews were certainly given too much land – about 30 per cent of the population were offered 54 per cent of the land of Palestine.

However, there are points nearly always overlooked by modern commentators. On 2 November, 1917, the British Government published a 'statement of policy' known as the Balfour Declaration. In this, the Government 'viewed with favour the establishment in Palestine of a National Home for the Jewish People'. Palestine, at that time included present-day Israel, the West Bank and Jordan.

---

6   The massacre of Deir Yasin was carried out by a rebel Jewish Brigade called the Stern gang, which broke away from another militant group (the Irgun). The main Jewish Defence Force – the Haganah – was not part of this atrocity, which acording to Martin Gilbert was in fact carried out by the Irgun and the Stern Gang together.

Subsequently, in her endeavour to placate the Arab nations, Britain largely went back on her promised support.[7] After being given the Mandate, following the end of the 1914-18 war, Britain limited the numbers of Jews entering Palestine while not limiting the number of Arabs. This had far reaching effects and greatly contributed to later problems.[8]

Her restrictions on the immigration of Jews to Palestine before and during the last war was responsible for thousands of Jewish lives being lost in the Holocaust. This is a dark chapter in British history, calling for repentance. It distressed and antagonised many Jews.[9]

Further, the Jews were only given about 15 per cent of the original British Palestine, and only a fraction of 1 per cent of the whole Middle East! This is a highly relevant comparison for two reasons:

1 After the European colonial powers left the Middle East the Arabs themselves ended up with 22 nations, some large and very rich in oil.

2 Jews in the Middle East were not confined to Palestine – there were large numbers in Iraq, Syria, Egypt, Libya, Algeria, Morocco. Although historically Jews had fared better in these countries than in Europe they were still officially classed a *dhimmi* people (second class citizens). This second class status was enforced with varying degrees of laxity or severity at different times in Islamic history. But by the middle of the 20th century these Jews were suffering terrible persecution with thousands killed or made homeless. They were forced to leave their Middle East homeland, and Israel provided a haven of security for them as well as those fleeing European persecution.

---

[7]   Joan Peters, *op. cit.* pages 335-357.

[8]   Winston Churchill said in 1939, 'So far from being persecuted, the Arabs have crowded into the country and multiplied till their population has increased more than even all world Jewry could lift up the Jewish population' (quoted from Joan Peters, *op. cit.* page 230).

[9]   'In its determination to prevent Jewish refugees from succeeding in their escape to the Jewish Nation Home and "offending the Arabs", the British Foreign Office cabled an order to its ambassador in Berlin in March of 1939, the British envoy was to inform the German Government about the means of escape being utilized by Jews, and to ask the German "Authorities" to "discourage such travel"...', *ibid.* page 347. For the text of the cable sent by the Foreign Office to Sir Neville Henderson, Treasury Papers, 188/226 see *ibid.* page 549 and Martin Gilbert, *Exile*, page 223. See also DVD 'The Forsaken Promise' produced by Hugh Kilson. Hatikvah Film Trust. Website: www.hatikvah.co.uk

After the UN partition of Palestine the Arab nations refused to accept partition, and vowed to destroy the Jewish part. Jordan invaded the Arab part of Palestine and occupied it, calling it its 'West Bank' (hence the name today). Jordan did not call for it to be a Palestinian state, for at that time much of the Arab world did not recognise the Arab people of the area as a distinct Palestinian people! Jordan said they were Jordanian, and Syria claimed that Palestine was simply the southern part of Syria (as it had been during the Ottoman period).

When the British finally withdrew from Palestine in 1948, they expected the Arab armies to wipe the Jewish State off the map. Within hours, the Jewish sector (just having called itself Israel) was bombed by Egyptian warplanes and invaded by several Arab armies. Language used at the time was not just about 'destruction of the Jewish state' but 'a war of extermination of the Jewish people'.

This was the context of the conflict in which Palestinian Arabs lost their homes in the late 1940s. Who started the war, and for what purpose? That is the question, which still drives Israel's fear of the Arab nations today. After the war, Israel found itself a little larger than the land given it by the UN plan – but still only nine miles wide at its middle-populated area. The land is about the size of Wales.

After the 1948 War, there was an exchange of refugees. Taking the whole Middle East context, more Jews than Arabs had lost their homes. All the Jews were given a place to make a new life in Israel, while the Arab nations refused to give new homes to the incoming Arab refugees from Palestine.[10] They were kept in camps so that they would be a propaganda weapon against Israel – a policy explicitly stated by leaders such as Nasser (President of Egypt). It is a policy, which has caused enormous suffering to Palestinians who are taught that Israel is the cause of their homelessness. The hatred for Israel grows – as it was meant to.

The question of refugees is an important part of any concern for a just settlement in the Middle East, and a more detailed treatment is given in Appendix 1.

Israel remained insecure for the next 19 years. Its civilian farmers were being killed in raids from Egypt, Jordan and Syria. The Golan Heights were a good staging post for rocket attacks against the Jewish farms below in the Galilee. In 1956 Israel invaded the Sinai to destroy bases used to attack it; they then withdrew, and the UN put a buffer

---

[10] Syria still bars Palestinians from owning agricultural land. In Egypt Palestinians find it hard to get work permits. Kuwait expelled 350,000 Palestinians in 1991. Libya got rid of 20,000 in 1995.

force between Israel and Egypt. During the 1956 war, Israel discovered that Egyptian soldiers had each been issued with Hitler's *Mein Kamph*. Israel technically fired the first shot in the 1967 War. Just beforehand, Nasser had expelled the UN buffer force and stated, 'Our basic objective will be the destruction of Israel'. President Aref of Iraq said, 'Our goal is clear: to wipe Israel off the map'. The chairman of the PLO said, 'The Jews of Palestine will have to leave... any of the old Jewish Palestine population may stay, but it is my impression that none of them will survive.' Much of the world's Press expected the Arabs to win and destroy Israel.

To their surprise, heavily outnumbered Israel won the war and occupied what is now the West Bank, the Gaza Strip, the Golan Heights and Sinai. After this 1967 'Six-day War' the UN passed resolution 242 calling on Israel to return the occupied territories and calling the Arab nations to live in peace with Israel.

In the 1970s in Israel's peace treaty with Egypt, about 90 per cent of the territories were returned, and it is clear from reports of the time that Israel expected to be able to negotiate the return of all the rest in exchange for firm peace. Back in 1968, Israel offered to give back everything except East Jerusalem on condition of peace. The reply from the Arab summit was not, 'Good, but we want East Jerusalem and more as well'. It was, 'No peace with Israel, no negotiations with Israel, no recognition of Israel.'

Israel continued to ask for face to face negotiations with the Arab nations. The Arab nations called for an 'international conference' so that they would not have to deal face to face with a nation whose right to exist they disputed.

Settlements inside the West Bank were started soon after the 1967 war under the Labour administration as a security measure. However, the voices in Israel calling for an extension of the country to the river Jordan became stronger, and the Labour Party eventually lost its power to the more right wing Likud. It was then that Israel began aggressively to put settlements on the occupied territories. For this there was a twofold reason – security, and biblical ideology. And it is this double concern that now makes resolution of the Middle East conflict so complex.

In 1973, on *Yom Kippur*, the Day of Atonement, Syria and Egypt attacked Israel again, taking Israel by surprise. At first the war went their way, but finally Israel won. A few years later, Anwar Sadat of Egypt decided to make peace, and Israel gave back the Sinai. However this is still a 'cold peace' for several reasons:

1 President Sadat was assassinated by opponents of any peace with Israel.

2 No public Egyptian map shows Israel's existence.

3 Old style Nazi propaganda still flourishes in the Egyptian media.

Later Jordan made peace with Israel. This was a warmer peace, which still continues, for, although there has been a change of regime, there has been no dramatic change of policy.

Just as the Syrians had used the Golan Heights to rocket Jewish farms in the Galilee, so the PLO, which had fled from Jordan to Lebanon, used the Lebanon Heights to rocket Israeli farms below. In 1982 Israel invaded Lebanon in an attempt to root out the PLO. This was a controversial move opposed by many Israelis. It was during this period that Sharon did not stop one of the Lebanese militias massacring large numbers of Palestinian refugees in one of the camps. (The PLO had themselves massacred many ordinary Lebanese Christian villagers, when they entered Lebanon in the late 1970s. This was the real start of the Lebanese civil war. Israel's invasion came later.) It was however an appalling revenge attack, and Sharon was widely blamed for not preventing it.

Withdrawal from Lebanon and the Oslo Peace Accord

Israel finally withdrew from Lebanon, and agreed to negotiate with Yasser Arafat. The Oslo Peace Accord, which was signed in 1993, was viewed by many as the way to a final settlement. It finally broke down when Arafat refused Ehud Barak's offer of 98 per cent of the disputed territories including East Jerusalem as the headquarters of a Palestinian State. Each side blamed the other, but behind the failure certainly lies the following:

1 The PA broke several of the clauses agreed, principally by smuggling in arms and building up an armed police force.

2 Israel did not trust Arafat, who had a history of duplicity and is well known to say different things in the Western and the Arab media. On the other hand, the 98 per cent offer was made verbally without showing any maps, and the Palestinian negotiators were afraid that the actual division of land would leave the new Palestinian State intersected by Jewish security zones.

3 Israel grew increasingly afraid for its security and the possibility of creating an armed and possibly hostile Palestinian State on its border.

4 After the start of the Oslo peace negotiations, many more Israelis were killed than during any other time of peace since 1948. The Palestinians failed to recognise that they had to convince the Israeli public, not just the politicians, of their desire for peace.

5 The PLO/PA, together with Hamas was and is still driven at least in part by the 'Palestinian Covenant', by the 'Hamas Covenant' and the view of fundamentalist Islam that Israel should not exist.

The question of the *intifada*, the PLO, Hamas and the involvement of terrorist organisations is complex as well as frightening, and is further described in Appendix 2. While the current wave of suicide bombers cynically uses the promise of paradise for its young recruits, it remains a sad commentary on the Middle East that many Palestinians feel there is no alternative.

In her concern for her national security, Israel has not acted, and does not act, in a way that is different from other states in the West. Every state would act to defend itself. Often she acts in a more restrained and principled way than other states, although the nations of the West seem to demand of her a higher ethical standard than they apply to themselves. Probably no state would accept the amount of provocation that Israel has experienced over the years, and during the present *intifada*, without going to war. Arik Sharon, now in a coma, described the situation presented by the *intifada* as a war against terrorism. It led to the wars against Hamas in Gaza and against the Hezbullah in Lebanon in the summer of 2006. Throughout these conflicts, because the Palestinian terrorist, or guerrilla forces often used hospitals and churches for cover, the Israeli army sometimes killed innocent civilians and destroyed essential infrastructure,[11] but, unlike her enemies, always unwillingly.

After much heart searching and under Sharon's leadership, Israel withdrew from Gaza in the summer of 2005 and dismantled the long established Jewish settlements there. In January 2006 a general election was held in Gaza for the first time. The result was a massive 77 per cent vote for Hamas. Mahmoud Abbas, leader of the Fatah movement is the Palestinian president. Although, according to Israel, he is a former terrorist, he has called on Palestinians to recognise Israel and

---

[11]   For example, on Jan. 24th 2003, an Israeli missile hit St Philip's Episcopal Church in the middle of the Ahli Arab Hospital compound in Gaza, and damaged the hospital. These buildings are not near government or military facilities. Apache helicopters not only fired the missile but returned to film the destruction which was shown on early morning Israeli television.

has called for negotiations with Israel to work for peace. Hamas refuses to recognise Israel or to negotiate. As a result of Hamas' position, her strong public support by Palestinians, and because of her strong terrorists links, Europe and the USA have cut off aid (although Europe not entirely) to the Palestinians in Gaza which has led to yet greater poverty and suffering. It has been impossible so far for the Palestinians to form and maintain a government of national unity. There has been frequent fighting between those loyal to the president Mahmoud Abbas and those loyal to Hamas, with many Palestinian deaths. In February 2007, talks between the leaders took place in the Saudi holy city of Mecca, and these seemed to herald a government of national unity, but at the time of writing the situation is closer to civil war, or perhaps a *de facto* separation of government with Fatah in control of the West Bank and Hamas in control of Gaza.

Since granting Palestinians control over Gaza, well over a thousand rockets have been fired from Gaza into civilian areas in Israel. On 25 June 2006 a faction within Hamas kidnapped an Israeli soldier. This led to a fresh invasion of Gaza by the IDF, with once again, considerable bloodshed in the loss of both Jewish and Palestinian lives. The IDF withdrew without recovering the kidnapped Israeli soldier.

Officially, a cease-fire was declared in late November. It held, but very shakily, because of Israel's restraint. According to the journal *Israel Today*,[12] in the few months since the 'cease-fire' (at the time of writing) more than 100 rockets had been fired into Israeli settlements, striking homes, schools and other Israeli communities.

Iran, which is Shiite, has over the years supplied arms to the PLO and Hamas, which is Sunni. On 3 January 2002, Israel arrested and took into custody a Palestinian ship, the Karine-A, carrying fifty tons of military weapons from Iran for shipment through Egypt to Gaza. Since the Palestinians were given control of Gaza, tons of military equipment from Iran have flowed in, through tunnels under the Egyptian-Gaza border. According to senior Israeli military officials 'hundreds of Hamas activists have recently been flown to Iran to receive military and terrorist training from Iranian Revolutionary Guards'.[13]

Brigadier General Sarni Turjeman, a senior Israeli security official, told the Knesset Foreign Affairs and Defence Committee on December 25, 2006 that IDF forces will soon have to grapple with improved fighting capabilities on the Palestinian side. 'In another few months

---

[12] *Israel Today* (printed in Israel), February 2007, page 2.
[13] *CFI Israel News Report* by David Dolan, January 2007.

in the Gaza Strip, we will have to deal with military capabilities of the terror organisations that we have not been familiar with until now, especially in the area of anti-tank missiles'. He added that Hamas' capabilities in particular are reaching a semi-military level.'[14] All this increases Israel's insecurity.

The present *intifada* commenced in September 2000. Stone throwing and suicide bombs have continued. To-date, several hundred Jewish civilians and Jewish servicemen (although fewer servicemen than civilians) have been killed, and thousands injured. Naturally, many Palestinians have been killed and injured. It is hard to be certain of exact figures. While stories of Palestinian children being hurt are commonly seen in the media, in fact more Israeli children have been injured and killed than Palestinian.

For Israel, it is all too apparent that the withdrawal from Gaza and the surrender of land has hitherto not lead to peace. Rockets fired into civilian centres, suicide bombs and stone throwing, have all continued. There was an increase in terrorist attacks and loss of life when Israel withdrew from areas in the West Bank, like Jericho and Bethlehem, as also when Israel withdrew from Southern Lebanon. Each of these withdrawals has given rise to a greater loss of Israeli lives and to an even greater loss of Palestinian lives. Most Israelis feel today, that to surrender the Golan Heights and the West Bank in order to create an independent Palestinian State, will make the whole country unsafe. It would open the possibility of every home and establishment being attacked. It is this desperate desire for security which, so often, makes Israel impervious to the pressures imposed upon her by Western States to negotiate further land for peace and makes her hesitate to create an independent Palestinian State, regardless of Palestinian impoverishment and suffering. Would our nation, or any nation in the world, given the same situation, act differently?

During the Gulf War, Israeli officials announced the discovery of a major bomb-making factory in the Arab-Israeli town of Jaljuya. They said three arrested Arab suspects confessed to making bombs for the radical Islamic Jihad movement, which announced that it was now sending suicide 'martyrs' to fight for Saddam. It was the first time that a factory connected to the Damascus-based radical group had been discovered inside Israel's pre-1967 borders.[15]

---

[14]   *Ibid.*
[15]   MessiNews, 1 April 2003.

Work on the wall between Israel and the West Bank started after the beginning of the present *intifada* and has continued. For the Palestinians the building of this wall has been cruelly unjust. It has cut through Palestinian settlements, destroyed Palestinian homes, cut off innocent Palestinian farmers from their orchards and farmlands, in some cases destroyed them, thereby taking away their income and reducing them to poverty and it has taken in more Palestinian territory. The erection of the wall has been condemned by the international community[16] and increased anger and hostility on the part of Palestinians and other Islamic states. Once again, in condemning Israel, the nations need to ask themselves, if they were in Israel's position, would they act differently? Israel argues that the wall has cut down the number of suicide attacks and reduced Israeli casualties by approximately ninety per cent and has said, if there is peace and security, it will remove the wall. Unfortunately the nations which are most vociferous in condemning Israel's action do little or nothing to secure peace and security for both Israel and the Palestinians.

When we consider that Israel is such a small country, about the size of Wales and that the Islamic states of the Middle East and North Africa together occupy land about 600 times larger and that one fifth of the world population is Muslim, that is over one billion, we can begin to understand Israel's preoccupation with national insecurity and why so often she acts as she does. The hostility of the Palestinians and the Islamic world and the declared intention of many Islamic leaders, to wipe out the state of Israel entirely, because they feel it is their religious duty and that they owe it to Allah to do so, requires to be taken seriously, by Israel and by the other nations. It threatens the peace of the world. As Israel has frequently said, 'How can you negotiate with (or consider the welfare of) those who do not want you to exist? Recently, one Israel politician said publicly, 'What would

---

[16] Israel is often accused of using the wall as an attempt to 'grab more Palestinian land' and 'to pre-empt final status negotiations'. In this connection it is worth noting that pro-settler Jewish opponents claim that the barrier is an attempt to create 'facts on the ground' that 'justify the mass dismantlement of settlements and displacement of over 100,000 Jews'. It is also worth noting that, as *Israel Today* (printed in Israel), February 2007 (page 11) points out, 'more than 1,200 acres of Jewish land around Jerusalem were cut off and now lie on the other side of the fence. Most of this land was bought (by Jews) before the establishment of the State of Israel . . . *In this case,* Demographic concerns determined the route of the barrier. Since the land is heavily populated by Arabs, the government decided to cede the legal rights of Jewish ownership'.

we talk about with them? Is it our own funeral arrangements?' Hamas, Hezbullah, Islamic Jihad, if not also the PLO, appear to want war, in the hope that the other Islamic countries will help them to destroy Israel.

In 2001, Syria,[17] Iraq and Iran signed an agreement, to co-operate in any military engagement. In 2002, both Kuwait and Saudi Arabia seemed to be making overtures of co-operation with Iran, although that more recently has changed with the arising conflict between Shia and Sunni Muslims and the increased power and influence of Shias.

Under Saddam, both Iraq and Iran seemed to be vying with each other as to which country would take the lead in attacking Israel. Iraq under Saddam claimed that it had a volunteer army of 2 (or even up to 7) million volunteers ready to fight Israel and on several occasions moved up army divisions to the Syrian and Jordanian borders seemingly in preparation for an attack on Israel. In December 1990, according to General Georges Sada, Air Vice-Marshall in the Iraqi Air Force, Saddam Hussein issued an order for 98 planes 'to proceed with a massive chemical-weapons assault on Israel', using 'three types of chemical weapons: the nerve gas Tabun, as well as Sarin 1 and Sarin 2'.[18] Before that command could be carried out, the Gulf War broke out, early in 1991, making that mission impossible.

The Saudis presented a peace plan in 2002 proposing that Arab nations should normalise relations with Israel in return for a return to pre-1967 borders. Israel's fear of a change of regime in Arab countries, and more recent events, involving Iran, Syria, Hezbullah and Hamas, and because of her settlements on the West Bank, have made that unlikely. It was then overtaken by the Iraq conflict.and then by both the war with Hamas in Gaza and the war with the Hezbullah in the Lebanon.

---

17   See article entitled *Rise and possible Fall of the Iranian Empire* by Paul Salem, Director of the Carnegie Middle East Centre in Beirut (Scotsman, 19 Feb 2007). Iran is Shiite and Syria is predominantly Sunni, but a minority Alawi regime dominates. 'The loss of Damascus' to Iran, because of a change to Sunni rule, would dramatically alter the situation in the Middle East; it would 'cost Iran its influence in Syria, Lebanon and Palestine in one fell swoop'.

18   Iraqi General Georges Sada, *Saddam's Secrets*, Integrity Publishers. Pages 1f. and 135f. General Sada was dismissed and imprisoned in 1992 for refusing to shoot coalition prisoners of war. Now retired, he is director of the Iraqi Institute for Peace and serves as spokesman for the elected Prime Minister of Iraq. He is an Assyrian Christian and president of a small group of evangelical churches.

Shortly after, or even before, the war with Iraq, Iran, with the help of Syria, supplied Hezbullah with a massive quantity of weapons including thousands of Fajjar-5 rockets, which were used in Israel's war with the Hezbullah in the summer of 2006. After firing hundreds of rockets into Israel, Hezbullah in July 2007, killed three Israeli soldiers and kidnapped two others, thereby provoking another war with Israel, lasting 34 days. Israel began by bombing all roads between Lebanon and Syria, in order to cut off supplies coming to the Hezbullah from Iran through Syria, and in order to try and prevent Hezbullah smuggling the kidnapped soldiers out of the country.

Israel bombed Beirut international airport, knocked out a good part of Lebanon's infrastructure and blockaded Lebanon by sea. The IDF then invaded south Lebanon. The war lasted 34 days. Both sides claimed victory. 119 IDF soldiers were killed, over 400 were maimed, 44 civilians were killed and over 1,3509 injured. Apart from the many Hezbullah fighters who were killed, over 1000 Lebanese civilians were killed and many more injured. The kidnapped Israeli soldiers have not been released at the time of writing.

For Israel, this was the most disruptive war since 1947/48 and the foundation of the State. Over one sixth of the population was evacuated from their homes in northern Israel. This accounts for the fact that not more were killed and injured, considering that the Hezbullah fired 3,900 rockets hitting almost every town and large settlement in the Galilee area.

The indecisive nature of the outcome of the war, with both sides claiming victory, left Israel confused and to an extent demoralised.[19] The more that Islamic militia sense victory, as they did on this occasion, the more they are encouraged to believe that Israel is not invincible and the more belligerent they become, with the threat of further war.

Since the cease-fire, and despite the agreement with the United Nations that the Hezbullah would be disarmed and that henceforth the only armed force in Lebanon would be that of the Lebanese army, Iran, with the help of Syria, has continued to supply the Hezbullah. As a result the Hezbullah, according to Israeli military intelligence, has regained almost all that it lost in the war with Israel and become a state within the state of Lebanon. It appears that the Hezbullah would like to control the whole of Lebanon. Whether it attempts to do so remains to be seen. With the help

[19]　Lance Lambert, *Middle East Update*, October 2006.

and training of the Iranian Revolutionary Guard, Hezbullah today is probably the most powerful and best equipped Arab army in the whole of the Middle East.

All this is a major threat to Israel.

During the early eighties Iraq tried to develop a nuclear bomb. After it was broadcast on the official Jordanian radio that the bomb being produced in Iraq would be dropped on Israel, Israel reacted by destroying the construction equipment in Iraq. Iraq then concentrated on developing large quantities of chemical and biological weapons, which it threatened and intended to use against Israel. Such weapons are cheaper to produce than nuclear.

These questions are now overshadowed by the increasing war-like activities and pronouncements of Iran that threaten the peace of the Middle East if not of the world. Iran, with the help of Russian scientists is almost certainly progressing rapidly toward the production of a nuclear bomb. It is anticipated that such a bomb will be produced within two or possibly three years and perhaps earlier. The former Iranian President Hashemi Rafsanjani, a man who continues to exert considerable influence, said recently that the first thing that Iran would do in the production of such a bomb would be to drop it on Israel. He said, 'On that day the strategy of the West will hit a dead-end since a single atomic bomb has the power to completely destroy Israel, while an Israeli counter-strike can only partially damage the Islamic world'.[20] The present President, Mahmoud Ahmadinejad has repeatedly said that he plans to wipe Israel off the map and it appears that he hopes to do so by using a nuclear bomb.

On 12 January 2007, Israeli newspapers published details of an official assessment by Israeli military intelligence, warning that a major regional war is likely to erupt in 2007, involving Lebanon, Syria, Hezbullah, the Palestinian authority and Iran. The possibility of nuclear weapons being used is very real, which could endanger the peace of the world.

Neither Iran in its threat to drop a nuclear bomb on Israel, nor Iraq with its earlier threat of chemical and biological warfare seemed troubled that in the process of destroying Israel they would kill Arabs as well as Jews.

So much for the political analysis, brief as it is. It would be possible to extend it almost indefinitely, with each side adding its own material. What makes the conflict even more complex, dangerous, and yet

---

[20] Julie Stahl, Jerusalem, *CFI News Digest*, February 2002.

ultimately hopeful, is the religious dimension. Those in the West are used to treating politics and religion as two separate things – politics are part of public debate, and religion a matter of private interest. This is a misunderstanding of Christian belief, but it is certainly true that the two things are kept separate in, say, the American constitution. This was not because the American Founding Fathers were not religious men, but because they did not wish to import religious conflicts from Europe into the New World. Nowadays of course it is made a justification for keeping such things as non-denominational Christian worship out of public schools.

Chapter 2 will introduce a Christian understanding of Israel and its significance today. At this point we need to look at the Jewish, and the Arab understanding of Israel – both vitally important dimensions today.

The Jewish Understanding

Many Jews would draw a line separating Jewish belief and the State of Israel – in fact a small group of Orthodox Jews regard the founding of the Jewish State as a theological mistake. Judaism has always been able to flourish outside the land, and up to the late 19th century, most Jews either went for assimilation to their host culture, or resigned themselves to ghetto existence. However, from the mid-19th century onwards, Zionism emerged as a possible viewpoint, associated with the name of Herzl in political Judaism, and Rabinowitz in what today we might call messianic Judaism (although many Jews reject this term).[21]

The link with the land was of course always somewhere underlying Jewish existence, as the toast 'Next Year in Jerusalem' implied. A moving tribute to this is given by Henry Tankel in Appendix 3.

However, for most Jews, religion is more a matter of culture and ethics than what Christians might call theology. Partly that is because Jews do not readily debate theology with Christians, they prefer to address customs and ethical questions – and maybe in turn that reflects a wish to distance themselves from 'triumphalist' Christian theology of past ages; partly that is because Judaism is more an ethic and a 'sense of who you are' than a theology. Witness the typically Jewish story from one of the concentration camps: the inmates have put God on trial and sentenced him to death for allowing such terrible things

---

[21]   See *Joseph Rabinowitz*, Handsel Press (Edinburgh 1995).

to happen. Then they turn to the Rabbi. 'What do we do now?' they asked. 'We pray,' comes the answer.

Most Jews, even in Israel, would call themselves non-practising – certainly not 'orthodox'. Many would say they were agnostic, or even atheist. Most would see the current situation in terms of security, although some would also challenge the Israeli Government's actions against the Palestinians on the ground of ethics. But a significant number would also invoke a biblical ideology of 'greater Israel', if not from the Euphrates to the Red Sea, certainly an Israel which included the 'Western Palestine' of the British Mandate era.

The combination of security fears, and biblical ideology, is well documented in the press and not hard to understand. What fewer people are aware of is the precise ideology behind what is often dismissed as 'Islamic Fundamentalism' (Muslims themselves prefer the term 'Islamism').

Arab Nationalism and Islamic Fundamentalism

These two forces are different, but they unite in opposition to Israel. The great hero of Arab Nationalism in the past was President Nasser of Egypt. It is chiefly represented today by the Baath (Arabic for 'resurgence') Party, which rules Syria (and formerly ruled Iraq). It is the movement responsible for overthrowing many of the corrupt Arab monarchies in the Middle East. It is fiercely nationalist, anti-colonial, and socialist. The presence of a non-Arab nation (Israel) in its midst is regarded as an insult to Arab honour, and their defeats at the hand of a smaller Israel have been doubly humiliating. (This is partly why 'Jewish cunning' is blamed for all kinds of disasters in Arab nations.)

Not all Arab Nationalists are Muslims. The founder of the Baath Party was in fact a member of one of the historic Arab Christian churches, and Christians in Iraq and Syria have more freedom than they would in an Islamic State. Some of the PLO leaders have belonged to an Arab church, even an extreme leader like George Habbash. Arafat tried to worship in Bethlehem on Christmas Day – an Islamic Fundamentalist would never do that.

In fact an Arab Nationalist like Saddam Hussein killed hundreds of thousands of Iraqi Shiite Muslims, and the late Assad of Syria slaughtered tens of thousands of supporters of the Muslim Brotherhood (in three days he killed over twenty thousand inhabitants of the town of Hama).

The PLO has even said that it could be reconciled to the existence of the State of Israel. But the more they come to rely on movements like Hezbullah, Islamic Jihad and Hamas, the more difficult it will be to hold to this. To understand that, we now turn to Islamism.

Islamic Fundamentalism

This unites some non-Arab nations in hatred of Israel and a desire for its elimination. Within the Palestinian territories, Hamas is now the main voice of Islamism. It sees a return to the 'purity' of original Islam as the solution to world problems. But whereas liberal Muslims can live with other forms of Government, even if they see these as simply a stage en route to an Islamic State, fundamentalist Muslims are utterly opposed, and increasingly call on the doctrine of *jihad* to justify armed action against Israel.

It is these religious reasons which explain why nations such as Iran, Pakistan and Malaysia hate Israel even though there are greater humanitarian injustices and tragedies closer at hand.

Muhammed, who lived 600 years after Christ, was the founder of Islam.[22] He was the writer of Islam's holy book, the Qur'an. The characters we meet in the Qur'an are mainly the same people we meet in the Bible, such as Adam, Abraham, Moses, Solomon, Jesus, his mother Mary. However the stories themselves are different from the Old Testament stories, and recent scholarship links them to versions of the story circulating among Jewish communities in the first few centuries AD.

Again, in the Qur'an the Bible stories appear in no particular order. The Qur'an has its longest chapters (*suras*) in the first part. These contain material from Muhammed's early days in Mecca – these parts are less political and contain much that Christians would accept.

These early parts speak of Jews and Christians in friendly tones. But the Jews did not accept Muhammed and his new writings, and so Muhammed became angry with them. Later sections of the Qur'an call on Muslims to fight and kill Jews, accusing them of twisting the word of God, and prophesy that they will live in permanent

---

[22] Muslims claim that Islam is a religion going back to Adam and Abraham, and that every human being is Muslim insofar as they live under the rule of God. However, the final revelation had to wait till Muhammed. The Jews, so Muslims believe, had distorted God's word when they wrote the Bible; Muhammed's reception of the Qur'an corrects these mistakes.

dispersion, poverty and misery. Thus the existence of the State of Israel is a contradiction to Qur'anic teaching. Without understanding this, we cannot understand what motivates Islamic hostility to Israel's existence.

Clearly, racial and religious violence can be found in the history of all religions, including Christianity (especially the Crusades). There was a significant element in the destruction of the Canaanites in ancient Israel – the command was directed against people who included child sacrifice in their religion.[23] This controversial area is examined further in Appendix 4.

But the main question at issue here is how Muslims understand the kingdom of God. In biblical teaching, there must be a relationship between priest and king, but they should not be united in one person. The only person who may unite the two offices is Messiah (interestingly, prefigured in the mysterious priest-king Melchizedek in Genesis), who is incorruptible.

In Islamic theology there is no separation of religion and state, sacred and secular. The Muslim struggle for God's kingdom must therefore involve a struggle to impose Islamic political, legal and military power on the world. Accordingly, the world is divided into two areas: the 'house of Islam' (*dar ul-Islam*) and the 'house of War' (*dar ul-Harb*). Indeed the name Islam means 'submission', i.e. the Muslim should only submit to God and God's rule expressed on earth through Muslim power structures (hence the imposition of *shari'ah* law).

Strands in Judaism are also territorial – but only claiming a small part of the Middle East. The Muslim claim is the whole world. Indeed Muslims divide God's purpose through time into three: first, the time of the Jews, from Abraham; then the time of the Christians, from Jesus; and finally the time of Islam, which is destined to triumph. It is part of Islamic theology that God will always give ultimate victory to the true Muslim,[24] never allowing a Muslim part of the world to revert to non-Muslim control. Muslims therefore feel deep unease about the loss of Spain, but even sharper unease about Israel. The existence of the state of Israel is a theological contradiction for Islam.

---

[23]   Ironically, the recruitment of young people as suicide bombers is a contemporary form of child sacrifice, done to please Allah and thus guarantee a place in Paradise! It should be remembered, however, that most suicide bombers are Palestinian men with political rather than religious motives.

[24]   It is this belief that God always gives victory to his prophets that lies behind the Qur'anic teaching that God did not allow Jesus to be crucified and die.

Chapter Two

TURMOIL IN THE MIDDLE EAST: ISRAEL AND THE OTHER NATIONS

The Spiritual Significance of Israel

The turmoil in the Middle East today, which is threatening the peace of the whole world, is both political and religious.

It has an important political dimension. The establishment of the state of Israel, the displacement of Arabs, the creation of refugees, the struggle by Palestinians for human dignity, freedom and independence, the demand by Jews and Arabs for justice and peace, together with the demand by Israel for national security and international recognition, is political. Every effort must be made to try and understand these issues and to solve them politically. That is the duty of each state and the nations of the world. Yet, in themselves, these issues cannot be understood purely politically and in their complexity have no purely political solution.

All these issues have a deep religious dimension. They have a spiritual significance which goes far beyond the political. That is what we need to recognise today and to attempt to grasp. Political and religious understanding need to go hand in hand. This is what the international community and the nations, including Israel, and even the Church, find so frustrating and seldom face up to.

Fundamentalist Islam accepts the basic religious dimension to these problems. Numerous Arab leaders have spoken openly of their religious dimension. Various Arab council meetings have affirmed it. For many Muslims, 'The Palestinian problem is a religious one'.[1]

For Western governments and Israel to accept that the present crisis is a religious one, would be to recognise that the Middle East crisis is beyond a purely human solution. They would have to reckon with God and what God is doing in his world today.

God has thrust Israel on to the front stage of world politics. He has made Israel the focus of world attention, so that what happens to

---

[1]   The Hamas Covenant, published 18 August 1988, Article 15.

Israel affects the world. Scarcely a day passes without Israel being mentioned in the public media and attention being drawn to what is happening in her relations with the Palestinians and her Arab neighbours. The Old Testament itself recognises that in a way as yet little understood, the fate of the surrounding nations is bound up with the destiny of Israel herself.[2]

So how does Christian theology understand Israel and her relationship with the nations?

God is not responsible for the injustices and the suffering, the fear and the bloodshed. That is the result of human sin, Jewish sin, Arab sin, all our sin. God loves every Jew, every Arab, everyone. In his love Christ died for the entire world and in Christ he offers his love and salvation to the entire world. All are special to him. That cannot be emphasised enough. What is important in the present crisis is that God, in a mysterious way is lovingly calling the attention of the world to himself, calling the world to acknowledge him and to submit to him as he works out the redemption of the world.

God has united the people of Israel in a very intimate way with himself. He has made with them an everlasting covenant, so that God is forever present with them and within them. Israel is God's servant, called to be his witness to the nations. Israel's relationship to the other nations, therefore, is different from the relationships that the other nations have between themselves. Israel's relationship with the other nations can never be just political. It is religious. The other nations in their relationships to Israel are in some way in touch with God. In what they do in relation to Israel, in what they do in response to what Israel is doing, they are responding to God, and being judged by God, as he is actively at work in the world today through his servant Israel.

This is made clear again and again in Scripture, perhaps particularly, in the Psalms. Israel, as a nation does not know, or accept, Jesus as the Messiah and she does not know what God is doing nor yet that she is God's servant. In her continued rejection of the Messiah she does many things which grieve the Lord and which are unjust, are wrong and which as Christians, trouble us. Yet, God is using Israel today. Through Israel God in a veiled but powerful way is confronting the nations, challenging them to acknowledge that he is the living God and calling them to submit to God in faith and obedience.

---

[2]   Isaiah 19:23-25.

Unless Christians appreciate this, we will never be able to understand what God is doing in his world today through the Jewish People, and we will not be able to pray, nor act, as God wants. We will not know how God wants us to pray for the Jewish People, for the Arab people, for all the Islamic peoples, and for the redemption of the world. Only in Jesus Christ and only as all people, Jews, Arabs, Islamic peoples, and all nations, come to faith in him, will justice and peace prevail. Only in Jesus Christ is there reconciliation and redemption.

The religious, or spiritual, dimension

In all the issues leading to and present within the Middle East crisis, there is a religious dimension. That is what makes the problems of the Middle East so intractable.

Islam, which lay like a sleeping giant for centuries, woke up with a severe jolt in 1948. The foundation of the State of Israel touched a religious nerve at the heart of Islam.[3] The Islamic revolution in Iran a few years later influenced almost the whole of Islam, arousing it still further. The sayings and teaching of the Ayatollah Khomeini influenced Muslims across the world so that recent years have seen an immense revival in fundamentalist Islam from Indonesia and Malaysia right across the Middle East to West Africa. Muslims in Asia or West Africa who could not read or write[4] and could not, if asked, have located where the land of Israel is on the map, have become aroused and set on fire. The establishment of the state of Israel has touched them at the heart of their faith.

Islamism or Islamic fundamentalism is not an aberration as some in the West would like to think. It is a return to the foundational tenets of Islamic faith. Islam has become militantly active and a threat not only to Israel but to the peace of the world, as is all too clear in the events of 11 September, 2001, when Islamic terrorists attacked the Twin Towers in New York, and the Pentagon or in the bombings which took place in Madrid, London and elsewhere.

Sayyid Qutb is one of the more influential of recent Islamic thinkers. He was executed by Nasser in Egypt in 1966. While in prison he wrote a commentary called *In the Shade of the Qur'an*, a passionate work written to provide a religious justification for *jihad* and what we today might call the Al Quaeda approach to life. Here is an extract:

---

3   See Chapter 7, Islam and Other Worldviews.
4   It is estimated that probably 50 per cent of Muslims throughout the world are illiterate.

Those who are prepared to lay down their lives for the cause of God are honourable people, pure of heart and blessed of soul. But the great surprise is that those among them who are killed in the struggle must not be considered or described as dead. They continue to live, as God himself clearly states.[5]

The American journalist Paul Berman challenges religious leaders in the West to give a religious rebuttal to philosophers like Qutb. He accuses Western leaders of responding to Al Quaeda with guns, instead of ideas.

Following the attack on the Twin Towers and the Pentagon, the Italian Prime Minister was the only European minister who had the courage to state that religion was an issue. Muslim writers had no such inhibitions. Sheikh Omar Bakri Mohamed of the British-based organization, *Al-Muhajiroun*, published on his organization's website on 13 September 2001 (two days after the World Trade Center attack) an interview in which he distinguished between civilian and military targets. He indicated that military and government entities were legitimate targets for Muslims to attack. On 31 August the Kuwaiti paper *Al-Watan* presented arguments to justify the killing of non-combatants by Muslims.

The article was concerned particularly with Jewish non-combatants, but the thrust of the argument would make it applicable to any non-Muslims living in a democracy. Citizens of a democracy have voted for their government and pay taxes to it, the author argued, therefore they can be attacked as if they were the government or military.[6]

In December 2002 a terrorist shot three American missionaries in a hospital in Yemen. He was reported in the Press as saying that he did it 'in order to cleanse the world and get closer to Allah'. This religious motivation is explained in Appendix 5 on '*Jihad* and Suicide Bombers'. Chapter 7 goes into more detail on how and why Islam is in theory and practice anti-Semitic.

Chapter 1 indicated the political dangers of the *intifada* escalating into regional war. As a religious comment on this, we believe that Israel will survive, not because of her ability, her military power or alliance with the USA, but because of the hand of God. There may be much suffering and, almost inevitably, considerable loss of life but God has said, 'I will plant Israel in their own land, never again to be

---

5   Cited by Paul Berman in the New York Times, 23 March 2003.
6   Information taken with permission from a 3 volume work on Islam by
     Patrick Sookhdeo.

uprooted from the land I have given them'.[7] That promise could not refer to the return of the exiles from Babylon because God again removed them from the Land. It seems clear that that promise refers to our day. It is certain that Israel will continue despite all adversity to live in the Land that was promised. They will also continue to be a nation[8] to the very end of the world. God has made that promise to Israel and it is a promise that he has made to no other nation. The reasons for this are explained and developed in later chapters.

Jerusalem

Muslims claim Jerusalem as a holy city. They call it *Al Quds*, the 'holy one'. During the years when it was under Islamic control, it was never a centre for pilgrimage or a focal point where Muslims gathered for prayer in large numbers. Once it came under the control of Israel, only then did it assume the important and prominent place in the Islamic world that it does today.

Jerusalem is the holy city for all Jews. It is for them the eternal city. It is desperately important for Islam to regain control of Jerusalem. For Muslims, it would substantiate their faith. Many times Arafat, the leader of the PLO said that their aim is to make Jerusalem the capital city of a Palestinian state and to fly the Palestinian flag over Jerusalem, over every synagogue, and Christian church and holy place.

His passionate aim was not merely political. It was religious. Compared to the capital city of other nations, Jerusalem has few assets in the way of an abundant water supply, industry and communications by land, sea and air. In all these it is lacking. Its real significance is religious. It is the spiritual centre for Judaism and (to a lesser extent) Christianity. For Muslims to control Jerusalem and fly over it the Palestinian flag would proclaim the supremacy of Islam over Judaism and Christianity.

The Dome of the Rock, built on Mount Moriah with marble plundered from Christian churches in Europe (there are no marble quarries in Israel/Palestine), with its statements in Arabic, affirming that God has no Son, stands as an open challenge not only to Jews but also to Christians, affirming the supremacy of Islam. An interesting point is that this mosque is one of the earlier ones, and does not have the *qiblah*, or direction of prayer, to Mecca.

---

[7] Amos 9:15.
[8] Jeremiah 31:36; see also Jeremiah 33:19f.

In the last few years, Muslims have attempted to remove from under the Temple Mount any historic trace of the first or second Jewish temple. They want to build on the Temple Mount, and in Bethlehem Square, yet larger mosques. This again is to try and demonstrate the supremacy of Islam.

The Vatican repeatedly has recommended that Jerusalem should become an international city, being, as they say, the centre of the three great monotheistic faiths. Many Western politicians have recommended the same or that Jerusalem be divided and become the capital city of both Israel and an independent Palestinian state. To fundamentalist Muslims a shared Jerusalem is impossible. For them, it must be clear for all to see that Islam is the only true religion. The battle for Jerusalem is not a political one. It is a religious, or spiritual, one.

A secular Palestinian State?

Some Arabs, and those who drew up the Palestinian Charter, advocated a 'secular democratic state'.

Article 16, of the Palestinian National Charter, reads: 'The liberation of Palestine, from a spiritual point of view, will provide the Holy Land with an atmosphere of safety and tranquillity, which in turn will safeguard the country's religious sanctuaries and guarantee freedom of worship and of visit to all, without discrimination of race, colour, language, or religion. Accordingly, the people of Palestine look to all spiritual forces in the world for support'.

Here a 'secular state' is being advocated. However, subsequent events, the present resurgence of fundamentalist Islam, and the many things that have been said by Islamic leaders make it clear that what is presently at stake in the struggle for a Palestinian state, is the supremacy of Islam.

In the areas which have come under Palestinian control, following the commencement of the Oslo peace negotiations, the Islamic attitude towards Christians confirms the desire for complete Islamisation. Previously the two communities lived side by side in peace. In 1948, 50 per cent of Jerusalem was Christian, and 25 per cent of Palestine was Christian. Now, about 2 per cent of Palestinians are Christian. The numbers of Arab Christians in the Bethlehem area have fallen from approximately 60 per cent to 20 per cent or less. In contrast, the numbers of Arab Christians within Israel have grown a little.

However, pressure from Muslim neighbours should not be exaggerated. Often communities on the ground are far more tolerant than their leaders whose statements are reported in the media. More important in this case is the fact that Christian Arabs have generally been better educated, more motivated towards material progress, and in a better position to emigrate. Many have, as the figures show. However the result has been that it is much easier for leaders who wish to do so to press the identity between Islam and the Palestinian cause.

Even in the West, the phrase 'the turbanning of the mind' has been used to underline the subtle change in political assumptions and limits to tolerance. In the Middle East, there has been a steady growth of pressure for Islamisation. To fundamentalist Muslims, the state of Israel, located in what they claim to be Islamic heartland, cannot be tolerated. They have no option. They must reject the state of Israel and seek its elimination. In this light, recent political history is significant.

Following the defeat of the Arab armies by Israel in 1967, *Sura* 47.35, from the Qur'an, was quoted in the Great Mosque in Mecca, 'Do not falter or sue for peace; you will be the upper ones'.

Afterwards, Israel made substantial offers to the Arabs and to Egypt, which were rejected. Israel offered back to the Arabs all the West Bank and to Egypt she offered back Gaza on condition of peace and the recognition and acceptance of Israel. Israel did not offer back Jerusalem. The memorable reply of the Arab League was, 'No negotiation (with Israel), no recognition, no peace'. On religious grounds, negotiations with Israel and the recognition of the state of Israel, believed to be located on Islamic soil, were not possible.

This view was stated clearly at a conference in 1968 at the influential Al-azhar University in Cairo. Sheik Abdullah Ghoshah, Supreme Judge of the Hashemite Kingdom of Jordan, speaking at that conference and with Israel in mind, presented a paper on *Jihad*. In it he said, '*Jihad* is legislated in order to be one of the means of propagating Islam. Consequently non-Muslims ought to embrace Islam either willingly or through wisdom and good advice or unwillingly through fight and *Jihad* . . . It is unlawful to give up Jihad and adopt peace and weakness . . . War is the basis of the relationship between Muslims and their opponents . . . The abode of Islam is the homeland which is subject to the rules of Islam'.[9]

---

[9]   Conference proceedings were published by the Egyptian Government Printing Office in 1970, in Arabic and English; quoted by John Laffin in *The Dagger of Islam*, Sphere Books Ltd, London, pages 54-55.

His Eminence, the Grand Imam, rector of Al-Azhar University, speaking against Israel, said, 'It is inconceivable that Allah would grant to the Unbelievers a way to triumph over the Believers. For this reason the setback that has befallen us is nothing but a sign of Allah's solicitude for our welfare, since we have certainly the genuine sentiment of religion, even if we have missed the way of the pious . . . The lingering spirit of the Crusades that was utterly routed by the feats of valour and heroic resistance of our forefathers, had made of the present-day Zionism a spearhead launched against Muslims by the enemies of humanity and advocates of imperialism . . .'[10]

As John Laffin says, 'Several speakers stated that it was outrageous for the Jews, traditionally kept back by Arab Islam in a humiliated inferior status and characterized as cowardly, to defeat the Arabs, have their own State and cause the "contraction of the abode of Islam". All these events contradicted the design of Allah and the march of history'.[11] The defeat of Arab armies by Israel was as it were 'a slap in the face to Allah' and as devout Muslims they owed it to Allah to wipe out this disgrace and sweep Israel into the Mediterranean Sea.

The Ayatollah Khomeini, on the other hand, as Lance Lambert has pointed out,

is the only Islamic theologian of repute that has recognized that Israel exists. He has said Israel exists and indeed before ever she came into being, he said, (quoting an ancient and revered Islamic tradition),[12] 'There is going to be a Jewish State', and he then explained it this way. He calls Israel 'satan'. In all his speeches he refers to Israel as 'satan' and the United States as 'the greater satan'. He says that because of the lack of devotion in the Islamic masses, because of their luke-warmness, because of the way they have behaved in their attitude to Allah, he has judged them by using satan to create a Jewish state, and he is going to use that Jewish state as a satanic instrument to bring out all the fury, all the anger and all the devotion, and all the commitment in the Islamic masses, until in the end there is a holy war, in which Allah will give the victory to the Islamic forces, and the Jewish state will finally be liquidated.[13]

The Ayatollah Khomeini said that, in the Holy Land, the Muslims, with the help of Allah, would kill all the Jews. 'He has said this for over forty years, and he has never changed his tune'.[14]

---

[10] *Ibid.* page 56.
[11] *Ibid.* page 56.
[12] The words in parenthesis are the authors'.
[13] Lance Lambert, *Islamic Fundamentalism: Is it a Threat to World Peace?* 1988, Christian Friends of Israel, page 6.
[14] *Ibid.* page 6.

According to the Ayatollah, and according to all fundamentalist Islamic teaching, all nations will in the end submit to Allah and to the truth of the Qur'an. It is foreordained.

It is very important for us to understand that the first stage is the reviving, renewing and returning of Islamic States to pure Islam, the second stage is the destruction of Israel and of the Jewish People, and the last stage is the conquest of the nations for Islam.[15]

It is in this context that we should understand Bin Laden, the Al-Qaeda terrorist training camps in Afghanistan, the attack on the Twin Towers and the Pentagon on 11 September 2001, other terrorist attacks throughout the world, including Madrid and London, and the present conflict in the Middle East.

Hamas is the largest of the terrorist organisations confronting Israel. Although it does not belong to the PLO hegemony, Gallup polls claim that the majority of people in the larger towns of the West Bank support Hamas. Documents, captured by the Israel Defence Forces in December 2002 in a raid on PLO offices in Ramallah, proved that Yasser Arafat, Chairman of the PLO, despite his claim to have adopted a more moderate position, contributed substantial sums of money, monthly, to Hamas to support their activities. The general election in Gaza in 2005 resulted in Hamas capturing a massive 77 per cent of the votes cast.

'The Covenant of the Islamic Resistance Movement – Palestine' (i.e. the Hamas Covenant) was published on 18 August 1988. What is said in the Covenant[16] is clear and represents the views of the majority of Palestinians. It is 'a comprehensive manifesto comprised of 36 articles'. The following are excerpts from some of them.

Preamble: 'Israel will exist and will continue to exist until Islam will obliterate it, just as it obliterated others before it'.

Article 11: 'The land of Palestine is an Islamic Waqf (Holy Possession) consecrated for future Moslem generations until Judgment Day. No one can renounce it or any part, or abandon it or any part'.

Article 13: 'Initiatives, and so called peaceful solutions and international conferences are in contradiction to the principles of the Islamic Resistance Movement . . . Those conferences are no more than a means to appoint the infidels as arbitrators in the lands of Islam . . .

---

15 *Ibid.* page 6.
16 A copy of the Covenant can be obtained from the Internet: www.fas.org/irp/world/para/docs/880818a.htm

There is no solution for the Palestinian problem except by *Jihad*. Initiatives, proposals and international conferences are but a waste of time, an exercise in futility . . . Renouncing any part of Palestine is equivalent to renouncing part of the religion, since for the Islamic Resistance Movement nationalism is a religious precept. It is to this goal that it educates its people, and they fight their Jihad in order to raise the banner of Allah over their homeland . . . '

Article 15: 'It must be impressed on the minds of all generations of Muslims that the Palestinian problem is a religious one and must be dealt with on these terms . . . '

In the West and in today's climate it is not 'politically correct' to say that in the present war on terrorism, the so-called Christian West is fighting Islam – or fighting Islamic fundamentalism. It is also not politically correct to say that Israel and the Palestinians, or Israel and the Arab states, are fighting a religious war. Politicians prefer to think, and persuade their people, that fundamentalist Mullahs, and Arab leaders who preach death to the Jews and to Christians and wish to wage war on America and the West are really out of step with Islamic thinking and are not representative of Islam. They fail to see that in Islam, fundamentalism is a return to foundational tenets of Islam and has swept through all Islamic countries.

It is folly not to listen to and accept what Muslims themselves are saying. We must face reality. The Arab League, and prominent Islamic theologians and teachers, have said repeatedly that the conflict is a religious one. Organizations like Hamas, Islamic Jihad, Hezbullah, the Popular Front for the Liberation of Palestinian (PFLP) and all the Muslim States, with the possible exception of Jordan, Egypt and Turkey, regard the conflict in Israel and the Palestinian territories as more than a struggle for a Palestinian homeland. They claim that it is a religious conflict, and many within Jordan, Egypt and Turkey claim the same thing. They believe, as mentioned in chapter 1, that it is their religious duty, which they owe to Allah, to wipe out Israel and many go further and believe that they should kill all Jews.

Despite all the issues of justice and peace for both Palestinians and Jews, if all that was at stake was the creation of an independent secular Palestinian State alongside of Israel, then an independent Palestinian State would have been established long ago. It would certainly have come about following the last Peace Talks in Camp David, USA, which ended in the summer of 2000.

It is the fact, as clearly stated in the Hamas Covenant, that the present conflict in the Middle East is a religious one, which places the conflict beyond a mere political solution. Islamic fundamentalism cannot accept Israel as a national, sovereign, independent state. 'If there were a nominal Islam, an Islam only in name, not puritanical Islam, or fundamentalist Islam, then it might be possible to compromise and negotiate. But Islamic fundamentalism, because it is a return to the foundational tenets of Islam, to the very heart of Islamic theology, cannot but reject the Jewish State'.[17]

Israel and Zionism

What of Israel's attitude to this conflict? For Zionists it is a religious conflict. Zionists believe that the land which God promised to give to Abraham is rightly theirs. They believe that God who rescued them from the persecutions and fires of the Holocaust has, in keeping with his promise, brought them back to 'the Land'. Even so, Israel does welcome and accept Arabs who are resident within Israel. There are many Israeli Arab citizens and it is noteworthy that since the granting to the Palestinian Authority control of certain areas of the West Bank, several thousands of Arabs have applied for Israeli citizenship, believing that they will have greater freedom and prosper better under Israeli rule. Arabs in Israel have equality in law, have a vote and are represented in Parliament. An Arab is a member of the Knesset.

What the ultimate boundary of the Promised Land should be today does not seem to be clear. Religious Jews would certainly believe that it embraces the whole of the West Bank and Gaza. That belief can blind many religious Jews to the rights and the needs of the Palestinians, make them blind or indifferent to their suffering and confounds any mere political settlement. Israel needs continually to be reminded, in a spirit of love and humility, of the teaching of their own Scriptures about God's command to live righteously, justly, and to welcome the stranger in their midst, although that is not easy for them do in the present crisis.

In the Old Testament it is clear that to continue to live happily in the Promised Land, Israel is required to trust in God. After her deliverance from Egypt it took forty years and another generation from those rescued from Egypt, to learn this lesson of faith. When living in the Land it was a lesson that they had continually to relearn[18].

---

[17]   Lance Lambert, *op. cit.* page 2.
[18]   2 Chronicles 16:7-9.

For protection against their foes they had to rely on God alone. It is the same lesson that Israel must learn today. God has graciously brought them back in unbelief. If they would enjoy peace and prosperity today they must put their sole trust in God, practice justice and live righteously.

Israel is called to be a nation (*ethnos*). As a nation she is entitled to act as do other nations. She is entitled to build up an army, air force and navy, and take all natural, reasonable steps for her own protection and security. At the same time, Israel is called to be a people (*laos*) set apart for God. As a people set apart for God her whole confidence must be in God, not in the strength of her armed forces, not in her military might, not in alliance with the USA or any other country, and she must live and walk in a way that is pleasing to God and live justly and righteously. God demands this of every nation, but none more so than Israel.

This call to be both a nation (*ethnos*) and a people (*laos*) has put Israel under incredible pressure, over the years. It created an almost unbearable inner tension in the state of Israel of old and it does so in Israel today. It is a tension with which Israel finds it very difficult to come to terms. Among other things it has meant that Israel is preoccupied with survival, instead of with its mission to the world clearly presented in the Isaiah 'servant songs'.[19]

In the present situation when Israel is attacked by stone throwing, by mortar attacks, Kassem-2 rockets, and by suicide bombers, the temptation is to use more and more force. She is tempted to rely solely on the superior power and skill of her police and armed forces, or to rely on the USA and on other nations to persuade the Palestinians to call a halt to the armed struggle and seek peace. Yet, the more Israel relies on armed force and military might, and the more she is tempted to rely on other nations, the more the cycle of violence and bloodshed continues, and escalates. According to an article in the London Times,[20] official statistics issued by Israel show that in the year 2001, (prior to the building of the wall separating Israel from the West Bank), there were 1,794 Palestinian terrorist attacks, which was an increase of 337 per cent on the number recorded for year 2000 when the second *intifada* began in late September. The Israeli police commissioner Shlomo Aharoniski, in a statement to the Israeli Press, Sunday 10 February 2002, translated the figure of 1,794 assaults. It covered 603 bombings, 367 mortar firings, 236 shooting attacks and 503 others (firebombs,

---

[19]   E.g. Isaiah 49:6.
[20]   London Times, Monday, 11 February 2002.

stabbings etc.). It left 208 Israelis dead and 1,563 injured. Violence has produced violence.[21] Terrorist attacks continue, but the number of attacks and casualties have decreased as the wall, separating Israel from the West Bank, began to be built and be extended. As mentioned in chapter one, Israel claims that, because of the wall, the numbers of both terrorist attacks and casualties have dropped approximately 90 per cent. This is apart from the many Palestinian bombings, and suicide attacks, that have taken place after Israel's withdrawal from Gaza, with an increase in the numbers dead and injured.

Attitudes on both the Palestinian and Jewish sides have hardened and become more united and more extreme. Words spoken by Asher Susser, when addressing members of the House of Commons and House of Lords, on 12 June 1989, during the earlier *intifada* are apt and relevant to the present situation.

> The higher the rate of casualties in the *intifada*, the longer the chances, the stronger the chances are of the *intifada* perpetuating itself. It is the casualties that fan the flames of the *intifada* . . . It is the sacrifice and loss of life in the *intifada* that is really the major asset, the oil on the wheels of the *intifada*. And it is for that reason that Yasser Arafat always has accounts of losses twice as high as the Israeli ones – and probably twice as high as the reality.[22]

Because the present struggle is a religious struggle, only God can solve it and bring it to an end and in the end he will only bring it to an end in his way. Israel is being called to put her trust in God. Israel cannot adequately do that without coming to acknowledge Jesus Christ as her Messiah and without putting her trust in him.

Here the Christian Church should be praying and seeking to help Israel to faith and trust in Jesus Christ, and to understand the great purposes of God. Sadly in this, the mainstream Churches are failing.

Most churches are doing nothing at all to present to the Jews or to the Arabs, the Gospel of Jesus Christ in whom alone is reconciliation, justice and peace. They have, to a large extent, succumbed to the

---

[21] Both sides take a different moral view on violence. For example, Mr Netanyahu, when he was the Israeli Foreign Minister, at a meeting with Heads of Churches on 30 December 2002 spoke of the teaching of Judaism about the value of individual life, and the convention that civilians should not be the targets of violence. In contrast, a Palestinian Centre has produced a monograph sympathetic to suicide bombing as a last resort.

[22] Asher Susser, The PLO and the Palestinian Entity, The Anglo-Israel Association, 1989, page 12. These words were spoken in an address to members of both Houses of Parliament. Asher Susser is from Tel Aviv University.

pressures of the world in their attitude to Israel and try to encourage Israel to seek only political answers to her problems.

Pronouncements by the World Council of Churches and the Vatican, reiterate views long held: if only Israel would withdraw from the West Bank (and Gaza, which they have done) and remove all settlements from Palestinian land, or if only there was a separate Palestinian State, sharing with Israel, its capital in Jerusalem, there would be peace! The Churches, like the secular states of the West are failing to recognise that, despite all the many real problems of justice that need to be solved, the real struggle is between the God of Abraham, the Father of our Lord Jesus Christ, and the god of Islam. It is a struggle between the living and true God, and the god of this world. What is involved in the Middle East is not just a struggle between human forces but with what Paul calls 'the powers of this dark world and… the spiritual forces of evil in the heavenly realms'.[23]

Israel, the Palestinians, the Islamic countries, and the other nations of the world, need all to come to a saving knowledge and faith in Jesus Christ. It is only in Jesus Christ that there can be healing of anger, mistrust and the desire for revenge. Every other way apart from Christ is ultimately futile.

Signs of hope in Israel

One of the signs of hope today as regards Israel, is the growing feeling of frustration with its present policies and the recognition of the futility of relying solely on its military strength.

Larry Derfner, a former Israeli Defence force (IDF) chief psychologist wrote an article in the 24 August 2001 Jerusalem Post in which he quoted Dr. Reuven Gal, another former chief IDF psychologist. He said, 'The situation today is different from anything that's gone before. This is the first time that the predominant Israeli attitude is one of hopelessness'. When we come to the end of our resources then, perhaps, we can turn to God.

Rachel Boskey, a Messianic Believer in Israel, wrote in a letter on Thursday 30 August 2001 about 'Signs of awakening in the heart of Israel'.[24] She said, 'Among the Orthodox Jewish community in Israel there is a real awareness that we are living in the times they call "the birth pangs of the Messiah". Many Orthodox know that what is now

---

23   Ephesians 6:12.
24   Rachel Boskey. Letter to CFI also circulated to Christian friends.

happening to Israel is somehow designed to accomplish redemption'. There is a soul searching that is affecting every level of society even those in government. Some are calling on Israel to pray.

Michael Freund, a former member of the Knesset, sent an article to the Jerusalem Post.[25] He said:

> There must be something more, something that each and everyone of us can do to directly affect the situation no matter who or where we might be. And in fact there most assuredly is. However you might define yourself - be it Jew or Christian, agnostic or simply confused - the key to Israel's victory may very well be in the palm of your hands or, more precisely in the words of your heart. Israel's best defence is the power of prayer, and it is time we unleash this weapon with all the fury and determination that we can muster.
>
> To modern ears, it might sound archaic, even simplistic. But modern solutions have failed us miserably in recent years, with diplomacy and statesmanship bringing us all to the edge of the abyss. For all our advanced technology and finely honed military prowess, Israel seems at a loss as to how to extricate itself from the current impasse. Perhaps it is time to put aside our cynicism and our doubts, and do what people in trouble have always done in their hour of need – turn to their father in Heaven and plead for help. The Palestinians are now openly declaring that we are all potential targets . . . Synagogues, churches and other places of worship should regularly recite specified Psalms on Israel's behalf, culminating in an international Day of Prayer at the Western Wall in Jerusalem. If tens of thousands or even hundreds of thousands, of voices are raised worldwide simultaneously, the echo will resound, not only through the corridors of power in Washington, Moscow and elsewhere but more importantly in the Heavens too.
>
> The fact is that for the past decade, we have given politics a chance and it has failed us. Now is the time to give God a chance, for unlike politicians, he can always be relied upon to keep his word.

Paul anticipated that many in Israel would finally come to faith in Christ. With the growing numbers of Messianic Jews in Israel today, in the USA, in Russia and elsewhere, together with what is happening as a result of the present troubles in Israel, it would appear that this turning to Christ on the part of large numbers of Jews may not be far distant.

---

[25] Jerusalem Post, Wednesday 29 August, 2001. Michael Freund served as deputy director of Communications and Policy Planning in the Israeli Prime Minister's Office from 1996 to 1999. Quoted by CFI.

Signs of hope in Islam

Following the attack of 11 September 2001, an Islamic university lecturer spoke on British TV of the need for Islam to undergo a reformation such as took place in the Church in the 16th century. She rejected violence as a true expression of Islam and rejected the attack on the Twin Towers as in agreement with the will of Allah. Many Muslims in the UK, the USA, Europe and in the white Commonwealth have also spoken in rejection of terrorism and the attack on the Twin Towers and the Pentagon on that date, and in rejection of the terrorist attacks in Madrid, London and elsewhere.

The London Arabic-language daily, Al-Sharq Al-Awsat, has published letters calling for a thorough self-examination in the Islamic world. On 21 December 2001 the paper published a letter by Dr Sahr Muhammad Hatem of Riyadh, Saudi Arabia, under the headline: 'Our Culture of Demagogy has engendered bin Laden, Al-Zawahiri, and their Ilk'. In her letter she criticised the triumphalism of Islam and many of their spokespeople who, without considering the consequences, have taught hate towards non-Muslims. She wrote:

> We began to turn to those who claim to be clerics, to rule for us on matters of medicine, engineering, space, and all the life sciences. Life moves on, (yet) we are stuck. We have begun to live an imaginary life that exists only in our heads, while the reality around us is entirely different. This is the (personality) split which engendered people like bin Laden. Since reality differs from (the picture) in his mind, he sets out as Mujaheed; whether he kills or is killed, he wins . . . We all focus on bin Laden and his ilk . . . but we have yet to focus on the more dangerous people, and I mean those who fill our heads with this rhetoric in the schools, the mosques, and the media, who disseminate words without hesitation and without considering the consequences or even understanding that in this era, the entire world hears what is said.

Dr Hatem's letter was warmly welcomed by the paper's liberal columnist Khaled Al-Qashtini, who said, 'This is the best letter of 2001, and this is the woman worthy of the title Woman of the Year 2001'.

Dr Hatem was also commended for her article by Abd Al-Salam bin Al-Hussein of Morocco, who wrote in another letter to the editor: 'She has put her finger on one of the causes of the disease – fanatical thought stemming from miscomprehension of (the Qur'anic verse that says Muslims are) "the best nation brought to mankind".'

There were other letters in support of what Dr Hatem said. In yet another letter, some two months later, Ahmad Othman of London said, 'By now it has already been proven beyond doubt that all those who participated in the suicide attacks on the WTC and the Pentagon . . . were Arab and Muslims. They are our sons, born and educated in our Arab societies . . . doubtless something in our society – not in the society of the American victims – is very wrong'. There have been similar sentiments expressed in the Egyptian government weekly Akhbar Al-Yaum.

On a world scale those calling for a re-think or a reformation within Islam seem to be in the minority. They are certainly a minority in the Middle East. According to news from Israel, a gallup poll in Saudi Arabia claims that 95 per cent of males between 16 and 41 years support bin Laden. Still, the present soul searching among some within Islam, and the call for reformation, is new and a sign of hope for Islam. One example of potential theological change is the suggestion that attention should be focused on the earlier Meccan suras in the Qur'an instead of the later Medinan ones.

Probably in the next few years there will come about a division between the more moderate Muslims and the orthodox fundamentalist Muslims. The rock on which God ultimately will break Islam, I believe, will not be the Church but Israel.[26] When that happens (and by the many conversions to Christ which are taking place in Islamic countries, perhaps it has begun to happen) I believe that we will see a vast number of Muslims turning to Jesus Christ. This would seem to be a fulfilment of the prophecy in Isaiah,[27] when we can anticipate that Jew and Arab (both children of Abraham) will become a blessing to the entire world.

Because this is the case, the responsibility is given to the Church to pray for Israel and to pray for the Islamic world. God loves the Jews and God loves those whose hearts and minds are at present captivated by Islam. The burden is to pray that they may come to faith in Christ Jesus and share together in his salvation, that they may be reconciled in Christ and together be a blessing in Christ to the whole world.

In order to pray like that, the Church must understand the mission of Israel, which is developed in Part 3 of this book.

---

26 See Zechariah 12:2, Jeremiah 51:20.
27 Isaiah 19:19-25.

Chapter Three

PEOPLE, LAND AND COVENANT

The subject of this chapter is a key to the whole book.[1] It has far-reaching theological and political implications. The subject arouses considerable feeling and controversy not only between Jews and Palestinians but also between people throughout the world. It causes division of opinion within the Church.

The first sort of division is a more general one, and should be mentioned briefly – the difference between 'liberal' and 'conservative'. There are many ways of stating this difference, but a relevant one is as follows. The liberal view believes in fundamental human principles of love and justice, which are illustrated in the Bible but stand on their own. Jesus, on this view, is a unique man whose life and teaching showed us the love of God. This idea of God's love can then be used to interpret and critique modern personal and world situations, not least Israel and the Palestinian territories. Justice is usually understood as 'love shared around', as well as a general human imperative. Biblical views such as the importance of the land of Israel are usually understood as one way of understanding Israel theologically, but not necessarily the only way or even the best way. On this view, the solution to the problem of Israel and the Palestinian territories lies in finding a just settlement, and in Israelis and Palestinians learning to forgive one another to the extent that they can accept a settlement. This is an important insight, but still leaves us with the two vital questions: what is just? And: how can I forgive?

The conservative view also has variations, but takes the view that Christianity is a revealed religion centred in the person of Christ; that the Bible is God's word as well as a series of books with their own human authors and contexts; and that Jesus is divine as well as human. Love and justice, on this view, are revealed in the way God relates to the world through his Son, Jesus of Nazareth. Love and justice are worked out in human situations as men and women receive and live

---

[1]   This chapter was presented on request in 1988 to a Church of Scotland Study Group on 'Land', as a basis for discussion. It is edited for publication.

by the good news of Jesus, his cross and resurrection. This of course still leaves us with the question: how can Jews and Muslims, how can Israelis and Palestinians (not one and the same) receive and respond to the good news? Whether you are liberal or conservative, there are no pain-free answers.

This book takes a conservative view, and this chapter therefore considers a second division, which occurs among those who claim to take the Bible equally seriously. All conservatives believe that Israel is important as the nation from which Jesus came, and that the Old Testament gives us a number of models for understanding the ministry of Jesus (well illustrated by the book of Hebrews in the New Testament), and many parallels – such as twelve tribes, twelve apostles. But what about the Jews, and the land of Israel in particular? Is the land important only up to the time of Jesus, so that when the Romans destroyed Jerusalem about forty years after the death of Jesus, that was the end; or, does the land have a continuing significance, and not least in our day when the Jews have been restored to it?

Some key texts and key ideas

Five writers who have in more recent times argued that the land of Israel has no more significance are Naim Ateek,[2] Colin Chapman,[3] Peter Walker[4], Gary Burge[5] and Stephen Sizer[6]. Much of their argument can be summarised as follows:

1 In the Gospels and Letters, the New Testament talks about a world-wide gospel that knows no particular boundaries of people or land. The kingdom of God is for all peoples, and it will reach its fulfillment in a heavenly, not an earthly Jerusalem. It follows that in the NT and therefore today, the OT special promises to Israel are no longer relevant.

2 The NT tells us that Christ is the fulfillment of Israel's destiny. His body is the new temple. It follows that a universal and heavenly message has replaced the particular OT promise to a people and a land.

---

[2]   One of the best known Israeli Arab/Palestinian Episcopal Church theologians.
[3]   *Whose Promised Land?* Lion, 2002.
[4]   *Jesus and the Holy City; New Testament Perspectives on Jerusalem.*
[5]   *Whose Land? Whose Promise?* Paternoster Press. 2003.
[6]   *Christian Zionism: Road-map to Armageddon?* IVP.

3 The book of Hebrews tells us that the true promised land is beyond this world and that the OT sacrifices are now obsolete. We must think of the OT promises about the land in the same light as the OT sacrifices.

4 In Romans 9-11 Paul may see some continuing unique significance for the Jewish people, but he is not concerned with the land.

Part 3, especially chapters 10 and 11, deals further with some of these issues. At this point, consider the following ideas and texts.

First, universal ideas in the NT do not replace particular ideas in the OT. In both testaments universal and particular are held together in creative tension. Centrally, it is the particular Jew, Jesus of Nazareth, who died and rose again 'to have first place in all things',[7] it is he who guarantees the promise of salvation for all people and all creation. Jesus remains a particular man in heaven even though through his Spirit he is universally present in his body.

In the OT, Isaiah's 'servant songs' combine the particular with the universal. The 'servant', who is both Israel and Israel's individual representative, has a universal call to bring light to the Gentiles.[8] Even the servant's blindness is used to enable the rest of the world to see. Now Paul picks this up in his letter to Romans, and speaks of the universal message which goes beyond physical Israel. He says that to be a true Jew, you must be circumcised inwardly.[9] It might seem that Paul is rejecting the continuing significance of particular Jewish Israel. But in the next verse he says that the Jews still have particular advantages and importance, even if they do not (at this stage) believe.[10] He expands on this in chapters 9-11, explaining why God does not change his choice of Israel's *earthly* ministry.

Now it is true that Paul does not specifically mention 'the land'. But he does say that the 'covenants' and the 'promise' belong to Israel, and claims that on this point he is inspired by the Spirit and speaking 'in Christ'.[11] So, do the covenants and promises include land?

From Abraham onwards, land is one of the most significant aspects of both. We are not talking of a few isolated texts but hundreds of references. It is a major theme of nearly all the prophets. Furthermore, a key thread runs through the Law, the Psalms and the Prophets – it is the scattering from, and regathering to, the land. Exile and return.

---

[7] Colossians 1:18.
[8] Isaiah 42:6.
[9] Romans 2:28-29.
[10] Romans 3:1-6.
[11] Romans 9:1-5.

When Paul wrote his letters, the Jews were still in the land. The Romans had not yet destroyed Jerusalem and scattered the Jews (though some had voluntarily, then and earlier, gone to live elsewhere). Paul had no reason specifically to talk of a restoration to the land, or to assume that the land no longer figured. The argument from silence is not valid.

Is the land like the temple and its sacrifices? No – the temple sacrifices were temporary signs of the covenant. God/people/land are the content of the covenant. Why did God choose a people? To represent in a particular way all peoples before God. Why did God choose a land? To represent the natural world in a particular way before God. That God is faithful to the people of Israel is a witness to his faithfulness to all peoples. That God is faithful to the land of Israel is a witness of his faithfulness to all creation. If God were permanently to break the relationship between Israel and the land, it would mean no hope for the redemption of humanity and the whole created order.

It is true that the Gospels say little about the OT themes of exile and return; but they are not silent. Jesus warned that Jerusalem would be destroyed, and trampled on by the Gentiles – but only 'till the times of the Gentiles were fulfilled'.[12] This indicates that Luke (and Jesus of course) knew that the OT promises of restoration were not only about the first return from exile in Babylon.

Scholars now recognise that John is a very Jewish gospel, in spite of its criticism of the Jewish leaders of Jesus' time. In chapter 4 Jesus encounters a Samaritan woman, and in conversation indicates that true worship is no longer a matter of 'on which mountain', but is universal, 'in Spirit and in truth'. But the same passage also says, 'You Samaritans worship what you do not know; we worship what we do know, for salvation is from the Jews'.[13] Particular and universal are held together – as they are in the death and resurrection of Christ.

What about the texts that speak of a return to the land which were not fulfilled by the return from Babylon and what about the inner logic of exile? Isaiah said: 'In that day the Lord will reach out his hand a second time to reclaim the remnant that is left of his people from Assyria, from Lower Egypt, from Upper Egypt from Cush, from Elam, from Babylonia, from Hamath and from the islands of the sea'.[14] *There have only been two exiles from the land, so that this prophecy must refer to today.*

---

[12] Luke 21:20-24.
[13] John 4:21-23.
[14] Isaiah 11:10-11.

At the same time this prophecy speaks of Jews returning 'from the islands of the sea', *which never happened in the earlier return from Babylon.* Again Isaiah said: 'But you, O Israel, my servant, Jacob, whom I have chosen, you descendants of Abraham my friend, I took you from the ends of the earth, from its farthest corners I called you, I said, "You are my servant"; I have chosen you and have not rejected you'.[15] *Here God brought back his people 'from the ends of the earth', not just from Babylon, and called them 'from its farthest corners'.*

1 God's judgement against Israel's sin means that her people will be scattered from the land.

> Then the Lord will scatter you among the nations, from one end of the earth to the other... Among these nations you will find no repose, no resting place for the sole of your foot. There the Lord will give you an anxious mind, eyes weary with longing, and a despairing heart. You will live in constant suspense, filled with dread both day and night, never sure of your life.[16]

2 God's forgiveness to Israel will mean that God will restore its people to the land.

> Then the Lord your God will restore your fortunes and have compassion on you and gather you again from all the nations where he scattered you. Even if you have been banished to the most distant lands under the heavens, from there the Lord your God will gather you and bring you back. He will bring you to the land that belonged to your fathers, and you will take possession of it.[17]

These are the principles laid down in the Torah, and therefore do not refer only to this or that event in the history of Israel. They describe how God deals with Israel in all of its history, and are discussed again and again by the prophets.

However, the return to the land is usually linked to Israel's repentance and spiritual return to the Lord. With the majority of Israelis today being agnostic, and many clear injustices perpetrated against Palestinians, it would be hard to argue that the present state of Israel has earned God's favour! This in turn raises an important question about God's grace and his promises – are they conditional on our good behaviour, or unconditional. The word 'if' is of course

---

[15] Isaiah 41:8,9. See also, Isaiah 42:14f., 43:1-9, 49:8f., 51:22, 51:1, 60:8,21. Jeremiah 31:1-9, 31-37; 33:6f. Ezekiel 36:16-36. Joel 2:18-27. Nahum 1:15. Zephaniah 3:14f. None of these prophecies seemed to have been fulfilled with the return from Babylon.

[16] Deuteronomy 28:64-67.

[17] Deuteronomy 30:3-5.

used in two senses: one is consequential, like the sentence: 'if we behave badly then a consequence will be that we bring trouble on ourselves'; the other is conditional, like: 'if we behave badly then God cannot bless us'. However both OT and NT argue that God's grace is in the end unconditional. If this were not so there would be no hope for any of us, for we all fall short and mess up.

[God] promises that as long as the natural order lasts, so long will Israel be a nation. Only if the sky could be measured... only then would he reject the people of Israel because of all they have done, declares the Lord.[18]

It is true that the enjoyment of the full *blessings* of the covenant were dependent on Israel's behaviour, but the fulfilment of his *purposes* through them and their land was not. However the chronology varies. Some prophets imply that restoration to the land comes before reconciliation with the Lord, and some, particularly the later prophets like Ezekiel,[19] that it comes afterwards. We might say theologically that peace with God and peace with the natural world belong together, but we cannot spell out how it actually happens.

When they met together, they asked him, 'Lord, are you at this time going to restore the kingdom to Israel?' He said to them, 'It is not for you to know the times or dates the Father has set by his own authority.... But you will be my witnesses in Jerusalem, and in all Judaea and Samaria, and to the ends of the earth.'[20]

Again, the particular and the universal are held together. The gospel is for all nations, but the kingdom will also be restored to Israel – only we do not know when.

O Jerusalem, Jerusalem, you who kill the prophets and stone those sent to you, how often have I longed to gather your children together, as a hen gathers her chicks under her wings, but you were not willing! Look, your house is left to you desolate. I tell you, you will not see me again until you say, 'Blessed is he who comes in the name of the Lord'.[21]

This implies that when the Lord returns, Jerusalem will be a Jewish city. It may be a mistake to argue from a passage like this for or against a particular political 'solution' for Jerusalem. What these passages do indicate, however, is that the particular status of Jews, Jerusalem, and the land remains beyond Bible times, and does not disappear into some 'universal message' or 'timeless truth'.

---

[18] Jeremiah 31:36-37.
[19] Ezekiel 36:16-38.
[20] Acts 1:6-8.
[21] Luke 13:34-35.

A biblical and theological analysis

As Professor Jurgen Moltmann has pointed out, the subject of the Jewish people, God's purpose for them and for the land, has been largely neglected by the Church throughout its history and neglected to the Church's own spiritual impoverishment. As Moltmann rightly says, 'According to the promise to the fathers, God, People, and Land belong together'.[22] Our understanding of God necessarily involves our understanding of both people and land. To think biblically, we must think of them both together. The God in whom Christians and Jews trust has entered into a covenant of grace both with Israel and the land – just as he has entered into a covenant of grace with all humankind and all creation. We understand God only in the context of his covenant of grace, which he made with Israel and the land, and with all people and all creation. This is made clear in the man Jesus Christ, who in fulfilling and confirming God's covenant of grace redeemed not only humankind but also all creation.

Sadly the history of Western thought indicates that far too many theologians have tried to distinguish between God's revealing and saving acts and the Jewish people. They have tried to separate God from his purpose for the world in and through the Jewish people.[23] They have tried to claim that they cling to the monotheistic faith of the Jews and yet, they reject the Jewish people and God's purpose for them. For them, God very largely ceases to be the God of the covenant. They have departed from the historic roots of their faith. Their theology ceases to be earthed in the historic, redemptive acts of God. They find difficulty in taking seriously the fact that the redemptive acts of God in Israel and in the Incarnation, Life, Death, Resurrection and Ascension of Jesus Christ, together with Pentecost actually occurred in space and time.

For them, as for the vast majority of philosophers, it is difficult to do more than pay lip service to the reality of space and time. Their theologies are not really grounded in space and time. They are spiritualised. As a result there enters into their thinking a dualism between the spiritual and the material needs of humankind and ultimately, in their thinking, a separation between soul and body. Their theologising becomes to a greater or less extent some form of humanistic rationalism which is chiefly concerned with general and eternal religious principles.

---

[22]   Jurgen Moltmann, *On Human Dignity*, page 213.
[23]   *Ibid.* page 213.

We escape this dualism between what is spiritual and what is material, this dualism of soul and body, when we hold as inseparable Israel and the land, humankind and all creation.

The God who has revealed himself in Jesus Christ and who has revealed himself in and through Israel is the God who has revealed himself in major historical and redemptive acts. He is the God who in and through his Church and through Israel, continues to confront the nations through historic happenings. He is the Lord of history who in and through the course of history is working out his purpose until he finally fulfils in Christ the renewal of all creation.

A theological consideration of 'God, People and Land' together in unity, carries with it far-reaching political considerations for Israel, for Palestinians and for other people living in the land of Israel, and in the end for all people of whatever country or nationality and wherever they are living on this earth. To seek to understand 'God, Israel and the Land' as belonging together calls from us a kind of holistic understanding to which we in the West are not generally accustomed. It calls for an understanding of Israel in wholeness as a people with great spiritual and political responsibilities. They are a people set apart for God and yet at the same time they belong to this world – they have earthly needs as much as any other human being. We are called to understand their role in the purposes of God both for the spiritual and material redemption of the world.

As a people and as a nation they are called to be a witness to God and his instrument in the outworking of world redemption. We may not deny to them the need to be a nation, else they could not be a representative nation, representing the nations before God, nor yet could they adequately witness to the nations, as nations. Political considerations, as such, are very important, things like justice and reconciliation between Israelis and Palestinians, Israel and the Arab States, Israel and the other nations of the world. However, a note of warning. Even if our theological and political understanding of Israel and the land belong together, and influence one another, our political considerations and our awareness of the need for justice for both Jew and Palestinian, for Jew and Arab, should not have priority over our theological understanding. We must first seek to understand God's mind through the witness of Scripture.

If we fail to take seriously the togetherness of 'God, Israel and the Land', this leads to a divorce between our theological and our political understanding. Our theology tends to become spiritualised in a wrong sense and is no longer earthed. Equally our political understanding, having lost its base in what God is actually doing in history in his world, tends to become a product solely of our own rationalistic thinking. Between our theology and our politics there comes an impossible divide. To state this is not to argue for a political religious party. The attempt to create a religious party arises when there is already a dualism between religion and politics and the religious party is simply an attempt to bridge that dualism. What is required is an attitude of humility, a readiness to listen to what God is saying through his Word and an openness of mind to what God is actually doing in his world through the Jewish people.

The Meaning of the Land

'Land' in this context refers to the land of Israel. It is the land that was promised to Abraham and to his descendants and which in Scripture is frequently called 'His Land'. We are not concerned here with the sensitive and political issue of the size or extent of this land and will not therefore be concerned with boundaries. Nonetheless by 'the land' is meant a particular geographic location on this earth. In the Genesis story of creation, Eden, the Garden of the Lord is 'a concrete terrestrial region'.[24] It is a genuine place on this earth, although it is not possible and not intended from the Biblical story to state its particular geographical location. In something of a parallel way 'the Land of Promise' is a particular concrete area of this earth. Of its location we can be certain, although we are not so certain of its intended geographical size and extent. The Promised Land is the land of Israel. It is not and never could be Scotland, Uganda or anywhere else.

The comparison between Eden, the Garden of the Lord, and His Land, Israel, is important because both can only be understood in the light of God's covenant of grace. By grace, humankind as represented by Adam and Eve is placed in the Garden of the Lord and humankind as represented by Israel is placed in His Land in order to tend it, to cultivate it and bring glory to God. Through sin, human beings are flung out of the Garden and Israel is removed from 'the land'. Removal from the Garden and from His Land is tantamount to a removal, a banishment from the presence of God. It tears at the very nature of human life and existence. It threatens an extinction, which is only thwarted by the gracious promise of forgiveness and return. God's restoration is the history of the covenant of grace, the unfolding of the biblical story, with its climax in Jesus Christ and the ultimate restoration of all things in Christ with his return to this earth.

---

[24]   Karl Barth, *Church Dogmatics* Vol. 3 part 1, page 252.

Creation and Covenant

God's purpose for the land, His Land, can only be understood in the context of the covenant of grace. His 'inner' covenant of grace with Israel and the land, points us to his wider covenant of grace with all humankind and with all creation. The inner covenant has cosmic implications. We can only understand his wider covenant with all creation in the light of his inner covenant with Israel and the land.

His covenant of grace, which is a covenant of redemption, for Israel and for all creation is fulfilled in Jesus Christ.

> He is the image of the invisible God, the first-born over all creation . . . For God was pleased to have all his fullness dwell in him, and through him to reconcile to himself all things, whether things on earth or things in heaven, making peace through his blood, shed on the cross.[25]

The doctrine of creation is a statement of faith. Through faith we affirm the reality and presence of God as Redeemer and Creator. In faith we affirm that he created the world in his freedom and love. In creating the world he did not limit himself in his Being and Reality nor yet in his will. In his freedom and in his love he chose to create the world out of nothing, and in creating it gave it meaning and purpose – a meaning and a purpose which it did not have and could not have in itself. Made out of nothing, it is solely dependent on the will, purpose and love of God who chose to create it and to preserve it for his glory.

Humankind, the last act of creation has a special place within creation. Men and women are also given meaning and purpose through God's creative word and will and love. He wills that we should live within creation to his glory. Our whole life and being is forever embraced and constituted by God's will and love; we depend continually on God's covenant of grace. Even when we are flung out of the garden, and removed from the immediate presence of the Lord, we are preserved along with all creation from the final consequences of our sin; we are preserved, because of God's covenant of grace, that is, by God's promise and purpose of redemption which unfolds in historic Israel and is fulfilled in Christ. God's covenant with humankind embraces the whole of the created world in which we are divinely elected to live.

Men and women are not aliens – we belong as creatures to God's created world. When humankind is blessed, all creation is blessed

---

[25] Colossians 1:15, 19-20.

and when humankind sins creation is spoiled and made to suffer. This is affirmed many times in Scripture, for example:

> Because you have listened to your wife and have eaten of the tree . . . cursed is the ground because of you; in toil you shall eat of it all the days of your life; thorns and thistles it shall bring forth to you . . . In the sweat of your face you shall eat bread.[26]
>
> The earth lies polluted under its inhabitants; for they have transgressed the laws, violated the statutes, broken the everlasting covenant. Therefore a curse devours the earth and its inhabitants suffer for their guilt; . . . for thus it shall be in the midst of the earth.[27]

The reverse also is true. When God chooses to bless his people the earth is blessed. 'The desert will rejoice and flowers will bloom in the wilderness. The desert will sing and shout for joy';[28] and again, 'The Lord says, "I am making a new earth and new heavens. The events of the past will be completely forgotten. Be glad and rejoice for ever in what I create".'[29]

The renewal of all creation is the message of the New Testament, for example in Ephesians 1, Colossians 1, and Revelation.

Humans differ from the rest of the created world and from every other creature in that into us alone God has breathed his spirit. We alone are created 'in the image of God'. At the same time, we remain very much part of the created world formed by God from 'the dust of the ground' and it is to dust that we return. Our physical nature is of the earth. In accord with God's will, we depend on the earth in order to live; we depend on the vegetable and animal order in a way in which they do not depend on us. At the same time, along with the whole of the created order, we are also completely dependent on the continuing creative and redeeming word and will of God. Without that, the universe (with us) would dissolve in non-being.

However, insofar as God has breathed his spirit into us and made us in his image, so we are given a position of special responsibility in the midst of creation. We are chosen to be the friends of God! Chosen to look after the earth, chosen to work so that everything might praise its Maker.

Because we sin, we fail to fulfil this calling. So, our calling and choice are gathered up and fulfilled in the man Jesus Christ. He, the Son of God, entered into our human created order and fulfilled the purpose

---

[26] Genesis 3:17f.
[27] Isaiah 24:5f.
[28] Isaiah 35:1f.
[29] Isaiah 65:17f.; 66:22.

of God for all humankind and for all creation. He redeemed the world and through him there will be a new, or renewed, heaven and earth where redeemed men and women will exercise their true roles, and live to God's glory.

The election of Israel

Israel is chosen in preparation for the coming of Christ and in order to be the instrument of God's redemption of the world. Because of her election she occupies a special place and carries a special responsibility within the world of nations to which she belongs. God has called her from among the nations, set her apart, taught her, and prepared her so that she might be before God a mediator on behalf of the nations. Like other nations she sins. She owes her preservation and salvation to God's covenant of grace that is fulfilled in Christ. In terms of her election however, Israel is called to be a light in darkness mediating the revelation and saving grace of God to the nations. She is God's servant and her hope is united with the hope of the world. Her election forever points beyond itself and points to Jesus Christ the man, whose coming to live on this earth was necessary 'for the perfecting of the earth: for the redemption of its aridity, barrenness and death: for the meaningful fulfilment of its God-given hope: and especially for the realisation of the hope of Israel'.[30]

The Land of Israel

As God's covenant with humankind embraces and includes his covenant with all creation, so his inner covenant with Israel embraces that particular part of the earth, His Land, in which Israel is elected to live and carry through God's purposes for her. God's covenant of grace with Israel is not a covenant solely with the people, in isolation from the land, any more than his covenant with all humankind is isolated from his covenant with the rest of creation on which we depend.

When Israel is removed from the land because of sin, neither her sin nor her removal from the land is able to break God's unalterable covenant of grace. Her removal represents a removal from the immediate presence of the Lord. It destroys, or very largely destroys, her national identity and threatens her very life and existence. As a result, the land is spoiled and ceases to enjoy the blessing of God.

---

[30] Karl Barth, *Church Dogmatics* Vol. 3 Part 1, page 239.

Israel is preserved only by God's covenant and his gracious promise of return to the land where alone his covenant purposes for Israel are able to be carried through. His covenant is not carried out, and was never intended to be carried out, in Israel in perpetual dispersion, as some in the Church today would wish to argue.[31] Israel's sin and dispersal from the land did not belong to God's covenant purposes for Israel, no matter how much his grace overrules and transcends Israel's sin and the sins of us all. His covenant is with both the people and the land of Israel.

God's inclusion of the land within his covenant with Israel was not a temporary measure. Scripture never regards it on the same level as the ceremonial law, as some today would wish to regard it.[32] The ceremonial law was fulfilled in Christ, and replaced, but the land was not replaced nor superseded, any more than the people were replaced or superseded in the purposes of God. The ceremonial law, like the sabbath, was a sign of the covenant, which God made with Abraham, long years before the giving of the law. The land is never regarded as a sign of the covenant. God's covenant with Abraham included the land. God said to Abraham, 'All the land which you see I will give to you and to your descendants for ever'.[33]

God's inner covenant with the people of Israel includes the land of Israel. It is to this land and no other that God called Abraham promising to give it to him and his descendants. It is to this land that God brought the people of Israel after his rescue of them from Egypt. It is in this land that God revealed himself in ways that he did not reveal himself elsewhere. It is to this land that God came in Jesus. As a Jew, Jesus lived and died in this land. In this land he was raised from death and from this land he ascended to heaven. It was in this land that God poured out his Spirit at Pentecost. It was from this people and from this land that we have been given the Scriptures of both the Old and New Testaments. This particular people and this particular land belong peculiarly together.

The word covenant (*berith*) occurs 253 times in the Old Testament and in the New Testament the word (*diatheke*) occurs 20 times. In the majority, and perhaps all, the occasions when the term is used it is impossible clearly to separate people from land. They belong together

---

[31]   Church of Scotland General Assembly Reports, Blue Book, 1985 page 364. Also Gary Bruge, *op. cit.* page 184. He quotes with approval Brueggemann, '*In the Christological logic of Paul, the Land, like the Law, particular and provisional, had become irrelevant*'.

[32]   *Ibid.*

[33]   Genesis 13:15.

in a way in which no other people and land quite belong. The land helped greatly to shape the religious character of the people. It helped shape their forms of worship. That is to say, their God-given worship accommodated itself to, and reflects the particular nature of the country, its climate and its agriculture, as Baruch Maoz has rightly pointed out.[34] It was a cultivated land that produced harvest seasons reflected in their religious feasts. It sustained flocks and herds which were offered in sacrifice, not to mention olive trees and fig trees and vines which figure in God's teaching of Israel through the prophets and figure in the teaching of Jesus.

The words used to express God's revelation of himself are intimately related to the land and cannot without grave injustice and injury to the biblical witness, be dissociated from the land. For example, the land is God's 'holy habitation'.[35] It is from this land that God reigns over all the earth. The Lord reigns from Zion.[36] His salvation is from Zion.[37] It is from his throne in Zion, Jerusalem, that he pours out his blessings on the world. Language with reference to the land has entered deeply into our worship and into our understanding of God and of Jesus Christ. For in God's purposes of grace and salvation the land of Israel together with the people of Israel have influenced, guided and directed our faith – and continue to do so, as we await the new Jerusalem and the return of Christ to Mount Zion.

The inter-relation between people and land is manifest in the way that people and land prosper or suffer together. When Israel obeys the Lord and is blessed the land prospers. The climate and its changing seasons are congenial. The land produces abundant harvests, flocks and herds multiply and the fruit trees are laden with fruit. When Israel sins and is condemned, the land shares the people's condemnation and suffers, the climate is threatening, the land becomes barren, the harvests cease and the flocks and herds disappear and the fruit trees wither. This warning is highly relevant to modern conditions.[38]

---

[34]　*Mishkan*, Issue No 5. 1986, page 59f.

[35]　Exodus 15:13.

[36]　Psalms 2:6; 68:35 etc.

[37]　Psalms 14:7; 46:4-5; 63:2. Also many passages in Isaiah. See Baruch Maoz, *op. cit.*

[38]　There was an article in the 21 March 2003 edition of Ha'aretz about the action of the Israel Lands Administration in pursuing its dispute with a Bedouin community in part of the Negev Hills: 'On March 4, in the early morning hours, two crop-dusting planes flew over the Negev Hills, spraying field crops with a toxin that cause them to wither and die. *(cont. over)*

The affirmation of this inter-relation between people and land runs right through Scripture.

> If you will not obey the voice of the Lord your God or be careful to do all his commandments and his statutes, which I command you this day, then all these curses shall come upon you and overtake you. ...The Lord will send upon you curses, confusion, and frustration, in all that you undertake to do, until you are destroyed and perish quickly, on account of the evil of your doings, because you have forsaken the Lord. . . The Lord will make the rain of your land powder and dust; from heaven it shall come down upon you until you are destroyed.[39]

> I looked at the earth – it was a barren waste . . . I saw that there were no people, even the birds had flown away; the fertile land had become a desert; its cities were in ruins because of the Lord's fierce anger.[40]

Again when Israel returns to the Lord or the Lord chooses to bless, both people and land prosper then:

> The spirit is poured upon us from on high, and the wilderness becomes a fruitful field, and the fruitful field is deemed a forest. Then justice will dwell in the wilderness, and righteousness abide in the fruitful field.[41]

> And I will make for you a covenant on that day with the beast of the field, the birds of the air, and the creeping things of the ground; and I will abolish the bow, the sword, and war from the Land; and I will make you lie down in safety.[42]

This is a theme, which is carried through into the New Testament. It is reflected in the parables of the fig tree.[43] The inter-relation of people and land is clearly manifest in the apocalyptic teaching of Jesus,[44] and in the teaching of the book of Revelation.

It is deeply significant that when Israel as a people was dispersed from the land in AD 70 the land itself suffered. For centuries it lay waste. Most of it became semi-desert and here and there, there were malarial swamps. What was anticipated by the prophets came about.

> Ten people, most of them children, inhaled the substance and required medical treatment. The farmers, whose crops were sprayed, are Bedouin who have been living in the region for generations . . . These farmers are Israeli citizens, who have been living in recognized villages since the establishment of the state.'

[39] Deuteronomy 28:15,20,24.
[40] Jeremiah 4:23,25,26. See also Jeremiah 9:12,13 etc.
[41] Isaiah 32:15,16. See also Isaiah 35.
[42] Hosea 2:18. etc.
[43] See chapter entitled, *Discerning the Signs of the Times.*
[44] Matthew 24:1-14; Mark 13:1-31; Luke 21:5-19.

None of the people who continued to reside in the land, nor the many other peoples who moved into the land, enabled the land to prosper. Only when the Jewish People returned did the land begin to become green again and prosper. No other people could be the instrument of bringing prosperity to the land. Great injustice is done to the teaching of Scripture when we fail to take seriously the inter-relation between the people of Israel and this particular land.

The Teaching of the New Testament

Some scholars have argued that the New Testament, in contrast to the Old, does not mention the land because the promises relating to the land have all been fulfilled in Christ and transcended and therefore the land ceases to have any particular significance in the purposes of God for his world. This chapter has argued for the inseparable relation between the people of Israel and the land and for the intimate relation between the inner covenant with Israel and the land and the wider covenant with all humankind and all creation in the ongoing redeeming purposes of God. In this the theology of the Old and New Testaments are in agreement – there is only one covenant of grace. It is worthy of note, for example, that there are fairly frequent references to the land in the New Testament. What is at stake is the way that we interpret these New Testament passages.

It is deeply significant that Jesus himself was, and is, a Jew who lived in the Land, who accepted, believed and perfectly fulfilled all the promises of the covenant, putting his eternal seal upon them. 'Think not that I have come to abolish the law and the prophets; I have come not to abolish them but to fulfil them. For truly, I say to you, till heaven and earth pass away not an iota, not a dot, will pass from the law until all is accomplished.'[45] Such was his commitment to the land that he did not chose to live and die elsewhere as he could so easily have done ministering to and teaching Jews in dispersion. His exile to Egypt in infancy and his return to live in the land emphasises his identity with Israel in her history and his identity with the land. His death in Jerusalem confirms God's reign from Zion. His resurrection and ascension with the promise that 'this same Jesus will come back in the same way that you have seen him go into heaven',[46] echo probably the earlier promise that the Lord would set his foot on the Mount of Olives.[47] The announcement of the angel to Mary reflects

---

[45] Matthew 5:17,18.
[46] Acts 1:11.

God's covenant with people and land and so also do the songs of Mary, Zechariah and Simeon.

The word 'kingdom' has for Jews, and for Jewish believers today, special reference to God's covenant with the Jewish people, with reference to them as a people, a nation and a state living in the Land. This is something to which only a few Christian scholars have given serious consideration. When the disciples asked Jesus, 'Lord, will you at this time restore the kingdom to Israel?'[48] Jesus did not say that this was an invalid or wrong question, as some scholars suggest that it is. He did not deny the restoration of the kingdom to Israel (and kingdom implies a nation and a state living in the land). What Jesus did say was, 'It is not for you to know the times and seasons which the Father has fixed by his own authority'.[49]

There is a similar reference in Luke[50] when Jesus, apparently anticipating either the return of the kingdom to Israel or the preparation for that return, said, 'Jerusalem will be trodden down by the Gentiles, *until* the times of the Gentiles are fulfilled'. His use of the word 'until' refers to a specific time in history.

There are also references to the land in some of Jesus' parables, like those of the fig tree and the vineyard. Surely also it is right to interpret the parable of the sower in the light of its Old Testament background with its four kinds of people: the faithful, the wider unfaithful household of Israel, the stranger within the gate who is not wholly committed to the God of Israel, and the unbelieving Gentile living outside the land. In like manner we should interpret the parable of the vine[51] and the olive tree[52] as having a physical, material dimension as well as a spiritual, and likewise Paul's anticipation of Israel's fullness.[53]

One of the principles of interpreting the Bible, which we have tried to demonstrate, is that the New Testament accepts the teaching of the Old Testament and confirms it.[54] Some things are transcended and replaced – but these are specifically mentioned, for example the laws of worship and the ceremonial law. Nowhere in the New Testament

---

47   Zechariah 14:14. See James B. Walker, *Israel, Covenant and Land*, Handsel Press, page 7.
48   Acts 1:6.
49   Acts 1:7.
50   Luke 21:24.
51   John 15:1-17.
52   Romans 11:16f.
53   See chapter entitled, *Israel in the Light of Romans 9-11*.
54   For example, consider how Jesus affirmed the Old Testament in full in Matthew 5:17-20. He then went on to explore the inner meaning of the

is it ever said or suggested that God's promises concerning Israel and the land are transcended or set aside. God's covenant of grace both with Israel, land and people and with all creation is unalterable.

Israel and Faith in God

Scholars have often objected that comparatively few Jews accept Jesus as Messiah. How then can God have a continuing purpose for Israel or be behind the creation of the state of Israel?

God's covenant is a covenant of grace. Jew and Gentile alike are only saved by God's grace. In the many passages of Scripture, which speak of God restoring his people to the land, his restoration of them is due entirely to his mercy and compassion. It is not dependent on Israel's repentance. The following passage from Micah is typical, 'The Lord says, "I am planning to bring disaster on you and you will not be able to escape it".'[55] Then after proclaiming the most fearful disasters at the hand of God, suddenly, and without warning the prophet as the messenger of God breaks in, 'I will surely gather all of you, O Jacob, I will gather the remnant of Israel; I will set them together like sheep in a fold, like a flock in its pasture, a noisy multitude … their king will pass on before them, the lord at their head'.[56]

The people return to the land because the Lord is gracious and merciful, not because they have repented or are righteous. God keeps his covenant. It is there in the land after their restoration that they turn to the Lord in repentance, in faith and thanksgiving. There are of course exceptions to this but this reflects the general pattern of their return to the Land. It is clearly the message of Zechariah 12 and Ezekiel 36 and 39. The land deeply affects Jewish understanding and faith in God.

> Come, let us go up to the mountain of the Lord, to the house of the God of Jacob; that he may teach us his ways and we may walk in his paths. For out of Zion shall go forth the law and the Word of the Lord from Jerusalem.[57]

Israel, for her faith, is more deeply dependent on the land than are any other people on the land, or country, in which they live.

Old Testament in the rest of the chapter, but without denying the importance of the outer meaning. Applied to the land of Israel, it means that we should seek the inner meaning of the land for all lands, but without denying the importance of the land of Israel.

[55] Micah 2:3.
[56] Micah 2:12,13.
[57] Micah 4:2.

People and Land, their meaning for world history today

The restoration of the Jewish people to the land and the creation of the state of Israel have placed Israel once again at the heart of world affairs. Names and countries, which were prominent in the Bible, have been resurrected. The world is forcibly reminded of Israel's past. From the Christian point of view this is surely deeply significant. Israel is mentioned in the Press and daily news, if only adversely, almost every day. The peace and welfare of this tiny state affects the largest nations. Events leading up to the Yom Kippur war in 1973, the threat of the Arab States that any country which helped Israel would receive no oil, precipitated a world economic crisis, which has affected literally every country in the world. Today, conflicts between Jews and Palestinians have escalated and threaten the peace of the world. War between Israel and her Middle East neighbours could envelop the world. All that would not be the case if the land were not the focus of world attention.

The creation of the State of Israel has deeply affected Islam. It has touched a religious nerve. The Church, entrusted with the responsibility of proclaiming the Gospel to all the world, has found Islam the hardest field in which to work. Over the years it has made little headway among followers of the Prophet. However, since the creation of the State of Israel, it is a remarkable fact that, despite all the wars and ensuing violence, with increased opposition to Israel and the West, there have been more conversions to Christ from Islam than there have been in all the earlier years.[58]

Likewise, the creation of the State of Israel has in a remarkable way affected the psyche of Jews and we have seen many Jews, in Israel, in the USA, in Russia and in other countries, come to faith in Jesus Christ.

It is also true of the other nations of the world, that the creation of the state of Israel has been most disturbing. God is surely calling the nations to account and testing them. Their attitude to Israel and the land largely reflects their attitude to God and his sovereign purposes of redemption for the world. The prophet Zechariah said, 'I am going to make Jerusalem a cup that sends all the surrounding

---

[58] Jeremiah 51:20.

peoples reeling'.[59] By the 'surrounding peoples', Zechariah is really speaking of all the nations of the earth.[60] In all of this we can see the remarkable way in which God is using Israel as his servant. Not only the people but also the land is embraced by God's purpose to humble and redeem the nations of the world.

God's covenant with all creation and the hope of the world

All that happens to Israel and all God's dealings with her are not only for Israel's own sake. They are also for the sake of humankind and the world. God is determined to rescue us and all creation. This is the glorious revelation that is made known in Jesus Christ. All history therefore moves toward that day when Christ will come, God will usher in a new heaven and earth. Men and women cleansed, forgiven and renewed will live with him sharing in the joy of his immediate presence and living to his glory. The resurrection of Jesus is a sign and pledge that all who believe will be resurrected. In a somewhat similar way the deliverance of this people from the holocaust and their restoration to the land is a further pledge of the new creation.

Israel and the nations are still sinful. Justice and reconciliation is required and demanded by God between Jews and Palestinians as between all other peoples. Our constant prayer should be that all come to share the one faith in Jesus Christ. Nonetheless, God's present care and concern for 'His People and Land' is a sign and proof of his care and concern for all peoples and all lands. The renewal and restoration of His Land is a sign and confirmation of his coming renewal of all the earth, even as the conflict within it is a reminder of the current 'groaning' of creation.[61] Under God the hope of 'Israel, People and Land', is forever related to the hope of the whole universe.

---

[59] Zechariah 12:2.
[60] Zechariah 12:3.
[61] Romans 8:18-25.

PART TWO

Chapter Four

UNDERSTANDING ANTI-SEMITISM

The nature and the meaning of anti-Semitism are subjects of fierce debate, now more than ever. The various allegiances of our politicians, the moral maze presented by the crisis in the Middle East, and questions about Zionism and anti-Zionism, are in danger of confusing the matter. Anti-Semitism is, after all, a powerful and pervasive force that has exercised a destructive influence over generations of people throughout the centuries. Christians themselves have often failed to recognise it. Before trying to explore the reasons for anti-Semitism, we should consider three important preliminary observations.

First, evil is irrational and anti-Semitism, which is evil, is also irrational. Those who are influenced by anti-Semitism are not necessarily aware of the reasons for their prejudice against and anger towards the Jewish people. It cannot be understood on the human plane alone, or scientifically analysed, or explained as something simply natural, although many have tried to do so. Anti-Semitism is demonic. In order to discern it and grasp its significance, our eyes need to be opened and our minds enlightened by the Spirit of God. Without God's Word and without faith, anti-Semitism remains hidden like a cancer in the body. When it goes undiagnosed it is able to flourish and exercise an evil influence over society and over nations. It grows more and more powerful until it breaks out with fearful onslaughts directed against Israel, God's elect people.

Second, anti-Semitism can take hold of us all, Gentiles and Jews, without exception. We should not assume that it is the preserve of the far right or of extremist Islam. Christians recognise that in drawing us into fellowship with God, the Holy Spirit causes us to 'put off' the old life[1] and to engage in a new life following Jesus Christ. Yet the old life continues to exercise some sway over us. As Paul says in his letter to the believers in Rome, 'I do not do the good I want to do; instead I do the evil I don't want to do'.[2] Or, in William Barclay's words, we are

---

[1]   Ephesians 4:22.
[2]   Romans 7:19.

each a 'walking civil war'.[3] In the same way that none of us can wholly escape the influence of our old lives, and continue to rebel against God in various ways, so anti-Semitism can persist in the attitudes and behaviour of Christians, and it often does.

Third, whilst anti-Semitism affects both Gentiles and Jews, it takes a different form for each. Amongst Gentiles we have seen it expressed as anger and violence against Jews and all things Jewish. It has resulted in the immense persecution of Jews throughout history, not least by the Church. It gave rise to the pogroms of Czarist Russia and the Holocaust of the Nazi era, which was explicitly an attempt to obliterate everything Jewish. Amongst Jews, anti-Semitism takes the form of assimilation. That is to say, it is the attempt by Jews to identify with a particular Gentile nation or people to the extent that they deny their Jewishness and deny that the Jews are God's 'covenant people'. Anti-Semitism amongst Jews has also been known to take a more overt form. It is one of the sad facts of history that Jews have sometimes suffered at the hands of fellow Jews, as in Soviet Russia after the 1917 Communist revolution.

Anti-Semitism is as strong today as ever it was last century.

In France there have been hundreds of anti-Semitic incidents in recent years. In Lyon, a car was rammed into a synagogue and set on fire. In Montpellier, the Jewish religious centre was firebombed; so were synagogues in Strasbourg and Marseille; so was a Jewish school in Creteil. A Jewish sports club in Toulouse was attacked with Molotov cocktails, and on the statue of Alfred Dreyfus in Paris, the words 'Dirty Jew' were painted. According to the police, metropolitan Paris has seen 10 to 12 anti-Jewish incidents per day since Easter 2002. Walls in Jewish neighbourhoods have been defaced with slogans proclaiming 'Jews to the gas chambers' and 'Death to the Jews'.

In Belgium, thugs beat up the chief rabbi, kicking him in the face and calling him 'a dirty Jew'. Two synagogues in Brussels were firebombed; a third, in Charleroi, was sprayed with automatic weapon fire.

In Germany, a rabbinical student was beaten up in downtown Berlin and a grenade was thrown into a Jewish cemetery. Thousands of neo-Nazis held a rally, marching near a synagogue on the Jewish Sabbath.

In Greece, Jewish graves were desecrated in Loannina and vandals hurled paint at the Holocaust memorial in Salonica.

In Holland, an anti-Israel demonstration featured swastikas, photos of Hitler, and chants of 'Sieg Heil' and 'Jews into the sea'.

---

3   William Barclay, *The Letter to the Romans*, Saint Andrew Press, Edinburgh, page 101.

In Russia, in the eighties and nineties, anti-Semitism declined after *Perestroika*. But whenever the economy turns down, there is a tendency for Jews to be blamed for Russia's economic problems. Scapegoating also happens in other Eastern European countries; in Hungary, Jews along with Gypsies are blamed although it is a delicate and controversial area as in public anti-Semitism is not supposed to exist. In Ukraine, skinheads attacked Jewish worshippers and smashed the windows of Kiev's main synagogue. Ukrainian police denied that the attack was anti-Jewish. In Slovakia, the Jewish cemetery of Kosice was invaded and 135 tombstones destroyed.

On a bus in London a young Jewish Yeshiva student was standing reading his *siddur* (prayer book) and was stabbed by a group of skinheads 27 times.

'Anti-Semitism', wrote a columnist in The Spectator, 'has become respectable . . . at London dinner tables.' She quoted one member of the House of Lords: 'The Jews have been asking for it and now, thank God, we can say what we think at last.' The London Times of 4 February 2002, carried a front-page article under the title '*Britain's sheikh of race hate calls for killing of Jews and infidels: Police fail to act against cleric*'. According to the article Shaikh Abdullah el-Faisal, a 38 year old Jamaican, has been touring the country urging followers to kill Jews. 'When a voice asks: "Should we hate Jews and when we see them on the street, should we beat them up?" Shaikh Faisal replies: "You have no choice but to hate them. How do you fight the Jews? You kill the Jews".' He was later arrested by the police and charged that he 'on or before February 18, 2002, within the jurisdiction of the Central Criminal Court encouraged others to murder persons unknown contrary to section 4 of the Offences against the Person Act 1861'.[4]

Israel is treated as a second class nation by the United Nations, judging by its participation in UN Committees. In 2002 no Israeli candidates were elected to the UN Human Rights Committee, the Committee on Elimination of Discrimination against Women, the Racial Discrimination Committee. Early in 2003 the only remaining elected Israeli on a UN body was Mayer Gabay, vice-chair of the UN Administrative Tribunal. By contrast, Egypt has members on all six of the UN human rights treaty bodies.

Israel is also the only UN member state denied membership in any of the UN's five regional groups, which elect UN bodies in Geneva. It is the sole nation prevented from winning a seat on the Security

---

4   *The Times*, Thursday 21 Feb 2002.

Council. So: Algeria, Bahrain, China, Cuba, Libya, Saudi Arabia, Sudan, Syria and Zimbabwe pass judgment on human rights, while Israel - a democracy - is excluded![5] The UN Commission on Human Rights examines alleged Israeli violations of human rights under a special agenda item during its annual meeting; the remaining 189 states are collectively examined under another agenda item.

1 Anti-Semitism is a rejection of God and his plans for our salvation

It has to be said clearly that we cannot account for anti-Semitism by laying the blame at the feet of the Jews themselves. Anti-Semitism does not really have its explanation in their practices or behaviour, but rather is a prejudice that runs deep in all traditions and quarters, and stems fundamentally from the way that humankind relates to God.

All nations, all peoples, have their faults, and whilst history shows that over a period of time we often forgive and forget, the Jews see their errors continuously dwelt upon and exaggerated. The Jews are distinctive in the hostility they attract. Similarly, whilst history is full of examples of savagery and, even in very recent times, acts of genocide, the extent and the nature of the persecution of the Jewish people means that it has to be placed in its own category. Anti-Semitism has manifested itself throughout the three-and-a-half thousand years of Jewish history. Eruptions of anti-Semitism have not come from a single antagonistic nation, nor are they limited to one place in the world. They have occurred in almost every nation, at the hands of almost every people in whose midst the Jews have lived.[6]

The Bible explains in many places that Israel is a people whom God singled out amongst all the nations of the world.[7] It teaches that God set them apart as a people so that through them he could provide redemption to the world. History has testified to this 'apartness', and it continues to be seen in the present day. In separating them out in this way, God nominated Israel to be a representative people. That is to say, God chose them to stand for all peoples and all nations before God. At the same time, God selected Israel so that through his peculiar identification with them, by being present in their midst, and through

---

[5] Taken from an article in Canada's National Post of 18 Feb 2003, written by Anne Bayefsky, international lawyer and professor of political science at York University, Toronto.

[6] The Jews claim that the only country in Europe where Jews have not been persecuted is Scotland.

[7] Numbers 23:9.

all that he said to them and did for them, they could represent God to the world. The very fact that, in terms of God's calling, Israel represents the nations to God and God to the nations, means that in them we encounter something deep, something beyond us, but something very real. We encounter God.

As human beings, even though we may not understand the nature of this encounter, we are nonetheless aware of it. It touches our inner being. We feel threatened by it, and challenged, and frequently withdraw in irritation or anger. Such resentment, even though not recognised as such, is a resentment of God, of God's election of Israel, of the way in which God deals with Israel, and of the way in which God deals with us.

In ourselves, because of sin, we do not want God, nor do we want his offer of salvation through the Jews.[8] We are at odds with God. When our rebellion takes the form of anti-Semitism, we attempt to deny God and to spurn the means whereby he offers his salvation. This fact is referred to again and again in the book of Psalms. For example, the Psalmist says:

> See how your enemies are astir,
> how your foes rear their heads.
> With cunning they conspire against your people;
> they plot against those you cherish.
> 'Come' they say, 'let us destroy them as a nation,
> that the name of Israel be remembered no more'.[9]

Here, the enemies of God are the enemies of Israel, and the enemies of Israel are the enemies of God. In seeking to destroy Israel, these enemies are trying to get rid of any reminder of God. Again, the Psalmist says, 'for your sake we face death all day long; we are considered as sheep to be slaughtered'.[10] We are able to see here something of the intimate relationship between the way the nations relate to God and the way they relate to Israel. In another Psalm he says:

> For I endure scorn for your sake,
> and shame covers my face.
> I am a stranger to my brothers,
> An alien to my own mother's sons;
> For zeal for your house consumes me,
> And the insults of those who insult you fall on me.[11]

---

8 John 4:22.
9 Psalm 83:2-4.
10 Psalm 44:22.
11 Psalm 69:7-9. See also Psalms 79:12,13; 88:15-18; 129.

2 The causes of anti-Semitism

In affirming that anti-Semitism is, at heart, a rejection of God and of his offer of salvation through the Jewish people, it is important that we go further and identify the causes of this destructive anger, this revolt from within sinful human nature. These causes can be located in a number of core resentments;[12] a resentment of the Jews as proof of the existence of God; a resentment of the way in which they depict our sinful nature; a resentment of the way the Jews testify to our dependence on God's grace; and a resentment of the way in which God has prospered and privileged the Jews at certain times.

(a) The Jews are evidence of God's existence

To start with, in ourselves we want to be like God. We want to be equal with God – to be the lord of creation and the master of our own destiny. This is how sin is defined and portrayed in the story of Adam and Eve in the Garden of Eden ('when you eat of [the tree] your eyes will be opened, and you will be like God',[13] says the serpent to Eve). Sin is depicted as the refusal to acknowledge that only God is God.

Men and women are simply creatures within God's creation, and the very existence of the Jewish people reminds us exactly who God is. Their presence draws our attention to their history, recalling to us the way in which God has set them apart, and the way in which he has made himself known to them – and through them to the world – as the living and true God. Their presence reminds us that we are not God. We are creatures and there is a living Lord and God who holds us, together with the whole world, and our destinies, in his hands. It is this truth that in our human nature we resist: we want to be free from the visible reminder of God, in the form of the Jewish people, in the vain hope that if we are rid of them, we will be masters of our own fate.

This 'reasoning', if we can call it that, is illustrated in many of the speeches and writings of Marxist Russia and Nazi Germany. Famously, when Frederick the Great of Germany asked Zimmerman, his private physician, whether he could give one proof for the existence of God, Zimmerman replied that the Jews constituted that proof. Neither Marxism nor Fascism can tolerate the existence of God, or even the

---

12 Karl Barth designates two causes for anti-Semitism. *Church Dogmatics*, Vol. 3.3, page 220ff.
13 Genesis 3:5.

reminder of God's existence, for if God exists, then neither Marxists nor Fascists are masters of their own fate. As soon as Communism took control of a country in the wake of the Second World War, atheistic propaganda was set in motion to try to persuade people that God does not exist. To become a member of the Communist Party a person was required to renounce all religion, and it is the same today.

When Nazi Germany embarked on what they called 'the Final Solution', their intention to annihilate the Jews was effectively an attempt to remove a manifest reminder of God's existence (although it was disguised through the fantasy of a master race). As a result of their core atheism, Marxist Communism and Fascism gave rise to the most destructive outbursts of anti-Semitism in history.

In 1960, after Adolph Eichman was apprehended by the Jews in Argentina and smuggled out to Israel, the BBC interviewed people who had met him in person. One of the interviewees had been the British ambassador to Austria shortly before Austria was invaded by Germany in 1939. He was asked what he remembered about his encounter with Eichman. In his reply to the BBC reporter, he recounted how one day Eichman had come into his office. A Bible was lying on the ambassador's desk. At the sight of the Bible, Eichman immediately became very angry. He asked the ambassador whether he believed in God. In learning that he did, Eichman said that he was more powerful than God and that he could prove it. Outside, he said, was a trainload of Jews. He proclaimed that with one word from him, everyone in the train would be sent to their death. Eichman's outburst reveals why the Nazis pursued the extermination of the Jews. They did not want to worship God. They wanted to worship man – superman.

Nations and governments often act as if God were distant and not concerned with how they behave. The Jews, by their presence, by their sacred heritage and traditions, and by the extraordinary things that have happened to them during their long history (not least in our generation with their return to the Promised Land), remind the nations that God is the God of history. We encounter him in the drama of everyday affairs, and as nations we are required to give account to him.

Against this too sinful human nature rebels – in our governments, institutions and nations. We wish we were not accountable to God. The nations have closed their eyes to what God has done and is doing in history. They are 'in denial' and vent the associated frustration and anger against Israel, against this covenant people, against God's servant for the saving of the nations.

(b) The Jews are evidence of our sinful nature

It belongs to the peculiar mystery of God's election of Israel, that in the Jews we can observe a perfect likeness of the general human condition: everything about man, who he is and what he is, is portrayed clearly in them. This is one of the ways in which God has used them as a representative people. Karl Barth describes the way in which the Jews provide the peoples of the world with a reflection to study: in them we see ourselves as we really are before God.

> The Jew is the man from whom the cloak has been torn off. The Jew stands before us as that which radically we all are. In the Jew is revealed the primary revolt, the unbelief, the disobedience in which we all are engaged. In this sense the Jew is the most human of all men. And that is why he is not pleasing to us. That is why we want him away... that is why we are so critical of the Jews. That is why we make them out to be worse than they really are... that is why we ascribe to the Jews every possible crime . . . Our annoyance is not really with the Jew himself. It is with the Jew because and to the extent that the Jew is a mirror in which we immediately recognise ourselves, in which all the nations recognise themselves as they are before the Judgement Seat of God. That is why we can never forgive the Jew. That is why we think we have to heap hatred and contempt upon the stranger. And obviously it is because the Jews are this mirror that they are there. The Divine Providence has arranged it.[14]

More than that, the Jews are a mirror which magnifies both our good features and our blemishes. For our benefit, everything in them is 'writ large'. In the Jewish people we see the very best and the very noblest of the human race, and we see faith in God at its highest level. In them we also see the worst of the human race, and it is the sight of how bad we all are that angers us. In the sin described and denounced by the Jewish prophets, we are able to recognise everyone's rebellion. Whether it is in the ancient decision of Israel to elect their own king in place of the Lord God their king, or in their desire, now as then, to control their own security, to take control of their own destiny, to assume for themselves the authority that belongs only to God, we are able to see the attitude of all governments and all nations. We see our human nature as we stand in relation to God. In short, we see ourselves, and we do not like what we see.

That is not to say that the mere presence of the Jews is in itself enough to impact us with these spiritual truths: we depend on the Word of God to enlighten our minds and to interpret the state we are

---

14   Karl Barth, *op. cit.* pages 221ff.

in. Even so, the nations of the world are in some way deeply aware of the disturbing example and the challenging testimony of the Jews in their midst. Something is being said to them, which they do not wish to hear. As they lash out against the Jews in response to this, they declare the reality of their confrontation with God and make manifest their anger and rebellion against him.

(c) The Jews are evidence of our dependence on God's grace

The presence of the Jewish people reminds the nations of the world, and each of us, that we live from day to day only by the grace of God – his unmerited favour. In his grace God has given us life; and we continue to live through his continuing grace. We have no other genuine support or security.

Plainly, Israel has only ever existed by the grace of God. That is one of the striking messages of the Old Testament. Only by the grace of God have the Jewish people survived through the centuries, through countless persecutions, pogroms and the Holocaust. Only by the grace of God has Israel been restored as a nation and allowed to live in the Promised Land. Only by the grace of God has Israel survived successive wars when fighting armies more numerous and more highly equipped than her own, and only by the grace of God will Israel survive the present crisis in which she is caught up in the Middle East; it will not be by her own efforts nor by the intervention of other powerful nations.

Even though modern-day Israel might not seem to accept it, and even though she does not trust in God as she should, her remarkable existence is a living reminder to us that we can only survive because God provides for us and sustains us. Our intolerance of the Jews shows that we do not like that idea. We believe deeply and invest heavily in our own earthly securities. We do not like to be reminded of our own ultimate powerlessness, or of the fundamental insecurities that persist in spite of our wealth, our sophistication and our achievements. We do not want to have to accept that our only true security in life is to be found in God's grace.

Israel makes us consider our future hope and our ultimate security. In terms of population one of the smallest nations on earth, persecuted through the long years of her exile, driven constantly from one country to another, Israel has demonstrated that we have no continuing city except by the grace of God. All of her literature, that of the Scriptures of the Old and New Testaments, carries that prophetic message. As the Jews in their dispersion have sought to return to Jerusalem as their eternal city, so we are taught to seek the eternal city whose builder and maker is

God. We look forward to a renewed heaven and earth that will be brought about by God. The hope of Israel is the hope of the world.

The person who wants to abandon God, to become his or her own god, is infuriated by the reminder that his or her only hope is in God. S/he cannot stand the idea and seeks time and again to get rid of the Jew, to confound God's promise of preservation, and to prove in turn that their own security and their own future are dependent on themselves alone. S/he sees in the supernatural perseverance of the Jew, an affront to his or her constructed security and hope, whether that is located in the Third Reich, planned to last for a thousand years, or in Marxism, which looked forward to a material kingdom without God which would embrace the world, or in the prospect of the whole world united under Islam. By the grace of God, the Jews continue to exist, and will continue to exist until the end of this world.[15] Their survival refutes the empty promises of our own schemes for salvation. It stands as evidence of God's grace and mercy, and a reminder that the hope of the world and its redemption lie in God alone.

(d) The success of the Jews

A further cause of anti-Semitism, and one which is perhaps more accessible because of its worldliness, is the resentment of the immense contribution that Judaism and the Jewish people have made to almost every area of modern life. Rather than responding in gratitude to God for the extraordinary impact the Jews have made on the worlds of science, the arts, politics and law, the nations are given to responding in envy and anger: consider Nazi Germany's public burning of Einstein's books.

It has been demonstrated by Prof. A.D. Ritchie in his lectures to students, by Prof. T.F. Torrance and by Einstein in their many books and by other Jews that modern science could not have developed without the contribution of the Jewish people. Their contribution to our modern world is a part-fulfilment of God's promise to Abraham: 'I will bless you; I will make your name great, and you will be a blessing . . . and all peoples on earth will be blessed through you'.[16]

In our alienation from God, we tend jealously to gather glory to ourselves, insisting that in our own strength and wisdom we can accomplish all things. We bitterly resent the fact that modern science and technology is so dependent on the contribution of Judaism because

[15] Jeremiah 31:35,36. Cp. Jeremiah 33:19-26.
[16] Genesis 12:2,3.

we resent the way in which the Jews testify to our reliance on the grace of God. Needless to say, Jewish people are as likely as anyone to let human pride overtake godly humility, but this does not negate the fact that their peculiar and wide-ranging contribution is a divine gift. It is a reminder that without God's involvement in this world we would be helpless.

The parts played by individual Jews have been hugely influential. Almost every major scientific advance in the twentieth century was either made by a Jew or was dependent on a Jewish contribution. Similar patterns can be recognised in the fields of education, psychology, economics and politics, as well as in music and entertainment. The greatest influences on everyday life in the twentieth century were exercised by Freud, Einstein and Marx. To these three we could add a host of others: Niels Bohr, who laid the foundation of modern atomic science; Levi-Civita, who paved the way for Einstein; Heinrich Herz, who pioneered in research on electromagnetic waves; James Frank and Gustav Hertz, who helped to develop the quantum theory and nuclear physics; J. Robert Oppenheimer, Edward Teller and Lise Meitner. We could also add Ferdinand Cohn, father of bacteriology; Waldemar Haffkine, pioneer of inoculation against cholera and bubonic plague; August von Wasserman who determined the syphilis test; Otto Warburg, the cancer researcher; Ernst Boris Chain, co-discoverer of penicillin; Selman Waxman, discoverer of streptomycin; and Jonas Salk and Albert Sebin, initiators of the anti-polio vaccine. Although numbering less than half a per cent of the world's population, Jews have been awarded a truly astonishing number of Nobel prizes, of which they hold proportionately more than any other nation, particularly in the fields of physics, chemistry and medicine.

In politics, commerce and society too, the nations often appear jealous of Jewish people, resenting the positions that they hold and their influence. The Jews constitute a minority in every society outside of Israel, yet in the UK and the USA, for example, an astonishing number are elected to Parliament and to the Senate. They occupy teaching posts in universities and colleges, serve in senior posts in law, science and medicine, and occupy top management positions in commercial enterprises. They do so out of all proportion to their numbers, and this evokes resentment now as it did in parts of Russia following the revolution of 1917 and in Germany in the 1930s, where it caused anti-Jewish riots and anticipated the Holocaust.

It is fair to say that the nations owe a unique debt to the Jews, although they are reluctant to acknowledge it and have often made every effort to stem the flow of Jewish success and excellence. At various times Jews have had fearful restrictions imposed upon them. In Czarist Russia, for example, Jews were not even allowed to proceed to advanced education. However, once restrictions against them were lifted and they were allowed to advance, as they were for a period after the Communist revolution in 1917, they made rapid progress.

This is seen time and again as Jewish people have outstripped their contemporaries in every area of commerce and the professional sciences, and people resent this bitterly. The godless person does not wish to recognise it, and in his or her jealousy will invent all sorts of spurious reasons why it should not be so. The Jews will be accused falsely, and will be blamed for conspiring to undermine and to hold back the rest of society. In Russia today, public voices can be heard blaming Jews for the downturn in the country's economy. What we find hard to acknowledge is that the extraordinary accomplishments of the Jews are intimately related to the hand of God. The Jews are party to a covenant in which God promises to bless the world through them.

3 Anti-Zionism is anti-Semitism

As we are seeking to clarify and comprehend our attitudes towards Israel, we need to be clear that anti-Zionism is anti-Semitism. Many people would initially disagree with this, claiming that they are anti-Zionist but are not against Jewish people, but to Jewish ears such a claim is impossible.

Zionism is not an abstract philosophy. It is the claim and the conviction on the part of Jews that they have the right to live in a country of their own, that is, in Israel. To be anti-Zionist, then, means to deny the Jewish people that right, and that is the stuff of anti-Semitism.

To agree with these principles of Zionism does not mean approving everything that the government of Israel says or does. By the same token, who would agree with everything that the governments of the UK or USA say and do? It is possible to be a loyal citizen of the UK or USA and yet disagree strongly with some of the policies of the governments of Prime Minister Brown or President Bush. Similarly, disagreement with certain policies of the Israeli government does not necessarily constitute anti-Zionism.

Nevertheless, when the United Nations declared that Zionism was racist, it was yielding to anti-Semitic pressure and was itself expressing anti-Semitic sentiments. Likewise, comparisons of the State of Israel to South Africa in the days of the apartheid are informed by anti-

Semitism. Although Israel is a Jewish state, Arab citizens are able to vote, are represented in government, are equal with Jewish citizens in law, and there is an Arab judge. That was certainly not the case with black South Africans living under apartheid, nor is it the case with Jews living in Islamic countries today. Since the Palestinian Authority was given control of areas of land in Palestine, several thousands of Arabs have applied for Israeli citizenship, believing that they have greater freedom in Israel than those living under PA control.

The strongest expressions of anti-Semitism today are voiced by Islamic fundamentalists. The Palestine National Charter (the 1968 Covenant of the Palestine Liberation Organisation) and the Hamas Covenant (the 1988 Covenant of the Islamic Resistance Movement – Palestine) call for the liberation of all Palestine and therefore the elimination of the state of Israel. According to the Preamble of the Hamas Covenant, 'Israel will exist and will continue to exist until Islam will obliterate it, just as it obliterated others before it.' Spokesmen for the Arab League and innumerable mullahs have repeatedly called for Israel's destruction. However, many people in Western society, in so far as they regret the establishment of the state of Israel or regret its continuance, are also effectively anti-Semitic.

Whether it is Islamic anti-Zionism or the kind of anti-Zionism more often expressed in the West, there is an urgent need to take to heart the words of Martin Luther King. He said, 'Let my words echo in the depths of your soul: You declare, my friend, that you do not hate the Jews, you are merely "anti-Zionist". And I say, let the truth ring forth from the high mountain tops let it echo through the valleys of God's green earth: When people criticise Zionism, they mean Jews – this is God's truth.'[17] Anti-Semitism can be subtle and it can take many different forms. We need to be constantly on our guard against it, not only in society at large, but also in the Church where, over the years, it has exercised a powerful influence. As Barth wrote in his *Christian Dogmatics*, 'Many of the best men in the Confessional Church still close their eyes to the insight that the Jewish problem [has] today become a question of faith... The question of the Jews is the question of Christ. Anti-Semitism is the sin against the Holy Ghost'.

---

[17] From M.L.King Jr., Letter to an Anti-Zionist Friend, Saturday Review XLV11, August 1967, page 76. Reprinted in M.L.King Jr., *This I believe: Selections from the Writings of Dr Martin Luther King Jr.* New York, 1971, pages 234-235. Quoted by Richard Gibson in the Herald. Christian Witness to Israel, Spring 2002, page15.

Chapter Five

IS THE NEW TESTAMENT THE SOURCE OF ANTI-SEMITISM?

In developing a right understanding of anti-Semitism, and of the means with which it can be overcome, it is necessary to address the charge that the New Testament is in fact responsible for historical animosity towards to the Jews and contemporary prejudice against Israel. Writing in 1978, in an article entitled 'Facing the Truth', Eliezer Berkovitz sums up the grave accusation:

> Christianity's New Testament has been the most dangerous anti-Semitic tract in history. Its hatred-charged diatribes against the Pharisees and the Jews have poisoned the hearts and minds of millions and millions of Christians for almost two millennia. No matter what the deeper theological meaning of the hate passages against the Jews might be, in the history of the Jewish people the New Testament lent its support to oppression, persecution and mass murder of an intensity and duration that were unparalleled in the entire history of man's degradation. Without Christianity's New Testament, Hitler's *Mein Kampf* could never been written.[1]

Similar sentiments are often voiced in Jewish circles. They are bound to create a desire amongst Jews to discredit Christianity itself, and to view the New Testament with fear and suspicion. The slander of the New Testament is troubling for a special reason: the best weapon against anti-Semitism is not the downgrading of the New Testament but a sound understanding of the heart of its message about the purpose and meaning of the death of Jesus. A fair reading of the New Testament, together with a commitment to Jesus as Messiah, Saviour and Lord, far from leading to anti-Semitism, leads Christians (by Jesus' own example) to a love and respect for Jewish people whether or not they believe in Christ. The Church's appalling record of anti-Semitism comes from a misreading or, more accurately, an abuse of the New Testament, driven not by the text, not by the word, but by a deeper bigotry towards the Jews.

---

[1] 'Facing the Truth', Judaism 27, 1978, p 325.

Although the New Testament has certainly been greatly misused by the enemies of the Jews, it cannot, in principle, be the only source of anti-Semitism. Prejudice against and persecution of the Jewish people is independent of misappropriated passages of the Gospels. The subject of the book of Esther (which was written a long time before the New Testament) is the attempted murder of all Jews because their 'customs are different from those of all other people' (Esther 3:8). Accounts of other pagan anti-Semitism have also been well documented.[2]

Similarly, Islamic anti-Semitism draws not upon any Christian texts, but upon the Qur'an itself, with its references to the permanent misery and dispersion of the Jewish people as a punishment from God. Whilst Jewish writers often compare the treatment of their people by Muslims in the Middle Ages favourably alongside their treatment by Christendom, the re-establishment of the State of Israel in modern times has re-awakened an inherent anti-Semitism in Islam. The Qur'an teaches that the Jews will live in dispersion forever; the thrust of the New Testament, in harmony with the Hebrew scriptures, is that Jewish exile would only ever be temporary.

Neither pagan nor Islamic anti-Semitism can be blamed on the New Testament. Rather, like anti-Semitism paraded under the banner of Christianity, they are a result of humanity's pride in the face of God's election of Israel as the gateway of salvation into the world. This was recognised in the Old Testament hundreds of years before the New Testament was set down:

> If we had forgotten the name of our God
> or spread out our hands to a foreign god,
> would not God have discovered it,
> since he knows the secrets of our heart?
> Yet for your sake we face death all day long;
> we are considered as sheep to be slaughtered.[3]

Now, here is the charge. Does the New Testament not place the blame for the death of Jesus supremely upon the Jews? Does it not attack Jewish religion as cold hearted legalism? Is it not anti-Semitic inasmuch as it claims that Jesus is the Messiah, and that Jews are wrong to reject that claim? Does it not command that Christians evangelise the Jews, and is that not a threat to the Jewish people? Does Jesus not prophesy the destruction of Jerusalem and the Jewish

---

[2]   See for example: Sevenster J.N., 1975, *The Roots of Pagan Anti-Semitism in the Ancient World*, published by Brill.

[3]   Psalm 44:20-22.

state? Does the New Testament not teach that the Church has effectively replaced Israel in God's purposes?

It is important to consider carefully the assumptions made about what the New Testament says. We cannot side-step the failure of the church in its stewardship of biblical truths about Israel (see chapter 6). Neither can we afford to jettison the Bible's message of hope and salvation because certain passages have been misappropriated and continue to be misunderstood: that message is pertinent, not only in terms of personal spirituality, but also in terms of public life, social development and international affairs.

The Assumptions People Make

1 *Blaming the Jews for the death of Jesus*

In many respects, the question of whether the New Testament holds the Jewish people solely responsible for the execution of Jesus is at the root of the matter. In a superficial sense it was indeed the Jews, Jesus' own people, who rejected him and demanded that he was crucified, but the New Testament, often drawing on the words of the Hebrew prophets, is clear in saying that behind it all is the hand of God.

All four of the Gospel writers, together with Paul and Peter in their letters, make it clear that Jesus came to this world with the express purpose of allowing humanity to do its worst to him so that he might bear its sin and forgive the world. The New Testament writers do not thereby excuse those who rejected Christ – for it was a heinous betrayal – but they do see the sins of the Jews as representative of all human sin. In other words, only if we ignore the very heart of the meaning of the cross of Jesus, as it is explained throughout the New Testament, as a means of atoning for the sins of the whole world, can we possibly be self-righteous about the Jews part in the rejection of Jesus. The concept of humankind's general blame for Jesus' crucifixion is well put by the hymn-writer, Charles Wesley: 'Died He for me who caused His pain, for me who Him to death pursued?' If we, as Christians, blame the Jews for the death of Jesus, how can we say that Christ carried our sins? To use the death of Jesus as an excuse for anti-Semitism is actually to deny the New Testament's message and reject the Christ it offers us.

If Christianity were merely devotion to a martyr – and in some traditions there can be a tendency towards this kind of attitude – then anti-Semitism might be explained as a vengeful response towards the murderers of a beloved leader. But the New Testament does not present the death of Jesus as a martyrdom. Likewise, where liberal Christianity denies the reality of the atoning death of Jesus, it lacks the theological backbone to resist a resurgence of anti-Semitism. Although at times it has seemed quite friendly to Jewish feelings, being willing to play down much of traditional Christian teaching, much of the vehement and irrational hostility that is currently emerging against Israel comes from proponents of liberal doctrine. Reminiscent of the anti-Semitism seen in the past, it puts a magnifying glass up to the sins of the Jews, whilst ignoring the enormous danger they face from very powerful, large, rich and fanatical enemies.

The New Testament, drawing on the Hebrew scriptures, sees God's election of Israel in two ways. Positively, Israel is singled out to be the bearer of God's revelation to the world and the vehicle for his redemption – to be a light to the Gentiles (Luke 2:32). Negatively, Israel is chosen to be the people who, in rejecting their Messiah, would unconsciously bring atonement and forgiveness to the whole world. Jesus and Paul, referring to passages such as Deuteronomy 29:2-4, Isaiah 6:9-10 and Isaiah 42:18-20, see the spiritual blindness of God's elect people as the way God chose to bring sight to the world. This unwitting but foreordained fulfilment of God's intention is also the theme of John 11:49-53, where Caiaphas the High Priest makes a decision to sacrifice Jesus for the sake of the people:

> As high priest that year he prophesied that Jesus would die for the Jewish nation, and not only for that nation, but also for the scattered children of God, to bring them together and make them one.

These positive and negative aspects of the election of Israel, both of which are used by God to bring mercy to bear on the lives of all peoples, are the main subject of the book of Romans in chapters 2, 3, 9, 10 and 11; here Paul presents these as the great reasons why God's ancient promises to Israel will never be set aside.

Those lifting lines from the Bible with a view to justifying their anti-Semitism, as well as those looking to discredit the New Testament as an anti-Semitic text, have fastened on the account in Matthew's Gospel of the words of the crowd at Jesus' trial: 'His blood be on us and our children'. Taken as a whole, however, Matthew's writings can hardly be accused of anti-Jewishness. This verse could only be an excuse for holding the Jews specifically accountable if there was any sense that God and Jesus agreed with them: on the contrary Luke (probably a Gentile – the only Gentile amongst the New Testament authors) reports that Jesus prayed: 'Father forgive them'.

2 Attacking Jewish religious practices

The New Testament certainly criticises the religion of the Pharisees as practised at the time of Jesus. However, the Hebrew scriptures are clearly revered by all of the New Testament writers. When it speaks of the inspiration of the scriptures, the New Testament is referring to the ancient Jewish texts. The apostles all counted themselves as Jews and continued to honour the Jewish customs. Paul, well after his own conversion, still refers to himself as a Jew and moreover a Pharisee (Acts 23:6).

Jesus himself tells his hearers to obey the teaching of the Pharisees because they 'sit in Moses' seat' (Matthew 23:2-3). He goes on to tell them not to behave as the Pharisees did because they did not practise what they preached. In other words Jesus accused the religious leaders of the day of failing to live up to their own standards. This is hardly an assault on their religion. It is much more a challenge to the way it was being practised.

In criticising the Pharisees' religious practices, Jesus continues the tradition of the Hebrew scriptures themselves, which strongly condemn the religious and political leadership of their time as unfaithful to God. The writings of Moses, Isaiah, Jeremiah, Ezekiel, Amos and Hosea provide strong condemnation both of the Jewish leadership and of the nation of Israel itself. Written by Jews, about the Jewish Messiah who limited his ministry, with a few exceptions, 'to the lost sheep of the house of Israel' (Matthew 15:24), written in many parts specifically for a Jewish readership, the New Testament claims only to be continuing that same tradition of prophetic criticism from within the family.

In particular, Jesus challenged the Pharisees about the apparently self-righteous and legalistic nature of their religious life. The reason that the Bible, as a whole, speaks about the self-righteousness of the Jewish religious establishment is because it was written by Jews in a Jewish context. That said, the New Testament also contains much that is deeply critical of Gentile leadership in churches such as those in Corinth, Galatia and Thessalonica. Paul warns that the same conceit and self-righteousness that afflicted Jewish religious leadership could also affect Christian leadership (Romans 11:17-25).

Church history has shown that his warning was well justified. The same sins that led the Jewish establishment to reject Jesus have deeply affected the Christian Church throughout the years. It is possible for the Church to acknowledge Jesus with its lips whilst its heart is still far from him.[4] It is part of human sinfulness to twist God-given doctrines and practices, to try to justify ourselves before God rather than acknowledge that we live only by his grace and mercy. The New Testament by no means teaches that the Jewish religion will be permanently legalistic or that the Christian religion will always be marked by a dependence on God's grace. Its denunciation of religious legalism is directed at Jewish and Christian leadership alike.

So, whilst the New Testament, like the Hebrew scriptures, takes issue with Jewish religious practice, it does not reject the God of Israel or his word, it does not seek to alienate the Jewish people, nor does it exempt Gentile believers from its warnings.

There are passages, such as some in John's Gospel, in which the writer first appears to be attacking the Jews as Jews.

> So, because Jesus was doing these things on the Sabbath, the Jews persecuted him. Jesus said to them, 'My Father is always at his work to this very day, and I, too, am working'. For this reason the Jews tried all the harder to kill him; not only was he breaking the Sabbath, but he was even calling God his own Father, making himself equal with God[5].

Here and in many other passages the villains are identified as 'the Jews'. Speaking to the same group of people Jesus says:

> 'You belong to your father, the devil, and you want to carry out your father's desire. He was a murderer from the beginning, not holding to the truth, for there is no truth in him. When he lies, he speaks his native language, for he is a liar and the father of lies.'[6]

Out of context, such verses could make for anti-Semitic reading. The problem is not one of the meaning of John's Gospel itself, but of the limitations and the generalisation of our English translations. The Greek word translated 'Jew' is the word *Ioudaios*. Whilst this is a legitimate rendering, in the setting of these passages it should really be taken to mean the Jewish leadership in Judea, or the Jewish inhabitants of Judea, as distinguished from the Jewish inhabitants of Galilee. Elsewhere John makes the deliberate distinction between the hostility of the Judean Jews to Jesus and the relatively friendly reception given by the Galilean Jews (John 7:1). In the context of John's Gospel, 'the Jews' of these passages refers to a particular group of people, and certainly not the Jewish people as a whole. John, after all, identifies Jesus himself as a Jew (John 4:9) and records him saying to the Samaritan woman: 'You Samaritans worship what you do not know; we worship what we do know, for salvation is of the Jews' (John 4:22).

---

4   See Isaiah 29:13 and Matt 15:8.
5   John 5:16-18.
6   John 8:44.

3 Asserting that Jesus is the Messiah of Israel

The New Testament presents Jesus of Nazareth as the Messiah, the redeemer promised in the Hebrew scriptures, the one born to assume David's throne. As such, it implies that those Jews that fail to recognise or respond to their rescuer are in error. This is a form of anti-Semitism only if anti-Semitism means refusing to agree with Judaism, and that would surely be to trivialise the meaning of the word. Of course, to say that Jesus is the Messiah, the only Lord and Saviour of the world, contradicts Orthodox Judaism. But it also contradicts Islam, Hinduism and atheism.

The Jewish claim that Jesus is not the Messiah is equally an anti-Christian statement. Its assertion that the Torah is the word of God is an anti-Islamic declaration because Islam teaches that the Torah was written as the result of the Jews distorting the true word of God which had been given to them. We simply have to acknowledge that religions do contradict one another in fundamental areas of belief. This should not be a cause for hatred but for dialogue in a spirit of humility and love.

4 Commanding the Christian to evangelise the Jews

The anti-Semitism of parts of the Church at various points in history, has caused evangelism to be bracketed with persecution as far as the Jewish people as concerned, and Jewish communities, organisations and media speak of proselytising in the harshest possible terms.

The New Testament does command Christians to evangelise the Jews, and not only the Jews, but the whole world too (Matthew 28:19). Similarly the Hebrew scriptures promise the Jews that the light given to Israel will convert other nations so that pagan idol worshippers may acknowledge the God of Israel as the true God (Isaiah 42:6-8, Isaiah 60, Micah 4:1-7). Incidentally, the writings of Moses and the prophets, together with the Psalms of David, are now known and loved throughout much of what was pagan Europe, the Americas, China and Africa, as a result of the missionary work of the Christian Church.

The real hostility to evangelism, and the thinking behind the charge of anti-Semitism, comes from the assumed threat of assimilation. It is crucial that Jews who do not recognise Jesus, as well as Jewish and Gentile believers, understand that assimilation is not part of the New Testament picture.

Whilst the New Testament is clear that when a pagan turns to Christ he ceases to be a pagan, the same terms can not be applied when talking about the Jewish people. The New Testament is equally clear when it shows us that when Jews became believers in Jesus they did not give up their Jewishness. Paul, who was so insistent that pagan converts to Christ must not become Jews in order to become Christians, did himself, as a Jew, continue to observe all the Jewish customs.

Christian evangelisation of Jews, as portrayed and encouraged in the Bible, could only be seen as a threat to Jewish people if a fundamental definition of being Jewish is not believing in Jesus. Why this should ever be the case is unclear: Jews who become Buddhists continue to be regarded as Jewish.

It remains to be said, in agreement with many Christian thinkers, that followers of Jesus can only speak to Jews about him in a spirit of sincere repentance for all the evil that has been done to the Jewish people in his name. It is the Church's appalling record of persecution which is the biggest single factor in hiding the true Jesus from the Jews.

5   Prophesying the destruction of Jerusalem and the Jewish state

The New Testament records Jesus teaching and prophesying on the future of the temple, Jerusalem and Judea. The time of judgement that he anticipates is often misunderstood as a sign of the Church somehow superseding the Jewish people as the instrument of God's grace in the world, leaving Israel forever scattered, abandoned and broken.

> Some of his disciples were remarking about how the temple was adorned with beautiful stones and with gifts dedicated to God. But Jesus said, 'As for what you see here, the time will come when not one stone will be left on another; every one of them will be thrown down'.[7]

> 'When you see Jerusalem being surrounded by armies, you will know that its desolation is near. Then let those who are in Judea flee to the mountains, let those in the city get out, and let those in the country not enter the city. For this is the time of punishment in fulfilment of all that has been written. How dreadful it will be in those days for pregnant women and nursing mothers! There will be great distress in the land and wrath against this people. They will fall by the sword and will be taken as prisoners to all the nations'.[8]

These words of Jesus are a reiteration of many of the themes that also preoccupied the Hebrew prophets, who were themselves drawing on the teaching of Moses:

---

[7]   Luke 21:5-6.
[8]   Luke 21:20-24a.

> Then the LORD will scatter you among all nations, from one end of the earth to the other. There you will worship other gods – gods of wood and stone, which neither you nor your fathers have known. Among those nations you will find no repose, no resting place for the sole of your foot. There the LORD will give you an anxious mind, eyes weary with longing, and a despairing heart. You will live in constant suspense, filled with dread both night and day, never sure of your life. In the morning you will say, 'If only it were evening!' and in the evening, 'If only it were morning!' – because of the terror that will fill your hearts and the sights that your eyes will see.[9]

However, Moses and the prophets always give a final hope for Israel and promise that exile will not be forever:

> Then the LORD your God will restore your fortunes and have compassion on you and gather you again from all the nations where he scattered you. Even if you have been banished to the most distant land under the heavens, from there the LORD your God will gather you and bring you back. He will bring you to the land that belonged to your fathers, and you will take possession of it. He will make you more prosperous and numerous than your fathers.[10]

The question before us is whether or not Jesus teaches that this latest scattering is in fact permanent. If that were the case, and the New Testament was seen to assert the disinheritance of Israel, the end of the Jewish state, then perhaps the charge of anti-Semitism could stand. In Luke's Gospel, however, Jesus says: 'They will fall by the sword and will be taken as prisoners to all the nations. Jerusalem will be trampled on by the Gentiles until the times of the Gentiles are fulfilled' (Luke 21:24). Whatever the phrase 'the times of the Gentiles' refers to, and it is widely and diversely interpreted, the fact remains that Jesus predicts an end to the trouble and the exile. Like Paul, who discusses the issue at length in Romans 11, Jesus gives us a clear indication that according to the plan of God, the fall of Israel is only temporary. 'I tell you the truth, this nation will certainly not pass away until all these things have happened. Heaven and earth will pass away, but my words will never pass away' (Luke 21:32–33): the Greek word often translated 'generation' is *genea*. In the context in which it is used, it is better and more correctly rendered as 'nation'. It is the same word used by Jeremiah in the Greek OT (the Septuagint of LXX) when he speaks of God's determination to preserve the family or descendants of Israel until the foundations of the heavens and earth pass away.

---

[9]   Deut 28:64-67.
[10] Deut 30:3-5.

This is what the Lord says, he who appoints the sun to shine by day, who decrees the moon and stars to shine by night, who stirs up the sea so that its waves roar – the Lord Almighty is his name: 'Only if these decrees vanish from my sight,' declares the Lord, 'will the descendants of Israel ever cease to be a nation before me.' This is what the Lord says: 'Only if the heavens above can be measured and the foundations of the earth below be searched out will I reject all the descendants of Israel because of all they have done,' declares the Lord.[11]

In the same vein, it has been accepted by many Christians, that, as the Church supersedes Israel, so an utterly abstract 'spiritual' kingdom completely supersedes the tangible, practical, political assurances God has made throughout the course of Israel's history. This is based not on what Jesus says, but on what he does not say, and that does not seem sufficient cause to write off the word of God in the Old Testament.

So when the disciples met together, they asked Jesus, 'Lord, are you at this time going to restore the kingdom to Israel?' He said to them: 'It is not for you to know the times or dates the Father has set by his own authority. But you shall receive power when the Holy Spirit comes upon you; and you will be my witnesses in Jerusalem, and in all Judea and Samaria, and to the ends of the earth'.[12]

Here the disciples ask Jesus if the promises concerning the final destiny of Israel are about to be fulfilled. Popular Christian teaching has concluded that Jesus is effectively, albeit indirectly, telling the disciples that they are wrong to ask such a question because the destiny of Israel has been overtaken by that of the Church. But that is not what Jesus says. He is simply saying that the restoration might not be accomplished in their lifetime, and that only God knows when he will bring it to pass. Their task, and their prime concern, instead ought to be the preaching of the gospel to Jews and Gentiles in all nations.

6 Replacing Israel with the Church

So, many Christians have assumed over the years that, in Jesus, they have somehow taken over the birthright of Israel; that the Jews were given a chance to follow God, failed, and so forfeited their covenant relationship, which was passed on to the Church instead. The implications of this 'replacement theology' require serious attention (see Chapter 10): here we want to determine briefly whether its conclusions are fairly drawn from the New Testament texts, and whether, therefore, the charge of anti-Semitism might be upheld.

---

[11] Jeremiah 31:35-37.
[12] Acts 1:6-8.

We should rightly note that, according to the preaching of the apostles, Gentiles were brought to Christ and so became spiritual descendants of Abraham (Galatians 3:6-9). Even though they were not physically circumcised, they became what Paul calls 'the circumcision' (Philippians 3:2-3; Romans 2:25-29; Colossians 2:11). By this Paul meant that the gospel had cut sin from the heart. This is the true 'circumcision of the heart' that matters in God's eyes, and the Hebrew scriptures themselves give the same teaching (Deuteronomy 30.6; Jeremiah 9.26; Ezekiel 44.7ff). The Gentiles were 'grafted into' Israel so that the Church began to inherit the many spiritual blessings that God had promised Israel of old (Romans 11:17-19); it was not that Israel was uprooted and the Gentile believers planted in their place.

The Apostle Peter notably uses the ancient titles given to Israel and applies them also to the Church: 'You are a chosen people, a royal priesthood, a holy nation, a people belonging to God' (1 Peter 2:9 – compare these titles with Isaiah 43:10,20; 44:1-2; 61:6; and Deuteronomy 4:20; 7:6; 14:2). He does not say that the Church is *the* chosen people.

Where the New Testament at first glance appears to contradict the Hebrew writings, it can often be found to be quite specifically faithful to the values and concerns of the Law and the words of the prophets. The New Testament writers, and Paul in particular, make it quite clear that the way of salvation is 'by faith' and not by the works of the Jewish law. Paul asserts that this is also the teaching of the Hebrew scriptures and is not a new concept at all (see Romans 2, 3 and 4 and the whole of the letter to the Galatians). In the same way, in the letter to the Hebrews we read: 'By calling this covenant "new" [God] has made the first one obsolete; and what is obsolete and ageing will soon disappear' (Hebrews 8:13).

In the context of his argument, the author is referring specifically to the system of animal sacrifices in the temple which had indeed been superseded by the sacrifice of Christ. Again, numerous passages in the Hebrew scriptures also tell us that animal sacrifice, though given by God, was not the essence of the religion of Israel, but was meant to point to something greater. In fact, the sacrificial system of the temple is seen as transitory and is even deprecated in such passages as 1 Samuel 15:22, Psalm 50:9-15, 51:16-17, 69:30-31, Isaiah 1:11-15, Jeremiah 6:20, Hosea 6:6, Amos 5:21-23 and Micah 6:6-7. It is also worth noting that Judaism has survived for nearly two thousand years without any Temple or animal sacrifices.

Plainly, the New Testament teaches that the Church, being grafted into Israel, does inherit much that was purposed for Israel, and there are new revelations and clarifications that impact upon Israel. None of them means that Israel is somehow cast aside. It is precisely because Gentile believers owe their salvation to the Jewish rejection of Jesus that God has not forgotten his promise to them: this is the reason Paul, in Romans 3 and 11, gives a resounding 'no' to the question, 'Has God cast them off?' The whole New Testament teaches that Israel's rejection of Jesus was not an accident. One of the reasons God chose Israel was in order that their sin would represent all sin, so that God might bear the sins of the whole world in the person of Jesus.

Conclusion

The New Testament attitude to God's ancient people, the Jews, or to those of them that do not believe in Jesus, is summarised by Paul:

> As far as the gospel is concerned, they are enemies on your account; but as far as election is concerned, they are loved on account of the patriarchs, for God's gifts and his call are irrevocable. Just as you who were at one time disobedient to God have now received mercy as a result of their disobedience, so they too have now become disobedient in order that they too may now receive mercy as a result of God's mercy to you. For God has bound all men over to disobedience so that he may have mercy on them all.[13]

He was passionately, lovingly concerned for his fellow Jews to come to Jesus Christ and be saved: 'I speak the truth in Christ – I am not lying, my conscience confirms it in the Holy Spirit – I have great sorrow and unceasing anguish in my heart. For I could wish that I myself were cursed and cut off from Christ for the sake of my brothers, those of my own race, the people of Israel'.[14]

In Romans 11, he reminds the Gentiles of their debt to the Jews and warns them of their responsibilities, believing that the day will come when 'all Israel will be saved'.[15] Far from being at root anti-Semitic, the New Testament presents a core message that is deeply preoccupied with the salvation both of Israel and all the nations of the world. The Hebrew scriptures and the New Testament alike reveal that God's singling out of Israel was not in any way favouritism, nor does it imply that he loves one people any more or less than another. Rather, God chose Israel for a particular purpose, to preserve them to the end as a sign to the world that his word is true.

---

13 Romans 11:28-32.
14 Romans 9:1-3.
15 Romans 11:26.

Chapter Six

ANTI-SEMITISM IN THE HISTORY OF THE CHURCH

Whilst it is not accurate or fair to say that the New Testament is a driving force behind anti-Semitism, it is true that the Church, throughout its history, has driven the persecution of the Jews.

In many respects, the Church is well aware of its guilt. There have long been calls (often from within the fold) for it to admit the error of its attitude to the Jews, and to demonstrably turn its back on it. In some instances services of repentance have been arranged and declarations made. In commending these as good examples of an appropriate response, it is still important to be clear about exactly what the Church needs to repent for. It is vitally important that the Church recognises the seriousness of its crimes and the need to make amends in a way that is proportionate.

1 The early Church

Racial anti-Semitism, as we would recognise it today – the hatred and oppression of Jews because they are ethnically Jewish – really began in the eighteenth century. Before then, prejudices were born of religious anti-Semitism, or what some Christian writers like Graham Keith,[1] would prefer to call anti-Judaism. The Church, almost from the beginning, was anti-Judaistic, not racially anti-Semitic. When Jews accepted Jesus as the Messiah, they were welcomed into the Church but, until very recent times, it went without saying that they would be expected to renounce their Jewishness. These attitudes not only laid the foundation for contempt for the Jews in wider society, but also corroded the Church's understanding of its Hebrew heritage, of what the Church itself should look like, and of God's purposes for Israel and the world at large.

---

[1] Graham Keith, *Hated Without a Cause?* Paternoster Press, 1997.

Very early on in the second century, if not towards the end of the first century, Christian leaders made serious mistakes. They lost sight of what was right as they tried to defend Christianity against those who were seeking to draw its members back into the practices and doctrines of Judaism. In what they said about those who practised the Jewish faith, they went far beyond the teaching of the New Testament writers. They failed in their preaching and teaching to distinguish between Judaism and Jews. At the same time, they failed to show any compassion for the Jewish people who did not embrace Jesus as their Messiah. They quickly lost sight of Paul's concern, and of the love and determination that Jesus himself showed in trying to gather Israel to himself.

Between AD 386 and 387, St John Chrysostom attempted to make a clear separation between church and synagogue, as he was anxious that many Christians in the congregation at Antioch, where he served as Presbyter, were participating in Jewish ceremonies. Delivering a series of eight homilies, he asserted that:

> the synagogue is not only a place of vice and impiety, it is a haunt of demons. The very souls of Jews are haunts of demons . . . Jews do not worship God but devils, so that all their feasts are unclean. God hates them . . . When it is clear that God hates them, it is the duty of Christians to hate them too.

He applies the words of Jesus recorded in John 4:44 – 'You belong to your father the devil' – to the whole body of Jews, men, women and children of every age. He seems to be unaware of Paul's words in Romans 9:3, where he writes, 'Theirs is the adoption as sons; theirs the divine glory'. He is unmoved by Romans 10:2, where Paul writes, 'They are zealous for God but their zeal is not based on knowledge'; and by the argument presented in Romans 11:12 where he writes, 'If their false step means riches for the world, and their falling short means riches for the Gentiles, how much more will their coming to full strength mean!'

Graham Keith does his best to qualify the harshness of Chrysostom's words, suggesting that he was simply seeking to defend the Christian flock from being led away from Christ:

> He was not directly addressing Jewish People. Nor was he interested in any violent action against them. Indeed, in the pluralist setting of Antioch he would have been happy for the Jews to continue their rites quite independently of Christians.[2]

---

[2]　*Ibid.* page 109.

On the basis of the way in which Chrysostom takes leave of Scripture, however, in the violence of his language and in his harsh criticisms of all Jews, Rosemary Reuter has a strong case when she says that his sermons are 'easily the most violent and tasteless of the anti-Judaic literature' of the Patristic period. Violent and tasteless they may be, but Chrysostom's sermons and pronouncements, along with others of the early fathers, have influenced the Church in its attitude to the Jews right down to the twenty-first century.

Tertullian, writing in the latter part of the second century, believed that God had become conclusively opposed to Israel because of their sin, and was determined to replace the Old Covenant with a new and better one. Melito of Sardis, writing at a similar time, was the first Christian to declare that Jews, in rejecting and crucifying Jesus, were guilty of deicide. He did not qualify his charge. He argued that the crime was not done in ignorance, but knowingly. He did not restrict the crime to the Jewish leaders of Jesus' day, but applied his charge to all Jews, apparently of that and every generation. The Gentiles in his opinion were totally absolved from any involvement in the crucifixion of Jesus. Although he accepted that, in an earlier period, the Jews were greatly blessed by God, he suggested that the Jews had been replaced by the Church who now became heirs of all the promises and blessings of God.

His charge of deicide was also taken up by later writers: Gregory of Nyssa described Jews as 'murderers of the Lord . . . rebels, and detesters of God . . . companions of the devil, a race of vipers . . . accursed'. Writing at the time of the beginning of Christendom, when the Church's priorities and those of the political powers of the day began to coincide, Melito's suggestion that the Church had superseded Israel, with all its associations with nationhood, divine appointment and territorial security, was an attractive concept.

Whereas some of the early fathers still believed in trying to take the gospel to the Jews, in spite of the divine judgement that was upon them, Chrysostom's beliefs were such that he abandoned any idea of the Jews being converted to Christianity.[3] He believed that the Jews had committed the unforgivable sin in crucifying Christ, and he did not hesitate to impute this sin to all the Jews of each generation. Whilst their sins as recorded in the Old Testament were grave, they were not sufficiently serious for God to altogether despair of them, he suggested. The sin of crucifying Christ, however, was of a different order altogether and would result in everlasting punishment and bondage for them:

---

[3]   *Ibid.* page 112.

You did slay Christ, you did lay violent hands against the Master, you did spill his precious blood. That is why you have no chance of atonement, excuse or defence. In the old days your reckless deeds were aimed against his servants, against Moses, Isaiah and Jeremiah. Even if there were ungodliness in your acts then, your boldness had not yet dared the crowning crime. But now you have put all the sins of your fathers into the shade. Your mad rage against Christ, the Anointed One, left no way for anyone to surpass your sin. That is why the penalty you now pay is greater than that paid by your fathers.[4]

Chrysostom was not a racial anti-Semite. He did not envisage physical violence against Jews, but taught that they, their synagogues and their homes should be avoided for religious reasons. But his sentiments went far beyond Scripture and contradicted the Bible in many ways. The venom with which he spoke, and his teaching of God's supposed hatred of the Jews and the Christian duty to hate them also, had a profound effect. From what he said were drawn serious political and social implications, particularly in later years.

For the early Church the proof of God's rejection of the Jews was the sweeping away by the Romans of the temple and all its rites, together with the destruction of Jerusalem and the scattering of the Jewish people. Undoubtedly, this chain of events has presented the Jews themselves with a grave problem. Whilst they have largely accepted that a time of exile was caused by the hand of God as a judgement against sin, they do not believe that it was because of the rejection of Jesus as Messiah. The Church widely believed that the scattering was a result of the Jews' failure to embrace Jesus, but there were also many who saw it as proof that Israel was actually guilty of deicide, and that God had consequently rejected them and rejected them entirely.

To these people, the Jews were seen as an object lesson, an idea that was elaborated upon by St Augustine in the fifth century. He asserted that unbelieving Jews fulfilled a vital role in witnessing to God and to the truth of what is promised in Scripture, that those who rebel against him will be punished. They were made an example of, Augustine suggested, both in their exile and in their social inferiority to other nations. In the years that followed, this view would have far reaching consequences and inform some bizarre ideas. The Church came to tolerate Jews in ways that they would not generally consider for pagans or heretics. The visible presence of the Jews helped the Christian cause, it was thought, because of the lesson that their

---

[4] *Ibid.* page 113.

unhappy position could teach mankind. It was in the Church's interest to encourage their political, social and economic repression, and to ensure that their humiliation was sustained. Simply expelling the Jews would not provide half as powerful and plain a testimony.[5]

2 The Middle Ages

In the period roughly between AD 430 and the First Crusade of 1096, Jews in Europe lived in relative tranquillity and prospered, with a few exceptions. Thereafter, things rapidly changed.

The Emperor Constantine had been converted to Christ in AD 327 and declared Christianity the official religion of the Empire. It took many years for the ordinary people to embrace the Christian faith, even nominally, but as Church power increased, so religious and social anti-Semitism increased. Jews were steadily impoverished and began to be treated as social outcasts. Stereotypes started to take shape of the Jew as a downtrodden, contemptible figure. Graham Keith notes that 'drawings began to depict Jews as physically distinctive, with long hooked noses, while the influential Fourth Lateran Council of 1215 took a major step in segregating Jews from Christian society by insisting that they wore special clothing'.[6] Their choice of work and where to stay also became restricted.

The Crusades then brought enormous suffering to Jews. The Crusades were called to free the eastern churches from Muslim oppression and to liberate Jerusalem from Muslim control. The Saracens were regarded as implacable enemies of Christ, servants of the devil, and, initially, the Crusades had little or nothing to say about the fate of the Jews. Once the campaign built up momentum, however, the hatred and resentment sewn in the earlier teaching of the church fathers, began to bear fruit. The Jews too were held up as enemies of God, on account of the crucifixion of Jesus, and large numbers were murdered in Mainz, Cologne, Speyer, Worms and throughout Germany and along the Crusaders' route to the Holy Land. All the lands stretching from the Danube to Jerusalem was bathed in Jewish blood. Jewish homes were pillaged, women raped and entire communities massacred. In Jerusalem itself, the whole Jewish community, men, women and children, were herded into a large synagogue, which was set alight while Crusaders knelt and sang the *Te deum*.

---

5   *Ibid.* see page 115.
6   *Ibid.* page 118.

In 1492, Ferdinand and Isabella of Spain, the 'Catholic Monarchs' as they liked to be called, heavily influenced by the Church, chose to expel all Jews from their realm. At the same time, the Inquisition employed the most brutal forms of torture, to try and root out Jewish belief and forcibly convert Jews to the Christian faith. Under their treatment, thousands and at times tens of thousands of Jews perished, and their property was confiscated.

Across Europe during the Middle Ages, anti-Jewish, anti-Semitic calumnies were manufactured. This propaganda developed under the influence of the Church, not so much by the official direction of the Pope or the bishops, but with the Church's knowledge and silent acquiescence, and often through the active involvement of clergy. There was 'the Blood Libel', for example, according to which Jews were accused of kidnapping and murdering Christian children in order to use their blood for the baking of *Matzah*, the unleavened Passover bread. Jews were also accused of poisoning wells from which Christians drank in order to cause disease, and were charged with causing or precipitating the plague. The calumnies had far reaching effects. They played no small part in cultivating an environment in which anti-Semitism could flourish, such as in England in the years from 1144 to 1290, which culminated in the first general expulsion of Jews from any country during the Medieval period.

3 The Reformation

Initially the Reformation brought a measure of relief to the Jewish people, as medieval traditions and beliefs came under careful scrutiny. In Germany, the outstanding figure of the period was that of Martin Luther. At first Luther advocated an attitude of love to the Jews: 'We must receive them cordially, and permit them to trade and work with us, that they may have occasion and opportunity to associate with us, hear our Christian teaching, and witness our Christian life'. At some point, however, Luther's attitudes changed.

The reasons behind what became his fierce anti-Semitism are much debated. Apparently he grew impatient over the lack of Jews converting to Christianity, and began to despair that they would ever acknowledge Jesus as the Messiah of Israel. At the same time, his protest against legalism in Christianity and his antipathy towards the Mosaic Law, caused him to take issue with Rabbinic Judaism. By 1543 he would write his second treatise, *Of the Jews and their Lies*:

> What shall we Christians do with this damned, rejected race of Jews? . . .
> set their synagogues on fire, and what ever does not burn up, should be

covered or spread over with dirt so that no-one may ever be able to see a cinder or stone of it . . . in order that God may see that we are Christians . . . their homes should likewise be broken down and destroyed . . . they should be put under one roof or in a stable . . . They should be deprived of their prayer books and Talmuds, in which such idolatry, lies, cursing, and blasphemy are taught . . . Their Rabbis must be forbidden to teach under the threat of death.

He went on to recommend that Germany should follow the example of other nations and remove every Jew from its soil. It is possible to see in Luther's extreme hostility to the Jews, how anti-Semitism was able to grow in Germany and in large areas of Europe unchallenged and even encouraged by the Church, the eventual consequences of which are frightening. Luther's fear of the Law and his dislike of the Old Testament dominated the German Church ever since. In Hitler's day there was considerable agitation to have the teaching of the Old Testament removed completely from the school curriculum, whilst Goebbels, his propaganda minister, launched the Nazi media campaign against the Jews with the republication of Luther's treatise *Of the Jews and their Lies* in its entirety.

The story is somewhat different in the Churches and countries more influenced by the Reformed movement of Calvin and his colleagues (like John Knox in Scotland). With a few exceptions, they manifested a very different attitude to the Jews, no doubt owing to the strong emphasis on the teaching of the Old Testament and the covenants. The same Reformed tradition was carried into the twentieth century by teachers such as Karl Barth, who helped to create a new and Biblical understanding of the place of the Jewish people in the purposes of God for the redemption of the world.

4 The Modern Era

During the Holocaust the official churches in Germany remained silent. Undoubtedly there were many individuals who became actively involved in trying to help the Jews. In Germany, particularly in the Confessional Church under the leadership of Barth and others, there were many who resisted the Nazi policies. In fact the number of individual cases, throughout Europe, in Holland, France, Italy and Hungary, in which people tried to rescue and protect Jewish people, helps to brighten a very dark picture. But officially and publicly, the churches said nothing and did very little indeed.

The Roman Catholic Church too remained silent, or, as some have suggested, silently acquiescent. Whilst, again, many bishops, priests, nuns and ordinary lay people risked their lives trying to help Jews, Professor Gunther Levy in his book, *The Catholic Church and Nazi Germany*, draws upon damning quotations that prove to what degree the Vatican and the leadership of various churches were aware of Germany's activities and intentions.

More than a million and a half people were involved in transporting and exterminating Jews during the Second World War, and this number is bound to have included many Church members. Michael Kaufman, writing in the *Jerusalem Post*, said:

> The Holocaust was largely the product of the incessant teachings of hatred of Jews and Judaism by the Church, and the Church's instigation of their legal, economic and physical persecution over the previous 1,500 years . . . teachings which conditioned people for the ultimate outrage . . . Hitler pointed out to German Bishop Berning and to Monsignor Steinman, that he was merely going to do what the Church had done for 1,500 years. Similarly, Hitler wrote to Pope Pious XII: 'We are continuing the work of the Catholic Church'.

The Orthodox Churches also have a terrible record of anti-Semitism, even in modern times, and particularly in Russia. In the pogroms which took place between 1880 and 1946, hundreds of thousands of Jews perished and over two million were displaced, compelled to flee the country (one million to Western Europe and one million to America). Many of these pogroms took place on Christmas Eve, Christmas Day, Good Friday, Easter or Whitsuntide, and were carried out under the sign of the cross.

The first known Messianic congregation in history was founded by a Christian Jew, Joseph Rabinowitz, in Kisinev, the capital city of Bessarabia. Rabinowitz and his followers continued to regard themselves as Jews – Jews who were fulfilled in Jesus Christ. The congregation encountered considerable opposition from both the Gentile Church and the Russian State. With Rabinowitz's death in 1898, the movement faltered. It came to an abrupt end four years later through a pogrom on Easter Day 1903. The rioting crowd did not discriminate between Christian and non-Christian Jews. Homes were plundered, women raped, young and old murdered, and babies hurled from second and third story buildings with shouts of 'Jesus has risen'.

5 Changing attitudes

The churches in Germany were the among the first to sound the call for repentance. The *Bruderrat* (the fraternal council) of the Confessional Church released a statement on 8 April 1948, which acknowledged on behalf of the German people their guilt regarding the Jews:

We acknowledge with shame and sorrow how much we have failed and how guilty we have become in respect to Israel. We are now under the judgements of God . . . so that in time of repentance we bow under God's mighty hand both as a Church and as a nation.[7]

The synod of the Evangelical Church of Germany, meeting in what was West Berlin in April 1950, declared in the name of the Church and the people that they were guilty of crimes of omission and commission against the Jewish people. They too warned of God's judgement, called for repentance, rejected all anti-Semitism, and asked that Jewish Christians be made welcome in the spirit of brotherly love.[8] The Provisional Committee of the World Council of Churches, which met in Geneva in February 1946, acknowledged 'with penitence' the failure of the churches to overcome anti-Jewish prejudice in the spirit of Christ. The First Assembly of the World Council of Churches, convening in Amsterdam in 1948 declared, 'We call upon all the churches we represent to denounce anti-Semitism, no matter what its origin, as absolutely irreconcilable with the profession and practice of the Christian faith. Anti-Semitism is a sin against God and man'.[9] The Third Assembly of the World Council which met at New Delhi in 1961 reiterated the statement of 1948 and renewed the plea to fight anti-Semitism. The World Lutheran Federation and other Christian churches in the USA and elsewhere have passed similar resolutions[10].

Vatican Council II also did a great deal to alter the thinking of the Church. Pope John XXIII made history and created a stir when he greeted a Jewish delegation with the words from Genesis,[11] 'I am Joseph your brother!'[12] Although his words can no doubt be interpreted in different ways, they do indicate that Pope John believed in both a historic and a spiritual connection between Israel and the Church. That marked a major change in the thinking of the Roman Catholic Church.

---

7 Jocz, *The Jewish People and Jesus Christ after Auschwitz* (Baker Book House, Grand Rapids, Michigan 1981), page 71.
8 *Ibid.* page 72.
9 *Ibid.* page 75.
10 *Ibid.* pages 75-77. See *also Stepping Stones to Further-Jewish Christian Relations: An Unabridged Collection of Christian Documents*, compiled by Helga Croner (Stimulus Books, 1977). See also David W. Torrance, *The Witness of the Jews to God* (Handsel Press, page 151 Appendix A entitled *Declaration of the German Roman Catholic bishops on the Church's Relationship to Judaism*).
11 Quoted from Jacob Jocz, *op. cit.* page 63.
12 Genesis 45:4.

The documents of Vatican Council II acknowledge, 'On account of their fathers, this people remain most dear to God, for God does not repent of the gifts he makes, nor of the call he issues'. They affirm 'the special bond, linking the people of the New Covenant with the stock of Israel'. The Council declared that the Jewish People were guiltless of the death of Jesus, thereby destroying one of the most entrenched notions of Christendom, which had for generations put Jews under a special curse and encouraged their persecution. Though Jews were involved in the trial of Jesus, the Council said, 'What happened in his passion cannot be blamed on all the Jews then living, without distinction, nor upon the Jews today'. The Jewish people 'should not be presented as repudiated or cursed by God'. This last statement was more far reaching than any other for Jewish-Christian coexistence. The Council also disapproved of all persecution.

These Vatican documents concerning the Jew probably owe most to the work of Pope John and Cardinal Bea, both men well ahead of their time, who died a few years after the Vatican Council. A Viennese Catholic scholar in his book *God's First Love,* cites a prayer that Pope John composed shortly before his death:

> We realize now that many, many centuries of blindness have dimmed our eyes, so that we no longer see the beauty of thy Chosen People and no longer recognise in their faces the features of our firstborn brother. We realize that our brows are branded with the mark of Cain. Centuries long has Abel lain in blood and tears, because we had forgotten thy love. Forgive us the curse which we unjustly laid on the name of the Jews. Forgive us that with our curse, we crucified thee a second time.[13]

The new thinking encapsulated in the work of the Vatican Council still has yet to permeate large sections of the Catholic Church. Some provinces and synods, however, have responded positively,[14] and many leaders from many Christian traditions have spoken out against anti-Semitism.

Like many Churches and Christian organisations, the Church of Scotland too has passed statements in successive years condemning anti-Semitism in all its forms, but, also like many Churches, it has not actually called for anything as concrete as a general service of repentance. Western Christianity is still struggling to know how best to respond to its anti-Semitic heritage.

---

[13] Quoted from Jacob Jocz, *op. cit.* page 63.
[14] David W. Torrance, *The Witness of the Jews to God,* page 151.

6 *The response of today's Church*

Christians and the Western Church need to learn from their past. Centuries of persecution by both Church and State have created within Jews a deep sense of insecurity and natural distrust. They have deep distrust about the motives behind the actions and policies of other states and a distrust of the Christian Church.

The Church needs to be aware of the terrible danger of going beyond the teaching of Scripture with reference to the Jews, as with any other issue. Its attitude towards the Jews needs to be shaped solely by the word of God, as do its attitudes towards all peoples and practices. In the same vein, it needs to confront some of the issues presented by churches such as those in the Middle East today (the Diocese of the Episcopal Church in Jerusalem, to name but one), which find it difficult to come to terms with certain passages of the Old Testament. In distancing themselves from Scripture, fellowships and organisations will struggle to resist the penetration of anti-Semitism into their ranks.

The *Spectator* of 16 February 2002 carried a chilling article about anti-Semitism in the Church of England ('Christians who hate the Jews').

The Church as a whole also needs to undergo nothing less than a Copernican revolution in its understanding of a series of key issues: the nature of judgement; the place of the people of Israel; the meaning of the covenant of grace; the authority and reliability of Holy Scripture; and the role of the State of Israel. The issues addressed by Vatican Council II need to be addressed by the whole Church. There can, ultimately, be no rapprochement in Jewish-Christian relations unless there is a complete theological reorientation in which the Church surrenders any suggestion of replacement theology.

It needs to recognise that through the anti-Semitic centuries it has helped to hide Christ from the Jews and has made it far more difficult for Jews to come to Christ. The Church needs to repent for everything wherein it has sinned against God and against its Jewish brothers and sisters. It needs to learn afresh to love the Jewish people as God loves them, and to long, as Paul did, that they come be saved by the recognition of their Messiah.

The Church needs to affirm with Paul that God's call to, and covenant with, the Jewish people is irrevocable. It needs to recognise God's ongoing purpose for them and accept their place in God's strategy for world mission. It also needs to grasp its dependence on the understanding, vision and faith of believing Jews. Their witness and heritage should play a crucial part in enabling the Gentile Church to grow in its knowledge of God and his word, and in helping it to carry out Christ's mission to the Jews.

Chapter Seven

ISLAM AND OTHER WORLDVIEWS

'In the mosque we had been taught that Jews were our greatest enemy, inherently evil, and that Israel should be destroyed.'
(Quoted from The Times, *8 January 2003, in an article by Ahmer Khokhar, a former British Muslim, now converted to Christ, describing his experience of conversion and its consequences.)*

At the time of writing there is much fear of Islam. It seems so militant and violent. Its militant wing seems bent on destroying Western society – and we must ask humbly whether we do not in fact deserve this kind of judgment. For example, when one considers the appalling pain to individual and society caused by the sexual chaos and marriage breakdown so prevalent in the West, we must ask whether God is bringing judgment upon us. As we read some of the biblical prophets it is clear that God uses outsiders, even wicked nations, to punish his people who were once close to him. Is militant Islam 'the rod of God's anger' against the West? It may be. However the purpose of this chapter is to consider other things.

Here we examine the underlying reasons why Islam is prone to fanaticism, and why certain powerful Islamic groups are so aggressive, particularly against Israel. Why among all the trouble spots of the world do they seem obsessed with hating Israel? Compared with other world conflicts the number of Muslims killed in the long running Arab-Israel conflict has been small. So why the special hatred for Israel?

At the same time, it recognises that the typical Western secular worldview has no real place for God, which is one reason why many Muslims hate the West as well as hating Israel. In order to understand these things we need to consider the basic worldview of Islam, comparing it with other religious worldviews.

Different world religions relate the physical world to the spiritual in very different ways. Consider some of the models.

Pantheism and Panentheism

Pantheism emphasises the immanence of God within nature but denies his transcendence – that is, he is to be found within nature but not beyond it. Pantheism has many forms, but it always means that God is not independent of nature, rather he is the spiritual dimension that holds nature in being. The Pantheist really has to believe that nature itself is eternal.

The spiritual is not usually seen as personal being but as mystical force. On this understanding, our spiritual quest is not to seek personal knowledge of God, but to harmonise ourselves with the impersonal spiritual principles of the universe. Eastern religions would be comfortable with this basic idea, although they have other important elements, and the very diverse New Age movement which influences western society also accepts this kind of basis for thought and action.

Westerners who realise the bankruptcy of materialism often seek solace in the spiritual without desiring or feeling the need to encounter any personal being who might call us to account. Many new-agers would say that we humans are the personal expression of spiritual reality, which is close to saying that we are God.

Panentheism is an attempt to combine what is understood to be the best in Pantheism with Christian theism. It asserts that there is indeed a personal Being who is greater that the material universe, but still sees the material universe as an expression of him (or her). It is as if God is related to the physical universe as human mind is related to its physical body. The physical universe is the means by which God makes himself known. Attractive as it may at first appear, panentheism has various problems. First, it must deny any real independence of action to the universe. If the universe (which includes ourselves) is an emanation of God himself, it is hard to see how there can be any real freedom and accountability. And second, if the universe is in effect God's body, how do we account for the enormous reality of evil?

Dualism

Here the physical world is considered negatively in relation to the divine. It is either unreal; a mere shadow of the eternal; evil; or unimportant. It is something from which to escape by the practice of religion. There is much in Islam, which teaches that this temporary earthly life, compared with an eternity of the afterlife, is unimportant. In this sense Islam contains elements of dualism – although as one of the three great monotheistic religions it has also elements in common with Judaism and Christianity.

Pantheism and dualism might seem to be inconsistent with one another; however, both are found in the eastern religions of Hinduism, Buddhism and Taoism. While these religions are not the subject of this book, it is worth noting that dualism has also had an adverse affect on Christian theology at different times in its history. For example, it has been taught that our eternal hope is 'immortality of the soul' (which comes from Plato), rather than 'resurrection of the body'; and especially in medieval times, a negative attitude to the body was common. Another example is the failure to have regard for the environment, in the belief that 'spiritual things' are more important. And maybe the failure to see the importance of the land of Israel in God's purpose is another example.

Duality

This is the biblical worldview. It is essentially 'relational'. The physical world is considered positively in relation to the divine. The physical world was created by God, separate from him, but nevertheless it depends on God for its continued being. Unlike the pantheistic view, it is not part of the divine. God gave it its own independent rational structure.[1]

This 'independent rationality', along with continuing reliance of God, is not easy to imagine. However, in the Christian doctrine of the Trinity (one God with a relationship of three) we also have a relationship which in our space-time cannot be imagined.[2] In the incarnation, God unites himself to our physical humanity. Again, this union of God with the physical cannot be described in ways that we can fully understand.[3] His thoughts are higher than

---

[1] Many would argue that this worldview (the belief that the physical world is governed by a rationality chosen for it by God, which nevertheless is not part of him) is necessary for the full flowering of experimental science.

[2] It is significant that as modern physics penetrates into the structure of matter it discovers that the fundamental constituents of nature only have their being in relation with other constituents of nature. Furthermore these relations cannot be pictured. They can be described by mathematics but not by diagrams or pictures.

[3] Perhaps we meet a related mystery every time we make a free decision to move part of our physical body. The decision itself cannot be merely part of the physical cause and effect chain of physical nature, because then it would not really be a free decision that we had initiated. So here we have a non-physical event (our decision) causing a movement of a physical thing. This 'mind over matter' relationship remains a great mystery but we witness it many times every day.

our thoughts.[4] God regards his creation as good and loves it. Although the physical creation has been negatively affected by human sin, the physical and the spiritual still belong together and are fully re-united in Christ's resurrection and ascension.

This means that the eternal world of heaven and the physical world are related. At the end of time the new Jerusalem comes from heaven to earth and God's dwelling place is with his people. There is both continuity and discontinuity between this world and the new creation. God does not merely destroy this world and start his creation all over again but creates the new from the old.

On the other hand this new creation involves a breaking in by God, into the old creation. So in the resurrection of Jesus we see that it is the same Jesus who died who is then raised; and yet there is something fundamentally different about him. He is no longer confined by the space-time of this world and is not always recognised by his disciples. The resurrection of Jesus is not just the miraculous resuscitation of a corpse, nor is it an entirely new Jesus. The tomb is empty and he is raised in a 'spiritual body', incorruptible and full of glory.

In this third model there is a clear interaction between the physical and the spiritual but they nevertheless remain distinct from one another. This means that we should highly value the physical world and physical life (however short). God loves the physical and so should we. This contrasts with the Islamic view of the world.

In the biblical view of the religion-government interaction, there should be a relation between the spiritual and the physical[5] but not a confusion. Something of this is attempted in the (unwritten) British constitution. The clergy of the two national churches are forbidden from standing for election to parliament. In the Bible the Priests and Kings were not allowed to combine their functions.[6] Only the one who would be free from sin – and therefore free from a tendency to corruption – could combine the roles of Priest and King. That person was to be the Messiah.

Nevertheless the State recognises that the Church's message and the behaviour of the leaders of the nation are linked. It does this

---

4   Isaiah 55:8-9 'For my thoughts are not your thoughts, neither are your ways my ways', declares the Lord. 'As the heavens are higher than the earth, so are my ways higher than your ways and my thoughts than your thoughts.'
5   The American Constitution mistakenly, we believe, makes a strict separation between religion and government.
6   In the Old Testament, when king Saul and later king Uzziah broke this rule they faced serious consequences.

explicitly by putting the power of the monarch under the authority of God in the coronation; by giving certain bishops seats in the House of Lords; and by the Sovereign always sending a representative to the General Assembly of the Church of Scotland.

The Islamic Worldview

Islam shares the biblical view that God created the physical world distinct from himself. However its view of the relation between the physical world and the spiritual world of paradise is very different from that of the Bible. So too is its view of the relation between religion and state.

(a) The physical world and the eternal worlds of paradise and hell.

In Islam there is no continuity between the life of this world and the life of heaven. This leads to the view that this life is of little value because it is infinitely shorter than the everlasting life that follows. As we saw, this aspect suggests that Islam is a dualistic religion. It means that Islam can defend those who kill and die to spread the power of Islam, because this life is of so little importance compared with the length of eternity – other than being the place where it is decided whether we live in submission to God or not. Thus it is not too difficult for fanatical Muslims to justify suicide bombing and slaughter in the *jihad* against non-Muslims. (The concept of *jihad* – meaning 'struggle' – is examined further in Appendix 5.)

Yet paradoxically the paradise of the next life is described very much in this-worldly terms! The service of beautiful virgin young women together with drinks to be desired is promised to the faithful.[7] In the Qur'an there is very little about fellowship with God, who does not seem to be present in the heavenly paradise.

Despite the teaching of the Qur'an, there have been developments, for example within the Sufic tradition, which do make room for intimacy. Sufism comes from the Arabic *safa*, meaning love. The *muhsin* (one who makes good) loves God without fear of favour. One Muslim prayer goes like this, 'If I worship you for fear of hell, then cast me in it. But if I worship you for love of you, then take me to paradise.' However sufism is regarded by the great majority of Muslims as a heresy, since to claim this kind of intimacy with God is a grave error. In Islam generally, God is only known through his will and his laws, not his heart.

---

[7]   The benefits of paradise promised in the Koran would seem to be more for men than women. A woman's reward is not mentioned.

In fact fear of hell is very real among Muslims. In Christianity we are warned of the reality of hell; however, this is balanced by the belief that God dearly loves the sinner and does not will that any go to hell. On the contrary God, in his grace, bears our sins in Christ and gives us forgiveness and a new life. If we finally go to hell it will be because we resisted and refused God's love for us. In Islam there is no corresponding confidence in the love of God for the sinner. On the contrary much Islamic preaching makes the imperfect Muslim believe that God hates him/her.

Thus the really dedicated Muslim spends his life worrying whether or not God will accept him/her and this can easily lead to a religious fanaticism as s/he desperately attempts to justify him/herself before God. However not even a fanatical adherence to religion will guarantee escape from hell. The only way to be sure is to carry this fanaticism to its extreme by dying in *jihad* – for example, by killing oneself in a suicide bomb attack.

(b) Religion and State.

Now here is a great paradox. Although this world is ultimately unimportant to Islam, God's rule on earth is something Islam must struggle for. In Islam there is no separation between religion and state, sacred and secular.[8] Religious leaders are also meant to be the political leaders who spread the rule of God, not only by persuasion and prayer, but also by political/economic and military power – all of which, they believe, are God's way of imposing his rule on nations and peoples. Islam does not make a separation between the rule of God on earth and political/military power. This means that Islam is a territorial religion. Not all states which have Islam as their main religion are prepared to accept this, of course. However it remains the Islamic ideal.

Since it is the duty of Muslims to spread the Islamic faith they will do so, if they think necessary, by political and military means.

Islam divides the world into two areas:

'House of Islam' – where God rules.

'House of War' – where it is the Islamic duty to spread the rule of God by force if needed.

---

8   Several nations where Islam is dominant have not followed this aspect of Islamic theology – especially Turkey and also some of the Arab nations whose ideology has been nationalist rather than Islamic. Islamic fundamentalism regards such nations as not truly Islamic.

'The abode of Islam is the homeland which is subject to the rules of Islam . . . the abode of war is the nation which is not subject to the rules of Islam'.[9] Muslims must promote Islam by reason and persuasion, and if that fail, by war. Those who will not submit must be killed. '*Jihad* will never end . . . it will last to the Day of Judgement'.[10]

Although Islam says it does not believe in compulsion in religion (i.e. forcible conversions) it does believe that everyone should be forced to live under the authority of Islamic rulers. Islam is a religion of submission to the will of God and by extension the submission of non-Muslims to the legal/political/economic/military rule of Islam.

However even here we can note two things:

Many times Islam has engaged in forcible conversion.

Toleration (as long as they submit) only applies to Jews, Zoroastrians, and Christians (the Peoples of the Book). It does not apply to idol worshipers such as Hindus who are to be converted or killed.

Of course it can be countered that many times in her history, the Church has confused its spiritual mission with political and military conquest and rule and used force to impose its will. However in doing so it was being untrue to Jesus who willingly, deliberately and passively, submitted to suffering and death and called on his disciples to take up their cross and follow him.

When Muslims use force they are being true to Mohammed. In the chronological table of Mohammed's life found in the popular Penguin Classics version of the Qur'an, we find a list of 21 of the main events in Mohammed's life. Many of these events are normal human occurrences such as birth, marriage, journeys and death. What is noteworthy is that not one act of kindness is mentioned, but eight battles are recorded. Several of these battles are against Jews who are defeated. For example we are told that in the year 627:

The Jewish tribe of Qurayza raided by Muhammed; some 800 men beheaded (only one Jew abjuring his religion to save his life) and all the women and children sold as slaves.[11]

Often present day Christians feel ashamed that their Crusader forebears attempted forcibly to remove Islamic rule from the Holy

---

[9]   Words spoken by Sheikh Abdullah Ghoshah, Supreme judge of Jordan. Quoted by John Laffin, *The Dagger of Islam*, page 55.

[10] Words spoken by Sheikh Zahra. Quoted by John Laffin, *ibid*, page 55.

[11] From the translation by N.J. Dawood in the Penguin Classics series, fourth edition, first published 1956. In later editions the report of the battle is shortened to: 'The Jewish tribe of Qurayza raided by Muhammed.'

Land and re-impose Christian rule. No doubt we should be ashamed. However what is sometimes forgotten is that the Muslims themselves first gained control of the Holy Land by military conquest!

It could be countered that in the Old Testament Israel was commanded by God to liquidate the pagan inhabitants of the Promised Land. For further discussion of this point see Appendix 4.

Muslims take the simple view that because God is all-powerful, he always gets his own way. This is the meaning of the words 'God is great' which are used in calls to prayer. They are called out with great vehemence by militant Muslims when engaged in their struggles with non-Muslims.[12] This means that once God (through Islam) has gained control of territory he can never relinquish it. When Islam loses territory to non-Muslims, it gives Islam a tremendous religious and theological problem. Such things cannot happen – but they do! So the loss of Spain (for example), even though it was hundreds of years ago, is still a source of anguish to devout Muslims.

Indeed, because God is on his side, the Muslim expects that Islamic nations should be the most powerful and prosperous. The existence of non-Islamic nations that are much more powerful presents the devout follower of Islam with a cause for real distress. Hence the modern fundamentalist Muslim attitude to America, the West and Christianity.

These things taken together with the continued existence of Israel (see below) lead to another fear the Muslim has – a problem hardly mentioned but certainly present – the fear that their religion, which makes such huge claims to universal truth and obedience, might be in fact untrue!

How does all this affect Islam's attitude to Israel and Jews?

Like Spain, Palestine was once entirely under the rule of Muslims. It was part of the House of Islam. Now it isn't. However the problem of the existence of Israel is much worse than the problem of a once Muslim Spain which is now non-Muslim. The reasons are as follows:

1 The Spanish are not mentioned in the Qur'an or the Hadith. The Jews are, and where they are mentioned, it is usually for criticism or cursing.[13]

---

[12]   When Christians speak of the greatness of God they should mean the everlasting self-giving love of God.

[13]   The Hadith says that to herald the Day of Judgement, Muslims will be called upon to kill all Jews. This text is quoted in the constitution of the Palestinian Islamic Group Hamas.

2 The Jewish Faith is believed by Islam to be a twisted version of the true Word that God gave their original prophets. Mohammed came to untwist the Scriptures. It is believed that the Qur'an is this untwisted version of the Scriptures. The Jewish faith should be dying! Any sign of new life for Judaism presents Islam with a major religious problem.

3 Tiny Israel's frequent victories over its huge oil rich Arab enemies who attacked it, gives the Islamic believer a burden hard to bear. Such things cannot happen – but they do!

4 The Qur'an itself prophesises the permanent wretchedness of the Jews who will live in poverty and misery forever.[14] Some Muslims are aware that the Bible prophesies the eventual return of the Jews to their original land where they will prosper. This is a deep problem for Islam.

5 The existence of Israel is, unintentionally,[15] like a sign saying: *Islam is untrue*. The devout Muslim cannot bear it. It is intolerable for him or her.

It seems that the violent anti-Semitism of the Nazi era has been transferred to the Islamic world. Since World War II, *The Protocols of Zion* and Hitler's *Mein Kamph* have been widely publicized and continue to be best sellers. Fundamentalist Islamic leaders, like the Ayatollah Khomeini, or Mahmoud Ahmadinejad, the present President of Iran, together with many of the terrorist movements, like Hezbullah and Hamas, financed and backed chiefly by Iran and Syria, have openly called for the destruction of all Jews.

The message of hatred towards Jews, as preached by Shaikh Abdullah el-Faisal (see chapter 4), is being preached today throughout the Middle East, in mosques, in newspapers and broadcast on radio and TV. That is why, during Arafat's time, Israel destroyed the PA's chief broadcasting station, in order to stop it broadcasting hate and encouraging Muslims to kill Jews. Israel does not appear on any Arab

---

14   The Koran teaches that: the Jews are the enemies of God, and of the prophet and of the angels (2:97-98); they have always been disobedient (5:78); they exercise unrighteousness (5:61-79); they attempt to introduce corruption (5:64); they are enemies of the believers (5:82); they have twisted the word of God (2:59, 75-79, 211); they lie against God (4:-50); they are damned by God because of their disobedience (2:88, 4:46, 52, 5:13, 60, 64, 78; they have killed the prophets of God (5:70); they will receive the punishment of hell fire (59:3).

    These texts are often approvingly quoted today in anti-Israel rhetoric. I owe this list of Koranic sayings to Terrance Prittie's book: *The Economic War Against the Jews*, page 147.

15   Most Israelis are unaware that Islam's faith prophesies the permanent poverty (and therefore dispersion) of Jews.

map or in any textbook in Arab schools. Children are taught in the classroom to hate and kill Jews and to welcome martyrdom in the killing of Jews. Yasser Arafat personally encouraged child martyrs. Suicide bombers are praised and their families rewarded, with promises of heaven.

An article by Fatma Abdallah Mahmoud in the Egyptian Government daily Al-Akhbar was entitled 'Accursed Forever and Ever' and makes chilling reading. It assumes the Holocaust is a myth backed by faked photos, exonerates Hitler and ends by imploring Allah to curse the Jews 'more and more, to the end of all generations, Amen'.

Anti-Semitism is an attack on God and on God's choice of the Jews to be his instrument for the redemption of the world. There are good and bad people in any nation, and good and bad people in the nation of Israel, but to attack the Jew as Jew and to attack Israel simply because it is a Jewish state, is to attack God. The anti-Semitism which lies in and behind the Palestinian and Arab opposition to Israel, is proof of the religious dimension of this struggle.

Lance Lambert, a Messianic Jew, writer and author in Jerusalem, has frequently said in his addresses and books that Islam claims to accept the writers and prophets of the Old Testament and to accept Jesus both as a prophet and Messiah. They claim that the Jews misinterpreted and corrupted the Scriptures. The Christian Church, which followed, they claim, also misinterpreted and corrupted the Scriptures. The true interpretation, they believe, was given by Mohammed through whom alone the light of heaven shone in purity and absolute truth. That is to say, Islam grew out of Judaism and Christianity, both of which, in Muslims eyes, are corrupt. Religiously, Israel belongs to the past. Judaism, in Lance Lambert's words, is for Islam, like a 'fossil'. To discover that what is supposed to be a fossil is alive and flourishing today, in the form of the present state of Israel, is a direct challenge and affront. It is a contradiction of Islam, and therefore must be destroyed. The Ayatollah Khomeini of Iran was recorded as saying that his worst nightmare would be to wake up and discover that a Jew was ruling the world!

Much of this seems extreme and is quickly dismissed as fanaticism. It is important to remember that it is supported by many Islamic writers, rooted in their interpretation of the Qur'an, and is a critique of the modern Western divorce between sacred and secular, and of the corrupting Greek influence on Christianity which, they believe, caused this split.[16]

---

[16] See Paul Berman's article on Sayyid Qutb in the New York Times, 23 March 2003.

And Finally

We must remember the following things:

1 Most Muslims are like the rest of us. Like us, their families are very important to them. They want the best for their children and hope to live in peace.

2 They are not necessarily glad to be Muslims. In interfaith meetings we must be careful not to strengthen the hand of the Imams and other Islamic religious leaders. Many ordinary Muslims fear their own religious leadership.

3 We must pray each day that the world of Islam discovers the love of God. Although we must be aware of what Islam is, we must never hate Muslims. The best way to make sure we don't fall into that trap is to regularly pray for them – those we may know personally and the world wide Muslim populations in their hundreds of millions.

4 Islam may be very militant just now. However it is very brittle. When it does finally collapse it will be not just because of military defeat but because, rather like Communism, it contains its own self-destructive tendencies and internal contradictions. Its collapse will come quickly. Its followers are greatly loved by God in Christ. We must love them too and be ready to help when they will need us most.

PART THREE

Chapter Eight

DISCERNING THE SIGNS OF THE TIMES

In Matthew 16:1–3, Jesus challenges the religious leaders of his day. He says that whilst they can interpret the signs of coming weather, they cannot interpret the signs of the times.[1]

In this chapter we will look at the signs Jesus spoke of in some detail, and will pose some questions which are important for anyone who wants to understand world history in the twenty-first century. Are there signs that we should be able to interpret today? What do they mean? How important is their interpretation for the Church and for society?

When we look at the world and see conflict and troubles, sometimes a result of natural catastrophe but more often a consequence of human invention and intention, should we discern – interpret – signs that speak of the presence of God? Are there signs of God at work in his world? Are there signs that he is Lord over the nations? Judeo-Christian teaching has always upheld the view that history is moving towards a goal, towards a final consummation, when God will come and renew the earth and the heavens, and when his will shall be done on earth as it is in heaven. Are there signs that we are moving toward this conclusion? Are there signs that the end may not be so far away?

The Bible indicates three signs in particular that we should be aware of and seek to interpret: the world-wide communication of the good news of Jesus Christ; the increase in upheaval and distress across the world; and the restoration of the Jewish people to their promised land.

First, a word of caution. Although the Bible refers to these signs, they are not supposed to be used to chart future events. The Bible makes it clear that no-one knows when the Lord will return, or when the final day of this present age will dawn. That is known only to the Father in heaven.[2] Jesus expressly warned against speculating and

---

[1]   Matthew 16:3.
[2]   Matthew 24:36.

making false predictions of when the end will come.[3] In the Bible, when prophecy relates to the future, it is not given so that we should try and map out exactly what will happen. Rather it is intended to encourage people to look to God in faith, to encourage them to believe that all things, including the future, are securely in his hand. When a word of biblical prophecy is cherished, then, as the future unfolds, people are able to recognise (or, again, interpret) what has happened, and acknowledge that things occurred as the Lord said they would in prophecy.[4]

1 The spread of the gospel into all the world

In Matthew 24:14 Jesus said, 'The gospel of the Kingdom will be preached in the whole world as a testimony to all nations, and then the end will come.'

Since those words were spoken, the gospel – the account of Jesus' life, death and resurrection – has been disseminated across the world. Churches have sprung up in every country. Some today are growing very rapidly. On average the churches of Central and East Africa have increased fourfold over the last twenty years. In Brazil and Indonesia the churches have grown by between four and ten times in thirty years. In South Korea the churches have grown four times faster than the population explosion. In China Protestant Evangelical churches have increased from under a million adherents as recorded in 1948, to what some government officials have estimated is a figure of more then 100 million.

What is more, over the last thirty years there have been more Jewish people acknowledging Jesus as the promised Messiah, in numbers that have not been seen since the days of the early Church. There are over 80 and possibly 100 Messianic congregations/fellowships in Israel; in most, Hebrew is the first language, and in some Russian or Ethiopian. In an increasing number of these, Arab believers meet alongside Jewish believers, a development, which is new, exciting, encouraging and promising, especially in the climate of heightened hostility and division in the land.

The decline of churches in the West is misleading. In the world as a whole, especially over the last thirty years, the Church has been growing at an unprecedented rate. Given the link that Jesus made between worldwide communication of the Christian message and the

---

3   Matthew 24:1-25.
4   Luke 2: 29-32.

end times, the rapid expansion of the Gentile Church internationally and the extraordinary groundswell of Jewish believers stands out as a startling sign.

2 A time of world upheaval and distress

The Bible anticipates wars, suffering, human crises and natural disasters that will escalate beyond anything that has gone before. It teaches that all of these signs of crisis will reach a climax before Jesus Christ returns. Whilst we may have a tendency to make out that things were better in the past, it is not exaggerating to say that no period of recorded history has witnessed more violence and bloodshed and suffering than the twentieth century.

This period of troubles could be said to have begun with the First World War in 1914. That marked the beginning of a 'shaking' which was to shatter whole ways of life and societies that had gone on for centuries. The Austro-Hungarian empire, the Ottoman empire and its sultans, the Russian empire and its czars, the German kingdom and its kaisers, the Chinese empire, the Japanese empire, the fascist empires of Hitler and Mussolini, the Marxist empire of Communist Russia, and the British empire all passed away within a matter of years. Some of these thrones and authorities had been in existence for more than a thousand years, and yet all were quickly swept aside.

Alongside this political upheaval, there has been dramatic social change. The common worldview has been shaped by a growth of secularism, agnosticism and atheism. Social values accommodate new attitudes towards marriage, divorce, the family and sexuality. A mainstream drug culture, new religious and political movements, and the relegation of traditional religion from the public realm to private space alone, all mean that many of what were accepted values, and Christian values at that, have been effectively discarded. The impact on individual life, family life and corporate life in the West has been immense.[5]

Upheaval has been coupled with widespread distress. Again, no period has seen more suffering than the century past. 1.25 million Armenians were massacred by the Turks in 1917. In the First World War some 20 million people died. In the Second World War of 1939-45, 55 million people perished – 20 million soldiers and 35 million

---

[5] See the research into the family carried out by, for example, the Family Matters Institute of the Centre for Contemporary Ministry (www.the-park.net).

civilians. China claims that almost 30 million died in the Sino-Japanese war. Millions more died violently in Vietnam, Laos and Cambodia (between 2 and 3 million); in India during the division between India and Pakistan (between 1 and 2 million); in Korea; in Bangladesh; in Nigeria; in Somalia, Eritrea and Ethiopia; in Mozambique, Sudan, Rwanda and Burundi; and in the Falklands, the Gulf, the Balkans and the various Middle East conflicts; and in Chechnya and the other countries of the former Soviet Union. 50 million people perished in Russia, and over 70 million in China following the Communist revolutions.[6] We are talking of more than 200 million people perishing violently during the last century. Further to these evidences of distress, it is estimated that 40 million abortions take place worldwide every year. Then, there are an estimated 23 million refugees in the world today, of which eighty per cent are women and children. And what happened to their men-folk?

Jesus predicted that there would be 'wars and rumours of war'– signs of the times – before the end came. In many ways the upheaval and the distress of the twentieth century is embodied in the suffering of the Jewish people. During the Holocaust, over 6 million – between one third and one half of the world's Jewish population – perished. And yet, whilst the Jewish people were at the centre of the twentieth century's suffering, so too the fortunes of the nation were restored in a remarkable way. This brings us to a third and most distinct sign associated with the return of Jesus Christ and the end times.

3   The restoration of the Jewish people to the promised land

The Bible records that God has made an everlasting covenant of grace with Israel. God says in Jeremiah 33:19-21, 'If you can break my covenant with the day and my covenant with the night, so that day and night no longer come at their appointed time, then my covenant . . . can be broken'. And in Jeremiah 31:36 he says, 'Only if these decrees [that is, his decrees concerning the ordering of the sun, the moon, the stars and the waves of the sea] vanish from my sight . . . will the descendants of Israel ever cease to be a nation'. With no other nation in the world has God made a promise like this. He has not made it with the Scots or English or Welsh or Irish. He has not made it with the French or Germans or Russians, or with the people of the United States of America. He made it only with the Jewish people, promising that they will still be a people, a nation, apart from all the other nations,

---

[6]   *Mao, the Unknown Story,* by Jung Chang (Jonathan Cape 2005) page 3.

to the end of history. Moreover, he ordained that Israel should be an everlasting witness to God in the midst of the nations.

Israel witnesses to the authority of the Bible, to God's word, in which we discover the living and true God, and in which through reading we encounter God face to face in Jesus Christ. Israel witnesses to the historic nature of divine revelation. Think of Israel, and we think of Israel's historic past. We think of a living God who entered into the world he created and its history to redeem Israel out of Egypt, who did mighty deeds at various points in time, who himself came physically into history in the person of Jesus Christ to save the world, and who is actively at work in the world today. We are forced to think about God, not in an abstract way, but as one whom we actually encounter on the plains of history. Israel witnesses to the fact that God confronts the nations today, in mercy and in judgement. We are not simply presented with a set of ideas or a marvellous system of teaching. We are confronted with a living personal God to whom all of us, individuals and nations, must give account.

Israel witnesses throughout her history and today, knowingly or unknowingly, willingly or unwillingly, to the mercy and judgement of God. The fact that the majority of Jews do not accept Jesus as Messiah, does not alter the fact that they are God's witnesses. Look at the amazing way that God has preserved Israel through the long centuries of wanderings and suffering. God has gone with her, suffered with her. He was with the Jewish people, suffering along with them even through the Holocaust.[7] Look at the way that he has restored the Jewish people as a nation in the Promised Land. In all this we see an amazing fulfilment of God's promises.

And Israel draws our attention to an actual end of human history, when Jesus Christ will come again to this earth, when 'his feet will stand [again] on the Mount of Olives and on Mount Zion', when he will call all nations to give account to God.

With that in mind, in 1948 the state of Israel was restored. After ceasing to be a nation nineteen-hundred years before, the Jews came together and a Jewish state was formed with its own government, its own civil administration, its own army, airforce and navy. After nineteen-hundred years Israel emerged with its own language intact. Although the terminology of politics and that of faith can be uneasy bedfellows, this is an astonishing miracle, an evidence of God's hand at work in history, a clear sign pointing us forward to Jesus' return. As a sign of God's activity and as an event that impinges upon very

---

[7]   Isaiah 63:9.

real personal dilemmas and political difficulties, its significance should be carefully considered.

The unique restoration of Israel is an event that was anticipated by the prophets of the Old Testament. Jeremiah said, 'This is what the Lord says . . . See, I will bring them from the land of the north and gather them from the ends of the earth'.[8] Ezekiel said, 'I will take you out of the nations; I will gather you from all the countries, and bring you back into your own land'.[9] The reinstatement of Israel in 1948 marks the true fulfilment of these prophetic writings. Whilst the Bible records that Israel was restored after its exile in Babylon, only during the events of 1948 were its people truly gathered from the ends of the earth and from all the countries. These and similar prophecies continue to be fulfilled as Jews from across the world return to the land that God promised to give to Israel.

In Luke 21:24, Jesus says that 'Jerusalem will be trodden down by the Gentiles until the times of the Gentiles are fulfilled'. In 1967, Jerusalem came under complete Jewish control for the first time since AD 70. In spite of continuing conflict and controversy about her future, Jerusalem is no longer trampled by the Gentiles. When seen in the light of world history and of biblical prophecy and revelation, the return of the Jews to the Promised Land and the restoration of the nation are remarkable events and distinct signs that indicate an important turn in world events.

In the gospel records, Jesus told three parables about a fig tree, which make for enlightening reading when considering the fate of Israel. The parables draw on the words and images of the Old Testament prophet Jeremiah. In Jeremiah 8:13 it says, 'There will be no figs on the fig tree and their leaves will wither. What I have given them will be taken from them'. Here the fig tree stands for Israel, the people and the land. By failing to follow the God of their forefathers, Israel had failed to bear fruit.

In the same vein, in Luke 13:6-7, Jesus was teaching his disciples, and told a parable of an unfruitful fig tree. In the parable, the owner of the fig tree says, 'These three years I have come looking for figs, but it has borne only leaves. Cut it down'. The dresser of the vineyard, the gardener, then responds, 'Let it alone for one more year. I will dig around it and manure it. If it bears fruit, fine! But if not, then cut it down'. The disciples would have well understood the pointed reference to the earlier scripture.

---

8   Jeremiah 3:18.
9   Ezekiel 36:24.

Then, in Matthew 21:18-20, and Mark 11:12-14 and 20-24, Jesus curses a barren fig tree, effectively acting out a parable with the same message. On his way from Jerusalem to Bethany in the evening, Jesus went over to a fig tree. It was not the season for figs. Nonetheless, he pretended to hunt for figs and, because there weren't any, he cursed the tree and said, 'May no one ever eat fruit from you again'. In the morning, on their way back to Jerusalem, the disciples saw that 'the fig tree was withered from the roots'. They were astonished and drew attention to it.

Many commentators say that these parables were fulfilled in AD 70, when Jerusalem, with its temple, was destroyed and burnt by the Romans and, after further war, Israel was utterly smashed and ceased to be a state, and its land devastated. Like the fig tree that was cursed, the state, the nation, the land, altogether withered.

However, in Matthew 24:30-34, Mark 13:28-31 and Luke 21:29-33, Jesus returns to the parable of the fig tree, this symbol of Israel. On the same afternoon of the day that the disciples had seen the fig tree 'withered from the roots', Jesus said, 'The trumpet will sound. The Lord will send his angels and gather together his elect people from the four winds, from one end of heaven to the other . . . Now learn this lesson from the fig tree [the tree that is withered from its roots upward], as soon as its twigs get tender and green again, and its leaves come, know that summer is near'.

Israel, the fig tree of the parable, had withered. In AD 70 Israel had ceased to be a state or a nation. It had ceased to be a nation for nineteen-hundred years and for nineteen-hundred years the land was desolate. But, in our time, we have seen God gather his people and bring them back from North, South, East and West (from some ninety different countries) and established them again in the Promised Land. In the words of Isaiah 27:6, Jacob has again taken root. Israel, although presumed dead, has begun to bud and blossom. Jesus said, when you see this happening, then 'know that summer is near'.

Israel's return to the land, and the accounts of Jews acknowledging Jesus as the Messiah, are remarkable signs which proclaim significant happenings under God. If the Bible continues to be proved right, God is about to do something very great in this world. Exactly what he will do and just when he will do it, we do not know. We are left expectant now, on tiptoes, holding our breath.

Chapter Nine

THE MYSTERY OF ISRAEL

The Church is at once excited by and anxious about Israel. In the current climate, questions of God's unfolding purposes in the world, and in particular the place of Israel in his plans, can be seen to polarise opinion amongst Christians. This blend of concern and disagreement stems from the inherent mystery of God's relationship with Israel and his role for them in the salvation of the world.

The Bible does not present us with glib answers, but nor does it confuse us with contradictions. The Hebrew Scriptures and the New Testament texts are in agreement that, as men and women, we are stretched when it comes to understanding God's ways. That does not mean that we cannot recognise his works and trust him in their delivery.

The people of Israel are the human subject of almost the whole Bible and therefore their identity, their calling and their destiny cannot be anything else but an important subject for Christians to study. There is room for learning and growth in such study, even if it leaves us feeling inadequate alongside some of the monumental mysteries of God's salvation.

1 The mystery of the Jewish identity

According to human observation, and according to the Bible as well, it would seem that Jewishness can be defined neither as simply racial, nor simply religious, nor a mixture of the two. The question, 'What is a Jew?' still puzzles the authorities in the State of Israel, as they agonise today about for whom their 'law of return' applies.

One of the points that the Apostle Paul makes in Romans 9:7ff is that ethnicity – mere physical descent from the patriarchs – was never a guarantee of belonging to the people of Israel. He uses the examples of Ishmael and Esau who were not seen as part of the chosen people, even though they were descended from Abraham to whom God's call and promise were given. The Hebrew Scriptures also record numerous examples of people who were not physically descended from Jacob being counted as Israelites – Ruth, Uriah the Hittite, Hushai the Archite and many others. This is still true today: Israel is one of the most racially mixed nations in the world. In Matthew 24:34ff, when Jesus says 'this *generation* will certainly not pass way' (apparently paraphrasing the Septuagint text of Jeremiah 31:36ff), he does not use the racial term (*ethnos*) but the family word for nation or household (*genea*). As the whole Bible makes clear, families include adopted children who are to be regarded as of the same worth and given the same privileges as their natural children.[1]

If we cannot define a Jew in racial terms, neither can we do so by religion. Many Jews today are secular. Even historically we would not be able to identify Jews just by their religious beliefs and practices. The Hebrew Scriptures are quite clear that there were many Jews who rejected and effectively rebelled against the God of their fathers.

So, although it is difficult to push Jewishness into a pigeonhole of race or religion, it cannot be denied that the Jewish identity has existed distinctively for thousands of years and continues to endure today. Jewishness is a startling fact of world history. In the letter to the believers in Rome, where Paul is discussing the history of the identity of God's people, he explains that 'it does not depend on human will or effort, but on God's mercy' (Romans 9:16). In other words, we cannot define Jewishness. It is something sustained by the grace of God. The extraordinary persistence of the distinct Jewish people provides the lesson that, good or bad, we live only by God's grace.

This existence by virtue of the grace of God is a difficult balance to find, even in the life of an individual. For a nation like Israel it causes enormous psychological tensions and dilemmas. If by 'nation', for example, it is meant a people–land relationship whose security is guaranteed by political and military power structures, then, at the deepest level, it is not true to say that Israel's vocation was or is nationhood.

Its dependence upon the grace of God for its continuing being means that the people–land relationship is secured by a deeper covenant of grace. The heritage of the Hebrew language encapsulates this. The word *'am*, meaning 'people' or 'nation', suggests personal interrelationships based on a common familial ancestry and/or a covenantal union. *Goy*, on the other hand, usually suggests a political entity. Although the two Hebrew words can each be used in both senses, the plural *goyim* came to refer to the Gentile nations as distinct from Israel.

---

[1]   Paul uses a parallel illustration in Romans 11.24 about Gentiles being like a wild olive grafted (contrary to the normal way) on to the native olive, Israel.

When Israel asked Samuel to appoint a king, they aimed to establish themselves as a political entity, trusting in the political power structures that other nations used for guidance and security. God made it clear to Samuel that this amounted to a rebellion against him who was their real King.[2] Nevertheless, when Israel insisted, God allowed them to have a king and to be a nation in the world's terms, accepting that legal institutional powers were necessary for a people living in a sinful world. God then laid down the laws that ought to govern the conduct of the King of Israel, and eventually promised that an everlasting King would come from the line of David.

Throughout the Hebrew Scriptures it becomes clear that, in order to keep this Messianic hope before Israel, their prophets had constantly to remind them that real security can come only from God himself, not from political and military structures and alliances. Israel's identity should be derived from their faithful relationship with God, not from the mechanisms of secular power. The tension in the heart of Israel resulting from their desire to be a nation 'like all other nations' and their calling to be a people of grace, is seen throughout history. It is a tension that will only be released when the connection is made between the Davidic line and the grace of God, when Israel realises its destiny under the Messiah.[3]

Israel struggles in the political world, and struggles with understanding its own identity. In fact, the mystery of Israel's ordeal is acknowledged even in the nation's name. The meaning of the word *Israel* is one of the most baffling philological puzzles of the Hebrew Scriptures. It combines the word for 'strong' or 'power' with the word for 'God'. Many different explanations of its meaning have been given. The footnotes of the NIV Bible suggest a direct translation of 'he struggles with God'. However, scholars do not fully understand what lies behind Genesis 32, the chapter in the Bible that records the origin of the name.

In many ways it is as well to accept the Bible's own explanation at face value. Jacob, the Bible tells us, was Abraham's deceitful grandson. The name *Jacob* means 'usurper'. After an adventurous life, Jacob found himself in a position of great danger, and as a last resort turned to God for help. Genesis 32 tells the mystifying story of how Jacob wrestled through the night with a man who he eventually realises is God himself. At first Jacob tries to free himself from his opponent but as the night goes on Jacob's struggle changes and he fights to hold on to the stranger until he is blessed by him. At the end of the story he

---

2   1 Samuel 8:7ff.
3   Isaiah 2:1-5.

emerges broken, with his hip put out of joint, but has also been given a new name. The reproach, signified by the name *Jacob* is taken away and he is given the name *Israel*, 'because you have struggled with God and with men and have overcome'. It is a remarkable name in so much as it describes the history of Israel to the present day, wrestling with God's calling and finding themselves striving for survival against numerous human enemies. Throughout that history God has persevered with Israel, drawing nearer and nearer to them as they struggle with him and against their special calling. In the very centre of that struggle, God reveals himself more deeply to his people.

In many places in the prophetic writings of Israel, this struggle at the heart of the nation seems fruitless, and is sometimes likened to a woman in labour who gives birth to nothing:

> As a woman with child and about to give birth writhes and cries out in her pain, so were we in your presence, O Lord. We were with child, we writhed in pain, but we gave birth to wind. We have not brought salvation to the earth; we have not given birth to people of the world.[4]

However, God reassures his people that, whatever the outward appearances of their situation, his purpose will be accomplished:

> But your dead will live; their bodies will rise. You who dwell in the dust, wake up and shout for joy. Your dew is like the dew of the morning; the earth will give birth to her dead.[5]

In particular, the struggles, the labour pains that will bring salvation, new birth and life from the dead, will be accomplished in the birth of that one Jew in whom all of Israel's destiny is gathered up and transcended. There are well-known verses from the Old Testament that Christians read each Christmas, in which are described the labour pains of the 'virgin daughter of Zion', the birth of the Messiah, the return of the exiles of Israel and the salvation of the world:

> 'But you, Bethlehem Ephrathah, though you are small among the clans of Judah, out of you will come for me one who will be ruler over Israel, whose origins are from of old, from ancient times.' Therefore Israel will be abandoned until the time when she who is in labour gives birth and the rest of his brothers return to join the Israelites. He will stand and shepherd his flock in the strength of the LORD, in the majesty of the name of the LORD his God. And they will live securely, for then his greatness will reach to the ends of the earth. And he will be their peace.[6]

---

4   Isaiah 26:17-18.
5   Isaiah 26:19.
6   Micah 5:25.

The Christian insight into this mystery lies in recognising that 'the Word of God' who had related to Israel throughout their long and painful history had now become one flesh with them.[7] The incarnation, the sufferings, the death and the resurrection of the Son of God, in whom God really does come face to face with Israel, are the great climax of the people's struggle. God was determined to bring salvation to the world through his people Israel, by bearing the sin of the world through them. In doing so he persevered until death.

Soon after Jesus' crucifixion, Israel too was broken and died as a nation. In AD 70, Jerusalem was destroyed and the Jews were scattered across the world. But after the death of Jesus came his resurrection, and Paul uses the language of resurrection to discuss the final salvation of Israel and the way that all nations would be blessed through them: 'For if their rejection is the reconciliation of the world, what will their acceptance be but life from the dead' (Romans 11:15).

The pattern of great suffering followed by renewal had fanned out into all of Israel's history, and is used in the New Testament as a template for the Christian life. It is seen especially clearly in the most significant example of Israel's deliverance, namely their rescue from slavery in Egypt, the crossing of the Red Sea, the receiving of the Commandments and the sacrificial system, their wandering in the wilderness and their eventual crossing of the Jordan into the Promised Land. It was during this time, that the call given to Abraham was spelled out in more detail to Moses, as God embedded his Word and his salvation more deeply into their consciousness. It was under Moses that they were taught the meaning of being a 'chosen people', not that it was an election that meant they were somehow God's favourites but that, being uniquely close to God, they would be required to serve God, and they would bear the glory and the pain of bringing salvation to the world at large.

2   The mystery of God's role for Israel

The book of Deuteronomy explains the way in which God's punishment and forgiveness of Israel are expressed in terms of their scattering from and re-gathering to the land (Deut. 28:64–67, 30:3–5). These principles are reiterated throughout the writings of the Hebrew prophets. They speak of a final restoration to the land at the end of the age, when Israel will be found at the centre of world hostility. Finally, the prophets write, Israel will be reconciled to her Lord, will

---

[7]   John 1:1-14.

be saved from her enemies, and will be used by God to bring blessing to all the world. The question of whether these principles and prophecies can be used to understand the latest re-gathering of the Jews to the Promised Land, is contentious, not least amongst Christians.

Many modern Post-Millennialists teach that the Church, having inherited much that was promised to ancient Israel, has now completely replaced Israel in God's purposes, Israel having lost her unique significance because of her rejection of Jesus. These ideas inform many of the assumptions that many Christians make. The central problem with the Post-Millennial view is that it seems to imply that God had not actually purposed that the Jews reject Christ for the salvation of the world.

Dispensationalists, on the other hand, accept that Israel's continuing existence and return to the land is a fulfilment of Biblical prophecy. Paradoxically, this Dispensationalism has a similar problem to the Post-Millennialist view, for it holds that God originally intended the Jews to accept Jesus. Only when they rejected him did God found the Gentile Church. This Gentile Church, according to Dispensationalism, is to be 'raptured' to heaven before God converts Israel to Christ who would then, through them, exercise authority on earth. The problem with both these theologies is that they implicitly or explicitly deny that the cross of Jesus lay at the centre of God's scheme of redemption from the beginning of the world.

There was an honourable non-Dispensationalist tradition among 17th century Puritan writers who, although disagreeing amongst themselves as to Post-, Pre- and Amillennialist eschatologies, held a common belief that in the last days the Jews would be restored to the Promised Land, acknowledge their Messiah, and bring great blessing to all peoples. This teaching also influenced the 19th century English Evangelicals. In 1858, J.C. Ryle commenting on Luke 1:32 ('The Lord God shall give unto him the throne of his father David and he shall reign over the house of Jacob forever') wrote:

> The literal fulfilment of this part of the promise is yet to come. Israel is yet to be gathered. The Jews are yet to be restored to their own land, and to look to Him whom they once pierced as their King and their God. Though the accomplishment of this prediction tarry, we may confidently wait for it. It shall surely come one day and not tarry.[8]

Karl Barth also believed in a God-given, unique destiny for Israel. Though he did not like so-called 'proofs from nature' for the existence

---

8   1969 edition of Ryle's *Expository Thoughts on the Gospels – Luke Vol. 1*, page 24.

of God, he did acknowledge that the 'mysterious story of Jewish existence' was proof of the truth of Biblical revelation.[9]

The only real clarity in these matters begins to emerge when God's original purpose behind the election of Israel is taken into account, and the meaning of the incarnation and atonement of Jesus Christ are recognised as taking place in the heart of Israel's life and destiny. In order for God to fulfil his purpose of grace and mercy, he was determined to bear the sin of humankind so that he might take them through death into life and glory. To make this real he needed to allow them to reject him in person so that he might actually suffer the full weight of their rebellion against him.

To accomplish this, he needed one people to represent all peoples, so that their sin could represent all sin. In the humanity of Jesus, God came face to face with this people and allowed them to reject him. In a mysterious but nevertheless real way, the whole of humanity was involved in the rejection of Jesus. It was not just the self-righteousness of the religious leaders of the day, nor the disloyalty of the disciples, nor the indifference of the passers-by that caused Jesus' death. In one way or another 'we were there when they crucified the Lord', as the song says. It is because of this that the Christian Church can teach that the atoning sacrifice of Jesus crucifixion is sufficient for all peoples, at all times, everywhere (1 John 2:1-2).

God began to draw near to the world when he called Abraham to be his friend. Through Abraham's descendants he planned to accomplish the painful but glorious purpose of redeeming humankind from its selfishness. Not only did he promise Abraham that his descendants would be a blessing, but he also led him to the Promised Land. This land too would play a central part in his plans, positioned as it was at the centre of the world, or, as we now know, at the junction of the continents of Asia, Africa and Europe: 'This is Jerusalem, which I have set in the centre of the nations' (Ezekiel 5:5).

Abraham's descendants were chosen, not for their own sake but for the sake of the world. Only if they were obedient would they enjoy the full blessings of God's covenant, but even if they were disobedient God would still fulfil his purposes through them and would never let them disappear until the end of the world (see Leviticus 26:3-43 and Jeremiah 31:35-37). Indeed, it was only in the context of the disobedience of Israel that God was able to reveal, through his prophets, his heart of justice and mercy for all humankind, who like

---

[9]   *Dogmatics in Outline* pages 75-76. Similar views were held by more recent well-known apologists such as Alan Richardson (see *Christian Apologetics* pages 141ff.)

Israel was sinful. The cross, the great climax of this process, was his pre-ordained way of revealing himself and saving the world.

The fact that God always had the cross in mind for Israel, is made clear in the records and prophecies that foreshadow it in the Hebrew Scriptures. God called Abraham to leave his father and his father's country and go to strange land. Two thousand years later another Son left his Father and his Father's home to come to this world to redeem it from sin. God commanded Abraham to sacrifice his son Isaac as an offering on Mount Moriah, before staying his hand, sparing the boy and providing a ram to take his place. From then on, the Bible explains, there came the saying, 'On the Mountain of the Lord it will be provided'.[10] This can also be translated 'On the Mountain of the Lord it shall become clear': in Genesis 22:14, the Hebrew *ra'ah* means, 'to see, observe, perceive, gain understanding, discover'. Two thousand years later, on the hills of Moriah, where Jerusalem is built, another Son, an only Son, loved of his Father, was sacrificed, and so the meaning of the story of Abraham and Isaac became clear. God had imprinted Golgotha, the mount of crucifixion, his means of saving the world, into the very heart of Israel.

Whilst God loves all people, his relationship with Israel was one of special intensity (Amos 3:2). As he drew near to them by his Word and Spirit, their history became distinct and different from that of other peoples. It is again the stuff of mystery, that although Israel was made separate from other nations because of their relationship with God, yet they become representative of those nations. The nations identify with Israel. They see their own histories encapsulated in Israel's. They relate to the Hebrew Scriptures, the Psalms, the writings of the prophets, as if they were written for their own people and churches.

The calling and the role of Israel, then, is twofold. Firstly Israel was chosen to be a vehicle of blessing, provision, enlightenment – chosen, in short, for a positive purpose:

> Theirs is the adoption as sons; theirs the divine glory, the covenants, the receiving of the law, the temple worship and the promises. Theirs are the patriarchs, and from them is traced the human ancestry of Christ, who is God over all, for ever praised! Amen.[11]

In other words, all the riches of God's self-revelation come to the world through Israel. The Old Testament is derived from their history. Not only that, but the humanity which God took to himself in the person

---

10   Genesis 22:14.
11   Romans 9:4-5.

of Jesus was Jewish. We could go on and say that all the disciples of Jesus were Jewish. Most of the New Testament was written by Jews. God chose Jews to be the bearers of divine revelation to the world: Abraham, Isaac, Jacob, Joseph, Moses, Samuel, David, Isaiah, Jeremiah, Mary, Jesus, Peter, James, John and Paul.

Yet the unfaithful of Biblical history also belonged to Israel. The corrupt and immoral kings who led Israel astray – such as Jeroboam, Ahab, Manasseh and Zedekiah – were denounced in the strongest terms by God's messengers. In the New Testament the chief priests and other members of the religious establishment were similarly self-serving and malicious. But here lies the wonderful paradox: it was the sin of Israel that enabled God to reveal even more fully the depths of his justice and mercy. The marvellous, profound, mysterious truths about the heart of God, to which the Hebrew prophets testify, could only be revealed in the context of Israel's sin. What is more, this type of revelation was also determined by the will and purpose of God. So, secondly, it has to be understood that Israel was chosen for a negative purpose.

Here we arrive at a conclusion that should make us apprehensive, awe-struck, humble in the shadow of God's ways. Israel was chosen so that it would reject its Messiah. In Romans 11 Paul cites the Old Testament with these words: 'God gave them a spirit of stupor, eyes so that they could not see and ears so that they could not hear, to this very day' (Romans 11:8, alluding to Isaiah 6:9 and 29:10). In Mark 4:12 Jesus quotes a similar message, from Isaiah 6:9–10: 'so that, "they may be ever seeing but never perceiving, and ever hearing but never understanding"'. They could have drawn on many other passages from the Hebrew Scriptures, including Moses own words:

> 'You have seen all that the LORD did in Egypt to Pharaoh, to all his officials and to all his land. With your own eyes you saw those great trials, those miraculous signs and great wonders. But to this day the LORD has not given you a mind that understands or eyes that see or ears that hear.'[12]

Likewise, in the servant songs of Isaiah 41 – 53, in which the prophet describes the world-wide mission of Israel, he asks his readers to consider: 'Who is blind but my servant or deaf like the messenger I send?'.[13] The strong implication of this message is that it is the very blindness and deafness of the servant of the Lord that brings light to the world.

---

[12]   Deuteronomy 29:2-4.
[13]   Isaiah 42:19.

The positive and negative aspects of Israel's calling have existed alongside one another throughout the history of the people of God. They existed together, that is, until the time when God confronted Israel face to face in Jesus. Through the people's encounter with Jesus, these two parallel vocations were broken apart and separated out. After his death and resurrection, Jesus' Jewish apostles became the foundation of what the New Testament calls the 'Israel of God' (Galatians 6:15-16). As a result of the preaching of the apostles, Gentiles too were brought to the Messiah, and so became spiritual descendants of Abraham (as Paul explains in Galatians 3:6-9). Though they were not physically circumcised, they became what Paul calls 'the circumcision' (Philippians 3:2-3; Romans 2:25-29; Colossians 2:11). The Gentiles were 'grafted into' Israel so that the Church began to inherit the many spiritual blessings that God had promised Israel of old (Romans 11:17-19).

This would not mean that the Church replaced Israel, for it is only through its continuity with Israel through Jesus the Jew, that the Church ever had any right to use the term 'Israel of God' for itself. But the Church, initially made up of Jewish and Gentile believers together, went out from the cross, in the power of the resurrection, with news of the salvation of the God of Israel, to fulfil Israel's calling to be a light to all nations. As a result, the Jewish Scriptures are now known all over the world.

But what of the negative side of Israel's calling? Israel, who had rejected Christ, went on into history, not from the resurrection side of the cross, but – to use T. F. Torrance's phrase – from the shadow side of the cross. One of the main conundrums with which Paul wrestled as he wrote the letter to the Romans was this: God chose Israel to reveal his Word to the world, but Israel rejected his final revelation in Jesus Christ, yet God – in order to save the world through the cross – had actually purposed that they reject him. How should this affect the Church's attitude to Israel and its understanding of God's role for Israel, past, present and future?

The account in the book of Genesis of Joseph and his brothers is very helpful in this. At the beginning of the story we read that Joseph is especially honoured by his father Jacob, and that this makes his brothers jealous of him. On one occasion, when his brothers had taken their sheep to distant pastures, Joseph was sent by his father to search for them. As they saw him approaching from a distance, the Bible describes their hatred for him growing in intensity. The situation anticipates the final approach of Jesus to Jerusalem, where the plotting against him was gathering momentum. Just as Jesus is rejected by his own Jewish brethren, so Joseph, 1900 years earlier, is rejected by his brothers. Initially conspiring to kill him, they eventually sold him into slavery in Egypt.

After many adventures in Egypt, Joseph achieved great success, so much so that he became a powerful and influential prince who saved the Egyptians from famine. So too, thousands of years later, Jesus, though rejected by his brothers, achieves greatness and glory as the saviour, the redeemer, in all the Gentile world where the Church bears witness to him. Through Joseph the Egyptians came to recognise the true God (Genesis 41:38-39). So too, through Jesus, the Gentile world comes to recognise the God of Israel as the true God. If Joseph's brothers had not sold him into slavery, the Egyptians would not have learned of the God of Israel. If the Jews had not rejected Jesus, the Gentiles would not have found the way of salvation.

As the story of Joseph in Egypt continues, it temporarily leaves his brothers behind in the land of Canaan. As history has continued through the centuries since Jesus' time, the Church likewise forgot the significance of his brothers, the Jews, who had betrayed him. However, the spotlight in Genesis eventually returns to Joseph's brothers. On travelling to Egypt to buy grain, the brothers encountered Joseph but they did not recognise him. They were fascinated by him, but he remained a mystery to them. They thought he was an Egyptian but he had an uncanny knowledge of them. For a long time many Jews have considered Jesus to be a Gentile figure. Many Jews, especially in Israel, are fascinated by him but he remains a mystery to them. Joseph behaved kindly and then harshly towards his brothers, alternating warmth and frost, bringing them around to recall with sorrow how cruel they had been to their brother. To them, Joseph seemed harsh, but his true feelings are revealed to the reader as he is said to keep turning away and weeping. Eventually the time came when Joseph revealed himself to his brothers. He put all the Egyptians out of the room, took off his Egyptian dress and drew them to him. It is a moving scene of reconciliation. But what of the fact that they had rejected him? What is Joseph's attitude to the betrayal?

> 'I am your brother Joseph the one you sold into Egypt! And now, do not be distressed and do not be angry with yourselves for selling me here, because it was to save lives that God sent me ahead of you . . . So then it was not you who sent me here but God . . . You intended to harm me but God intended it for good to accomplish what is now being done, the saving of many lives.[14]

---

[14]   Genesis 45:4-5, 8; 50:20.

As God continues his painful but infinitely loving struggle with his ancient people Israel, the day approaches when Jesus will draw near to them and say, 'I am Jesus, your brother, whom you handed over for crucifixion. Don't be afraid; you meant to harm me but God had purposed it for good for the salvation of the world'.

Chapter Ten

THE CHURCH IS NOT THE NEW ISRAEL!

A Critique of 'Replacement Theology'

According to Replacement Theology God has cancelled his covenant with Israel because of their sin and the rejection of Jesus the Messiah, and because Israel's purpose has been fulfilled in the person of Jesus. The Church has replaced Israel as the elect of God and as God's instrument for the salvation of the world.[1] This theology and the worldview that is derived from it, has the weight of much of the Church's historical thinking behind it, and also the backing of many of its people. Scripture, however, is unanimous in affirming, with the Apostle Paul, that God's election of Israel is a permanent fixture: 'God's gifts and his call are irrevocable'.[2]

The Church, made up as it is of believing Jews as well as Gentiles, is appointed by God to be the means with which he engages with the world, making known salvation. Unbelieving Israel, nonetheless remains God's covenant people, bound by the covenant with Abraham and his descendants for ever.

The words 'New Israel' do not occur in the New Testament and are unbiblical. The phrase 'the Israel of God' used in Galatians 6:16, refers

---

[1]   Among the more influential books written in recent years and advocating Replacement Theology are, *Whose Promised Land?* by Colin Chapman, 1983, Lion Publishing and *Israel in Prophecy* by William Hendriksen, 1968, Baker Book House. Both books have undergone several editions. See also Samuel Hosain's booklet *Israel Reassessed,* 1988, Handsel Press, and *Whose Land? Whose Promise?* by Gary Burge, 2003, Paternoster Press. Burge differs from the others as he seeks to hold to 'a middle position' (page 188), in that he believes that Israel, despite her unbelief 'remains unique, honoured, and beloved because of God's commitment to Israel's ancestors'. With its fulfilment in Christ, however, the particular land of Israel has lost its significance. It has been spiritualised and transformed to represent the whole earth and the Church, embracing believing Jews and Gentiles has replaced Israel.

[2]   Romans 11:29.

to a Church comprised of Jews and Gentiles. There is no suggestion anywhere in the New Testament, that the Israel of God (the Church) replaces historic Israel, the covenant people of God. The majority who argue that the Church has superseded Israel, stress Israel's sin and their rejection of Jesus as the Messiah. They argue that God's covenant with Israel and his promise to bless Israel and make them a blessing to the nations of the world, were conditional on Israel's faith and obedience. They zoom in on passages such as Deuteronomy 28, which speaks of the relationship between blessings and obedience on the one hand, and curses and disobedience on the other. In the view of Replacement Theology, Israel's sin and betrayal of the Messiah necessarily entailed the end of God's covenant with them, and their being overtaken by the Church as the vehicle for God's purpose of world redemption. It is difficult to overstate the seriousness of this misunderstanding of the Biblical doctrines of the covenant and of grace.[3]

1   God's covenant of grace

The covenant with Israel and with all creation is God's covenant. God initiated it. Its continuance depends entirely on God. It does not hinge on men and women, nor on what they do or don't do. Sin and disobedience cannot invalidate it. God does not cast off what he has created nor does he depart from his plan and determination to redeem Israel and the world. Nor does he ditch his plan to redeem through Israel, 'for salvation is from the Jews'.[4] God is faithful in all that he promised, first to humankind through Noah[5] and then to Israel.[6]

Although two parties are present in a covenant and participate in it, in the Hebrew Scriptures, a covenant is altogether different from a contract. A contract is between two mutually contracting parties. Both lay down prior, mutually agreed conditions. Each party then depends on the other fulfilling their side of the agreement. God's covenant

---

3   The theologian who has written and contributed most in this area, expounding God's irrevocable covenant with Israel as an integral part of his salvation for Israel and the world, is Karl Barth in his *Church Dogmatics*. See Vol. 2, part 2, pages 3-506, particularly pages 195-305: and vol.4, part 1, pages 3-78. See also for the relationship of Creation and Covenant, vol.3, part 1, pages 42-329.

4   John 4:22.

5   Genesis 5:8-13.

6   Genesis 12:2,3; 17:1-8.

with Israel and with all humankind is entirely different.[7] God alone initiates it. He makes his covenant with Israel in order that he may work out and fulfil his wider covenant for the redemption of all creation. God chose to set Israel apart from the other nations of the world. He chose to make himself known to them in a distinctive way, to unite them to himself in a unique bond of everlasting love, so that in and through them he could reveal himself to the world and restore the relationship between the world and himself. He promised to bless Israel and to make them a blessing to the world.[8] Israel was called to respond to God's will in submission, obedience and faith, but their response, whether it is obedience or otherwise, would not alter God's decision for them and for the world. It does not alter his covenant with Israel.

Many Christians will recognise that this principle is exactly the same in God's wider covenant with humankind and all creation. God's covenant does not depend on human response nor on human sin. Neither Israel's sin, nor the world's sin, can alter God's determination to deliver redemption.

God did not make a covenant with a holy people or with a perfect world, nor lay down the condition that a chosen people remained perfect. In fact he did quite the reverse. God made a covenant with a sinful, 'stiff-necked', rebellious people (see Deuteronomy 9:5ff). Israel was no less sinful than the other peoples of the world, and they were not more so either. God chose to make his covenant with them so that they could serve as representatives of all the other sinful peoples of the world. Likewise God deliberately chose to enter into covenant with the world that rebelled against him and was estranged from him. His covenant and his offer of salvation is one of unconditional goodwill and unmerited favour.

---

[7]   God's love in Christ is a covenant love of grace, which is unconditional and embraces both Israel and the world. It differs from a contract, which is legalistic and where there is a business agreement with conditions, entered into and accepted by two contracting parties. A covenant is based not on law but on love. There are, however, two kinds of covenant, mentioned in the Bible. There is a mutual, two-sided covenant, such as between man and wife, who promise to be faithful in love to one another. There is also a unilateral covenant initiated and established by one party. God's covenant with Israel, and with all people, is a unilateral covenant where God in his love pledges himself to be forever their God and Father and in which he binds them forever to himself, as his children. God's unilateral all-embracing covenant of grace does not impose conditions but it does impose obligations both on Israel and the world to love and obey him.

[8]   Deuteronomy 7:9; 1 Kings 8:23; Psalms 25:14 and 105:8 etc.

God's partnership with Israel, as the instrument for world redemption, would make very costly demands on them. It meant pain and suffering and change on the part of Israel. As God pressed more deeply into the inner life of the people and sought to draw his collaborator in the world's salvation into closer communion with himself, Israel rebelled. God was not dissuaded by their resistance. He was not thwarted in his determination to redeem the world through them. As a father disciplines the son whom he loves, so through the years God disciplined Israel, in order that they might be properly equipped to deliver God's revelation and his message of reconciliation. No matter what Israel did, God said that he would never reject them or break his covenant with them.[9] Israel is forever hedged around by God's unconditional grace and his unrelenting purpose to redeem the world through them.

God disciplined Israel to cleanse and renew them and to make them a suitable vessel for his salvation. He promised that if Israel responded in love and obedience he would greatly bless them. They would be given 'the strength to go in and take over the land'. They would 'live long in the land that the Lord swore ... to give ... a land flowing with milk and honey' (Deuteronomy 11:8-9). The Lord said he would bless the land and give abundant harvests (Deut. 11:13-15): 'Then all the peoples on earth will see that you are called by the Name of the Lord, and they will fear you' (Deut. 28:10). By the same token, God promised that if they 'turn away and worship other gods . . . then the Lord's anger will burn against [them]' (Deut. 11:16-17). And again, 'The Lord will send fearful plagues . . . harsh and prolonged disasters . . . the Lord will scatter [them] among all nations' (Deut. 28:15-68).

God also promised that whenever they returned to him, then he would restore their fortunes and have compassion and gather them again from all the nations where he scattered them (Deut. 30:1-10; 1 Kings 8:34,46f; 2 Chronicles 6:36). God's disciplining of Israel, then, was an outworking of his love and his efforts to cleanse and purify them. Far from suggesting a breakdown in the covenant, it was a sign that God was seeking to draw Israel always closer and more fully into his partnership of mission to the world. When Israel responded to God in obedience and faith, Israel enjoyed God's covenant and rejoiced in all the blessings of the covenant. When Israel resisted and rebelled against God, Israel suffered. Their enjoyment of God's blessing and their suffering were conditional upon their response to God. It is important that the conditional nature of receiving the

---

[9]   Jeremiah 31:37.

blessings associated with the covenant, is not confused with the unconditional nature which defines the covenant itself. That confusion lies at the centre of Replacement Theology's teaching that the Church has superseded Israel.

Christians draw on the same principles in their personal spirituality. God blesses believers even when they do not respond in obedience and faith. He blesses them when they least deserve it. It is in terms of his prior blessing of them that they learn to respond in faith and obedience and love: 'We love because he first loved us' (1 John 4:19).

God continually takes the initiative in bestowing the blessings of his love. This is true in his dealing with the world and with the Church, and it was true throughout his entire dealings with Israel in the Old Testament era. God did not deliver Israel out of Egypt because of their repentance and obedience and faith. He delivered them through his grace and love. He trained and disciplined them for forty years in the wilderness, to teach them to live by faith. Even so, he did not bring them into the Promised Land and establish them because of their faith (Deut. 29:4), but by grace. Within the land, time and time again, despite Israel's sin, God graciously blessed them. After he had removed them from the land, it was by grace and mercy that God later restored them from exile in Babylon. When God said, 'Comfort, comfort my people, speak tenderly to Jerusalem . . . her sin has been paid for' (Isaiah 40:1), there is no indication that Israel had repented.

God's action of grace always preceded Israel's response. Their restoration to the land led them, through an understanding and experience of God's grace in achieving it, frequently to respond in repentance and faith. This same reaction of God's grace evoking human response is seen most clearly in God's demonstration of love for the world in Jesus Christ. God loved us long before we were born, or thought of him or loved him. He took the initiative. He came into the world in Jesus Christ. He was born of the Virgin Mary, within the context and environment of Israel, and he made atonement for our sins. He forgave us and offered us his love, new life and all the blessings of his Kingdom. God's forgiveness in Christ anticipates our repentance, a point made by J.B. Torrance in a number of places:

> Repentance is our response to the Word of the Cross, our submission to the verdict of guilty to those sins which Christ has already borne away. It is the word of forgiveness, the word of the Cross which, through the Spirit, converts and heals and reconciles.[10]

---

[10] J.B. Torrance, 'Theses on Grace for the Mission of the Church'.

God in his great love has already spoken his word of forgiveness and Grace in Jesus Christ and now summons us to receive this word in repentance. Faith and repentance are our response to Grace, not conditions of Grace.[11]

Faith and repentance are exceedingly important, because without them there is no partaking in the salvation of God. Yet, God's gracious offer of salvation is always prior to repentance and conversion. His offer does not depend on a person's response. His grace is unconditional.

By grace people are saved, called and made to share in the covenant blessings and privileges, to witness to God and serve him. It is remarkable that a Church which seems to hold firmly to the gospel of unconditional grace and forgiveness described in the New Testament, suggests that a different gospel of conditional Grace is presented in the Old Testament. But this is the assumption that lies behind the idea that Israel's failure to meet the mark rendered the covenant null and void. Is it likely that God experimented with a gospel of conditional grace in the Old Testament, found that it did not work, and so replaced it in the New Testament with a gospel of unconditional grace? Was Jesus an afterthought in God's plan to redeem the world? Is he not the one through whom God created and redeemed the world? Is he not the Lamb slain from the beginning of the world?

If we pursued this line of thinking, which is advocated by the adherents of Replacement Theology, then Jesus Christ could not be understood fully within the context of Israel as the one who both fulfilled and confirmed all the promises; the message of the Old and New Testaments would not be not fully one; and the understanding of grace as it is explained in the New Testament would be in danger of being deficient. If the gospel is seen as forgiveness upon repentance, then Christian assurance is weakened immeasurably. But God does not change. The message of the Hebrew Scriptures and the New Testament is the same. Salvation is by grace. God offers his grace and love to us despite all our sins. There are no conditions.

2   The continuing role of Israel

Israel, despite their resistance and sin, has witnessed to God throughout history and continues to witness to him before the nations. God made his covenant with Israel not simply for their sake, but for the sake of the whole world.

---

[11]   J.B.Torrance, 'The Covenant Concept in Scottish Theology and Politics'.

Prior to his covenant with Israel, God had made a covenant of preservation, or salvation, with all humankind and all creation. Within that wider covenant, he made his particular covenant with Abraham and his descendants in order that he might work out his purpose of salvation for everyone. Everything that God said and did in Israel, his labour to shape and mould their inner life, calling them into covenant partnership with himself, he did not only for Israel but with a view to world redemption. God blessed Israel, brought them into the Promised Land, scattered them abroad and restored them to the land in order that other nations could witness the intervention of the Lord God and acknowledge him.[12] God testified about himself through Israel. Therefore, no matter what Israel's response to him was, whether it was obedient or disobedient, willing or unwilling, they bore witness to God among the nations. The history of anti-Semitism (see Chapter 6) indicates that the other nations, although they do not wish to admit it, recognise themselves in Israel. In Israel's resistance and sin, other nations see their position before God and recognise their behaviour. In the way in which God deals with Israel, other nations are reminded of the way in which God deals with them.

The Hebrew Scriptures are wrapped up in the very life and soul of Israel. They stand as a record of the saving grace of God, and equally as a record of men and women's resistance to God. They record God's mercy and his judgement. They also make it clear that Israel, despite everything, remained God's servant: 'You are my servant: I have chosen you and have not rejected you' (Isaiah 41:9); 'Only if the heavens above can be measured and the foundations of the earth below be searched out will I reject all the descendants of Israel because of all they have done, declares the Lord' (Jeremiah 31:37).

The Church, theologians, commentators all need to be careful about speaking too much, too judgementally about Israel's sin, getting ahead of themselves in declaring Israel rejected by God. Israel has never been any more or less sinful than the other nations of the world. The message of the book of Job is relevant and sobering and sets things in perspective: the attitudes of the nations and of the Church towards Israel have often resembled those of Job's friends who sat around him, misunderstood his misfortunes and sufferings, accused him falsely, and in doing so incurred the wrath of God.

Because of Israel's calling as a witness to God, so Jesus, according to his human line, was a member of this chosen servant people. As a Jew, as the 'Holy One of Israel', as the long expected Messiah, he

---

[12]   Ezekiel 36:23.

fulfilled all God's promises to Israel, but far from setting aside Israel's calling and election, he confirmed and sealed it for all time. This, clearly, is the view of the apostles. Paul writing in Galatians is saying that the covenant, far from being cancelled by Jesus, is centred and confirmed in him.[13] Peter when preaching in the Temple courts, said to the people, 'You are heirs of the prophets and of the covenant God made with your fathers'.[14] Peter is speaking here after the resurrection and ascension of Jesus Christ. Although the Jewish people had rejected Jesus, Peter nonetheless identifies them as heirs of the covenant. Paul would not have written as he did in Ephesians,[15] if God's election of the Jewish people was not still relevant.

The Gospel writers also make it clear that there is a future for the elect people of God, as we have seen in the lesson of the fig tree.[16] The parable anticipates Israel's ultimate return to the Land of Promise and affirms that the nation will survive and will not pass away until Jesus Christ returns at the last.

The main problem with the Replacement Theology assumption that Israel has been passed over because of their sin, is the Bible's teaching that Israel's sin and resistance to God were knitted into the very fabric of God's salvation, both for Israel and for the world. There are a number of references to Israel's blindness in the Hebrew Scriptures, many of which on their own (or in themselves) appear to be simple statements of fact. Moses says: 'But to this day the Lord has not given you a mind that understands or eyes that see or ears that hear'.[17] Isaiah says, 'Who is blind but my servant, and deaf like the messenger I send? Who is blind like the one committed to me, blind like the servant of the Lord? You have seen many things, but have paid no attention; your ears are open, but you hear nothing'.[18] However, this blindness is given new significance in the passage chronicling Isaiah's commission:

> He said, 'Go and tell this people: Be ever hearing, but never understanding; be ever seeing, but never perceiving. Make the heart of this people calloused; make their ears dull and close their eyes. Otherwise they might see with their eyes, hear with their ears, understand with their hearts, and turn and be healed.[19]

---

[13]   Galatians 3:16,17.
[14]   Acts 3:25f.
[15]   Ephesians 2:11-15 and 3:6.
[16]   Matthew 24:32-35; Mark 13:32-37; Luke 17:26-30,34-36.
[17]   Deuteronomy 29:4.
[18]   Isaiah 42:19,20.
[19]   Isaiah 6:9,10.

Here Isaiah is given an unusual commission. He is asked to do the
opposite of what you would normally expect of a prophet. Isaiah is
often called the evangelist of the Old Testament, but on this occasion
he is not called to warn, exhort to repentance, or threaten. He does
not have a joyous message to proclaim but only hopeless hardening.
What would normally appear to be an unintended and undesirable
effect of the preaching – namely, the listener turning a deaf ear to the
message – appears in this passage as something directly intended by
God. These verses are cited five times in the New Testament, and
need to be taken seriously.[20] Whilst it is not right or accurate to say
that God is responsible for the sin of Israel, God used, deliberately
and by design, their stubbornness and selfishness in his plan to
reconcile and redeem the world to himself.

If Israel had not been continually resistant to God, they would not
have been a representative people, the Hebrew Scriptures would not
have the same appearance, the nations would not have received the
revelation of God's holiness, judgement and mercy. If Israel's sin was
an integral part of God's plan to redeem the world, then, far from
causing God's covenant with them to cease, it played a part in
confirming the covenant. Therefore God says, 'You are my witnesses
. . . that I am God . . . No-one can deliver out of my hand . . . I, even I,
am he who blots out your transgressions' (Isaiah 43:12,13,25). 'I have
made you, you are my servant; O Israel, I will not forget you. I have
swept away your offences like a cloud, your sins like the morning
mist. Return to me, for I have redeemed you' (Isaiah 44:21–22). 'Only
if the heavens above can be measured and the foundations of the earth
below be searched out will I reject all the descendants of Israel because
of all they have done, declares the Lord' (Jeremiah 31:37).

The passages in the New Testament which quote Isaiah 6:9 are
deeply significant. Jesus used the prophet's teaching to explain why
he spoke to the people in parables.[21] The passage is also quoted in
John's Gospel, in which Jesus cites it to explain why the Jews could
not believe in him despite all the signs or miracles he performed.[22] In
Acts, Paul refers to the same passage in order to explain the general
lack of susceptibility of the Jews to the preaching of the Gospel.[23] In
Mark[24] and Luke[25], when the verses read, 'In order that seeing they

---

[20]   Cp. Isaiah 29:9,10.
[21]   Matthew 13:14; Mark 4:12; Luke 8:10.
[22]   John 12:40.
[23]   Acts 28:25f.
[24]   Mark 4:12.
[25]   Luke 8:10.

may see and not perceive' the Greek word rendered 'in order that' is *hina*. *Hina* is a strong word that does not permit of any variation of meaning. This leaves us with a profound and mysterious teaching. The sins of humanity put Jesus on the cross. Everybody, without exception, is responsible for his death. God, however, determined that the Jews would represent the world in its sin. He chose them to be his means by which Jesus' sacrificial atonement would be carried out.

Here we must clap our hands upon our mouth and speak only in fear and trembling within the forgiving love of God – Israel was elected to reject the Messiah. If the covenant partnership of Israel with God meant not only that the conflict of Israel with God became intensified, but was carried to its supreme point in the fulfilment of the covenant, then Israel under God could do no other but refuse the Messiah. And as Peter announced on the day of Pentecost, that is precisely what God intended, in his determination to deal with our sin at the point of its ultimate denial of the saving will of God.[26]

The advocates of Replacement Theology fail to understand the connection between Israel's sin and God's atonement in Christ. Through God's over-ruling grace, Israel's sin plays an integral and necessary part in God's salvation of the world. Their sin, however, is not for ever. Paul wrote in Romans, 'Did they stumble so as to fall beyond recovery? Not at all! Rather, because of their transgression, salvation has come to the Gentiles'.[27]

3 The Church's relationship to Israel

With all this in mind – the location of Israel in the unconditional grace of God, and their role in God's sovereign purpose of salvation – the Church needs to reconsider its relationship with the Jewish nation.

The Church is the community of all who believe in the living God. It is God's special creation. Jesus Christ is its foundation stone. It was through his atoning sacrifice that the Church is brought into being. He is the head over the Church and the Church – the community of the redeemed – is his body on earth. He lives in the Church and in every member through his Holy Spirit. In these terms, the Church has existed from the beginning of Israel's history. Abraham, the Patriarchs and the saints of the Old Testament era lived long before the days of Jesus Christ, but his sacrifice was effective for them as it is effective for all who would come after. It is through the once-and-for-

---

[26] T.F. Torrance, *The Mediation of Christ*, T & T Clark, 1992, p.34.
[27] Romans 11:11,12.

all sacrifice of Jesus that Abraham and the saints of the Old Testament are a vital part of the Church of Jesus Christ. Paul says in Romans:

> Abraham believed God, and it was credited to him as righteousness . . . so then he is the father of all who believe . . . Abraham and his offspring received the promise that he would be heir of the world . . . through the righteousness that comes by faith.[28]

The Church reached back in time to Abraham and it embraced all who believed in the Lord and obeyed him, whether Jew or Gentile. The faithful were often a minority in Israel, the inner few, the remnant, the seven thousand in Elijah's day who refused to worship Baal. But from the beginning it was intended that the Church of the faithful which arose within Israel, should embrace Jew and Gentile alike. In the Old Testament era, believing Gentiles were comparatively few – people like Rahab the harlot, Ruth the Moabitess, Ittai the Gittite and Uriah the Hittite in King David's day – despite the great spiritual visions of the prophets and psalmists and the prayer that people living at the ends of the earth might turn to the Lord, bow the knee, confess his name and be saved.[29]

It was with the coming of Jesus and the unfolding revelation through God's Holy Spirit, that it became more clearly recognised by Peter, and by the other apostles and leaders of the Church, that Jews and Gentiles are one in Christ Jesus. Gentiles 'are no longer foreigners and aliens, but fellow citizens with God's people and members of God's household, built on the foundation of the Apostles and Prophets with Christ Jesus himself as the chief corner stone' (Ephesians 2:19,20; 3:4,6). Peter says of the Church, 'You are a chosen people, a royal priesthood, a holy nation, a people belonging to God' (1 Peter 2:9). He uses the titles that were given to Israel and applies them to the Church to affirm that the Church shares with Israel in the covenant promises. The Church in Jesus Christ is God's inheritance. It is loved by God, in Christ, as he loves his only begotten Son. He calls the Church to share in the covenant promises to Abraham and, in Christ, to share in all the treasures of the everlasting Kingdom.

Even so, the Church has not replaced Israel. Israel remains embraced by the covenant. The Church arose within Israel. Apart from Israel the Church would not have emerged and could not exist. The Church, founded on Jesus Christ, needs Israel as the environment into which Jesus Christ would come, incarnate, and to which he would belong.

---

[28]   Romans 4:3,11,13.
[29]   Isaiah 45:22-23 and 49:26 etc.

The Church needs the revelation that was given to Israel and the Scriptures of the Old and New Testaments to which Israel, under God, gave rise. The Church needs God's reconciling action in the heart and life of Israel and needs to participate in Christ's atoning sacrifice, which took place within the history and life of Israel. The Church needs Israel, even today, in order truly to be the Church to which she is called by God. In a similar way – in a mysterious way – Israel also needs the Church. As the unbelieving wife is sanctified by her believing husband and vice versa,[30] so Israel is sanctified by the Church, in Christ Jesus. Christ was, and is, the Holy One of Israel in and through whom both Israel and the Church are sanctified.

The great schism that has taken place between the Church and Israel has had far reaching consequences. When an individual's relationship with God is broken, his relationship with other people becomes fragmented and corrupt. That individual is flung back upon him or herself. In the same way, as a result of the schism which took place between the Church and Israel, the Church lost much of its roots and became divided within itself. All of this has deeply affected its faith in God, its Christian understanding and its effectiveness in mission to the world. In recent years the Church has tried to build bridges through the ecumenical movement and through joint missionary action, so that divisions might be healed and that it might present a united witness to the world, but without Israel coming to faith in Jesus and a binding of the break between the Church and the Jewish people, the divisions will not be properly healed and the witness to the world will always be marred. Only if all the branches are grafted in to the original olive root can there be a Holy United Catholic Church. The Church which loses its roots in Israel, or is indifferent to Israel and to God's continuing purpose for the Jewish people, is wide open to anti-Semitism. The Church which loses its roots in Israel suffers from a loss of faith. It cannot engage fully with Jesus the Jew.

The Church is called to bear witness throughout the world to Christ and his saving work. The Church in her mission, however, must not deny or forget or belittle God's mission for unbelieving Israel. The Church needs the witness of the Jews in order to fulfil its own mission. The mission of the Church and the continuing mission of Israel are mutually interdependent. According to Karl Barth, the Church witnesses to the joyous aspect of the cross, to the resurrection of Jesus Christ. Jesus the Messiah is alive and present in the Church giving resurrected life to all who come to him in faith. Israel witnesses to the

---

[30] 1 Corinthians 7:14.

shadow side of the cross. Israel is a living testimony to the words of Jesus, which are yet words of hope: 'Look, your house is left to you desolate. I tell you, you will not see me again until you say, "Blessed is he who comes in the Name of the Lord"' (Luke 13:25). Both witness to the mercy and judgement of God; But primarily the Church witnesses to the mercy of God, and primarily Israel witnesses to the judgement of God. The witness of both are required, for the world will only accept the mercy of God if it grasps the reality of the judgement of God. In a mysterious and powerful way, Israel witnesses to Christ's atoning work, as T. F. Torrance explains:

> The Christian Church went out from the resurrection side of the Cross into history as the Church of the Lamb who had been slain but is for ever triumphantly alive; but the Jewish Church went out from the dark side of the Cross into history as the scapegoat cast out and scattered over the earth under the shadow of the crucified Jesus. Each had its distinctive mission to fulfil in bearing witness to the nature of atoning reconciliation provided by God, but each in ways that were the obverse of each other and thus mutely and unknowingly supporting each other.[31]

4 The Land, the Church and Israel

The assertions of Replacement Theology mount up and come to a head to confront the issue of God's purposes for the Promised Land. (Or, perhaps, Replacement Theology stems from an attempt to reconcile the difficult and challenging issues associated with God's material and territorial promises.) Colin Chapman in his book *Whose Promised Land?* affirms a position held by many Christians today. He suggests that in terms of God's purpose for the nation and the world, the Old Testament writers anticipated a political and spiritual restoration of the nation to the Promised Land, but that New Testament writers were concerned with a purely spiritual interpretation of the covenant. The promises concerning the land are all fulfilled in an abstract understanding of the Kingdom of God: 'In the teaching of Jesus, the theme of the Kingdom of God takes the place of the theme of the Land and everything else associated with it in the Old Testament'.[32]

George A. F. Knight, a very different writer and theologian, comes to a similar conclusion in his article, *Israel – the Land and Resurrection*.

---

[31] *The Mediation of Christ*, T & T Clark, page 37.
[32] Colin Chapman, *Whose Promised Land?* 1989 ed., p. 153.

He says, 'The Risen Christ is the eschatological significance and ultimate outcome of God's ancient promise of the Land'.[33] For Gary Burge the land has been fulfilled in Christ and spiritually transformed 'to include the entire world'.[34]

Certainly, Jesus in his person fulfils and confirms all the promises about the Promised Land. He did so during his earthly ministry and he will do so in a yet more manifest way at his final coming, when he will usher in a new heaven and a new earth. But the view which divests the Kingdom of God of the material dimension of the land raises serious difficulties. It means that with the coming of Jesus the covenant made with Israel came to an end, or came to an end in the form in which it was made with Abraham. It means that Christ transformed the promise of the land, a material reality, into something quite different – a purely spiritual Kingdom. It means that the word 'everlasting' does not mean 'for ever' but only 'a long time'.

> I will establish my covenant as an everlasting covenant between me and you and your descendants after you . . . the whole Land of Canaan, where you are now an alien, I will give as an everlasting possession to you and your descendants after you; and I will be their God.[35]

It suggests that God said something misleading. It might even raise doubts about the way in which the word 'everlasting' is used in the New Testament, when Jesus says, 'I give you everlasting life', for example. Not many Christians would want to say that in this context 'everlasting' means only a very long yet limited time-span.

It also means that a distinction is drawn between the Hebrew Scriptures and the New Testament. To affirm that Old Testament writers anticipated a political and spiritual restoration but that New Testament writers looked to a purely spiritual renewal, is to draw an unnecessary distinction between the message of the Old and New

---

[33] *The Witness of the Jews to God*, p. 41.

[34] Gary Burge, *op.cit.*, page 182. Burge says, pages 188 and 189, 'I prefer a middle position that harmonizes Paul's double commitment. Israel has fallen and has been utterly disobedient. Christians have been grafted into their place. Indeed, Christians are the heirs of Abraham. And yet fallen Israel in its unbelief remains unique, honoured and beloved because of God's commitment to Israel's ancestors. Things have not changed'.

We would reply, that for Burge, things have changed in that according to his view, the land and all the promises relating to the land have been spiritualised to include the whole earth and 'the Israeli attempt to take land and forge a nation is religiously misdirected'.

[35] Genesis 17:7-8.

Testaments. This distinction does not exist in the texts. The New Testament reaffirms the Old Testament, although it carries it to a higher level. Their gospel is the same. In trying to create distance between the gospel proclaimed in the Old Testament and the gospel delivered in the New Testament, an unscriptural dualism emerges, and with it a series of misunderstandings that has troubled the Church for years. The (one) gospel is concerned with men and women in their entirety as body, soul and spirit. By developing a kind of disembodied idea of 'the spiritual' and trying to transform the promise of land into something abstract, the Church is in danger of undermining its hold on the resurrection of the body, and the renewal of visible, material creation in the form of a new heaven and earth.

God's covenant with the Jewish people, with its material dimensions and his promises concerning the land, witnesses to the material renewal of all creation. God has not altered or annulled his covenant with Israel. His covenant was not made within the sphere of the land, but rather embraced the land, just as his covenant with all humankind was not made within the sphere of creation, but embraced creation. God's promise of the land to Israel helps us to understand God's concern for all lands. His concern for the land of Israel witnesses to his concern for all the earth. The restoration of the land of Israel anticipates the ultimate restoration and renewal of all creation. Unlike circumcision and the Law which came over 400 years later,[36] the land was not a sign of the covenant for it was embraced within the covenant. With the coming of Jesus Christ, circumcision, the ceremonial law and the sacrifices were replaced by the sacraments of Baptism and Holy Communion. The promises relating to the land and the moral law were not abrogated nor replaced. They were confirmed.

The gospel has a spiritual and physical dimension in space and time, and will have a literal fulfilment in Jesus Christ. Any understanding of the gospel becomes greatly impoverished if we try and affirm that it has only a spiritual dimension or we try and work with a dualism between spiritual and material things or between soul and body. In order to escape this we need to seek to understand the New Testament, the Person and work of Jesus Christ, his teaching, the parables, the preaching and teaching of the Apostles in the light and with the guidance of the Old Testament. It is certainly hard for the Gentile Church to understand the New Testament through anything other than Gentile, secular eyes. Yet, it is extremely important to endeavour to understand the New Testament with the God-given

---

[36] Galatians 3:17.

tools of the Old Testament. Likewise, it is necessary to approach the Old Testament and seek to understand its message through the God-given tools of the New Testament. In order to do this properly the Church today desperately needs the help of the Jewish people, in particular the help of Jewish believers, and their understanding of God and his purpose of redemption. Especially it needs the help of Jewish believers.

God's purpose for the Jewish people and for the Church belong together. The hope of Israel is for ever bound up with the hope of the Church and all creation, just as the hope of the Church and all creation is for ever bound up with the hope of Israel. The hope of all is Jesus Christ.

Chapter Eleven

ISRAEL TODAY IN THE LIGHT OF ROMANS 9 – 11

In chapters 9 – 11 of his letter to the Romans, Paul explores in great depth many of the taxing questions that arise when the Church re-evaluates its relationship with Israel. Not least, Paul provides a very clear refutation of any doctrine that suggests that the Church has been called to replace Israel. These chapters, as Professor Charles Cranfield argued,[1] are integral to the main theme of Romans and to the Christian understanding of salvation, and they must not be skated over on the assumption that they are a parenthesis.

Romans opens with Paul identifying himself as an apostle, 'set apart for the Gospel of God' (Romans 1:1). This gospel is the revelation of God in the person and work of Jesus Christ. This revelation is inseparable from God's revelation to Israel in the history of the Jewish nation and in the Hebrew scriptures. Because of that continuity, Paul is deeply concerned that his readers interpret the Old Testament in the right way. The majority in Israel rejected Jesus, as they do to this day. In proclaiming the gospel, Paul took up the theme of God's faithfulness to his promise of salvation through Abraham and his seed, and explained the position of unbelieving Israel in God's plan. God does not cease to love Israel because of her unbelief, nor does he cease to love the unbelieving Gentile world. 'Who shall separate us from the love of Christ?' (Romans 8:35).

It is important to consider these three chapters together, as a whole. There is plenty of opportunity for misinterpretation and failure to understand the thrust of Paul's argument by looking at striking verses in isolation. There are strong temptations to try and build a doctrine or a theology out of single chapters or even single passages, especially when it comes to the perplexing subject of election. This has frequently happened.

---

[1]   Charles E.B. Cranfield, *Romans: International Critical Commentary,* T. and
        T. Clark, Edinburgh, page 445f.

That said, in Romans 9-11, Paul is concerned with the election of the community of Israel, not the election of the individual. He is not teaching on the subject of eternal salvation or damnation. He is speaking about Israel being elected, 'to make the riches of his glory known'. He is explaining Israel's call to service. In God's relationship with Israel, there is an election within an election. There is the singling out of the whole of Israel as a distinctive servant people, on the one hand; and there is the calling of those who through faith are the spiritual children of Abraham, on the other. Again, the Church has long made the mistake of failing to recognise that both kinds of election are included in the election of Christ. In Chapter 9:4-5, Paul affirms that the Jewish people, despite their unbelief, are fellow-members of the people of God: 'Theirs is the adoption as sons; theirs the divine glory'. His language is clear and emphatic. Nothing can alter the fact that Israel continues to be the elect community, not even their unbelief. These are words that ought to be kept before us as we ponder the crisis in the Middle East today.

In the first few lines of Chapter 9, Paul introduces the subject with which he is concerned by declaring his 'great sorrow and unceasing anguish' (Romans 9:2) for his fellow Jews who have not accepted Jesus as the Messiah. As he has been setting forth in the letter up to this point, without Christ they cannot share in the righteousness of God, they cannot share in the wonder of his salvation. Paul's sorrow is not that of a Jewish nationalist, but of an apostle and a pastor who is deeply concerned for the eternal welfare of his people. Paul is so possessed by the Messiah that he is able to identify with his fellow Jews and to feel for them in their rejection of Jesus. Full of love, he would do anything if it would mean them sharing in the blessings of Christ. His words echo Moses' prayer in Exodus 32:32, when Moses prayed for Israel over their worshipping a golden calf: 'Please forgive their sin – but if not, then blot me out of the book you have written'. Neither Moses nor Paul felt that they could enjoy God's salvation unless they were able to enjoy it with others. This attitude informs the whole of the discussion of Romans 9-11.

1 Romans 9:6-29 Election and belief

In Romans 9:6 Paul broaches the issue with which he will wrestle until verse 29. That is, God's word has not failed because of Israel's continuing unbelief. His promises to Abraham, his plan for world redemption in Jesus, by means of Israel, has not failed nor been frustrated. There is no clash between the righteousness of God that comes through faith (the doctrine he has been developing in Chapters 1 – 8) and the promises and election of Israel. Paul has affirmed God's election of all Israel and their right to sonship, glory and the covenants. Now he goes on to affirm that within that wider covenant, there is an inner covenant, an inner Israel. These, through faith, are the true spiritual children of Abraham: 'For not all who are descended from Israel are Israel. Nor because they are his descendants are they all Abraham's children' (Romans 9:7). From the beginning God's promises were given to the spiritual children of Abraham, not necessarily to his natural children. Through the inner covenant, the spiritual remnant within Israel, God's promises and plans for world redemption in Christ are fulfilled.

There has always been a process of selection in Israel's history. There was a selection of Isaac in place of Ishmael, of Jacob in place of Esau, of those to whom the promise was given and those to whom it was not. Likewise, there has always been a selection between those in Israel who believe and in believing form the inner remnant, in place of those who do not. We might well ask on what grounds this selection was made, but the answer given suggests that it rests on nothing in people or in what people do. It does not even rest on their faith, for that would turn their faith into works. Jacob was chosen in place of Esau before either was born. God will have mercy on whom he will have mercy, and compassion on whom he will have compassion: 'It does not, therefore, depend on human desire or effort, but on God's mercy' (Romans 9:16). If those within the inner covenant were to ask, 'Why are we so privileged, why do we believe?', Paul would simply point to God's mercy.

This is the foundation for Christian confidence and comfort. Spiritual security does not depend on people's faith or in any work that they do. Everything depends on God and his mercy in Christ. As Paul writes in his letter to the Galatians, 'I live by faith *of* the Son of God',[2] that is, by Christ's faith, not his own. Paul does not attempt to explain the implicit mystery of freedom and election. He certainly does not deny freedom. Instead he is set on exalting the sovereign mercy of God.

When he turns to the subject of those who do not believe, Paul's emphasis shifts from God's merciful election, to the unbelief of the unbeliever. He does not say that God elects people to unbelief and destruction, as some have wrongly affirmed. Whilst he talks about God 'hardening' Israel, Paul is clear that their unbelief and subsequent

---

[2]   Galatians 2:20; here the KJV translates correctly (cp. Greek text of Gal 2:16, Rev 2:13 and 14:12).

rejection by God is entirely their responsibility: 'Who are you, O man, to talk back to God?' (Romans 9:20). The majority in Israel chose not to believe.

However, those who do not believe and those who become vessels of wrath, are still embraced by God's mercy. Although, in the end, not all will be saved, God 'does not want anyone to perish, but everyone to come to repentance' (2 Peter 3:9). This again is a challenging principle when applied to modern-day Israel, still living in unbelief, or militant fundamentalist Muslims, or suicide bombers intent on killing as many Jews as possible, or unbelieving Gentiles. All continue to benefit from God's mercy and love, which is set out as an unconditional gift to invite repentance and faith.

Israel, who does not believe, will nevertheless fulfil the purposes of God. Paul makes reference to the way in which God used Pharaoh during the Exodus, to illustrate Israel's position (Romans 9:17). The comparison in and of itself would have made an impression on the Jewish reader, and would probably have been quite offensive. The point is, however, that the Bible teaches that Pharaoh in his own freedom hardened his heart; at the same time it says that God hardened Pharaoh's heart. The Bible does not explain human freedom, but it accepts it and takes it as a given. At the same time it describes, overarching human freedom, the sovereign will of God.

Faced with the immovable object of God's sovereignty, Paul is aware of people's concerns and intellectual objections. Why does God blame those who do not believe? Why does he not take into account human works and character in bestowing his promises? Paul will not answer these kinds of questions: 'Does not the potter have the right to make out of the same lump of clay some pottery for noble purposes and some for common use?' (Romans 9:21). He only affirms the righteousness of God in all that he chooses to do. He effectively denies that such questions have merit. He disallows them. He will not encourage people to judge God according to human standards. Suffice to say, God in his 'sovereign mercy gives and withholds it to whom he will'.[3]

As he did towards Pharaoh, God exercises great mercy and patience toward unbelieving Israel. Verses 22-23 are linked to verse 17 by the preoccupation with God's glory. Paul indicates that God had a twofold purpose in raising up Pharaoh, and by implication, unbelieving Israel. First, he wanted to make known his power and his wrath. Second, he wanted to make known 'the riches of his glory' throughout the world.

---

3   Anders Nygren, *Commentary on Romans*, SCM Press, page 364f.

As a result many Jews and many Gentiles have come to believe in him. Those who believe are the elect of God. They are spiritual Israel, which gathers together both believing Jews and believing Gentiles. Paul quotes from the Old Testament to prove that this was always God's purpose: in Christ, in the Messiah, there is no barrier between Jews and Gentiles.

2 Romans 9:30 – 10:21 Israel's rejection of God's salvation

Israel missed a window of opportunity in respect to the righteousness and salvation of God, which the Gentiles received as a free gift (Romans 9:30–31). In their freedom the people of Israel tried (and still try) to pursue a righteousness of their own, dependent on good works. They stumbled on the cornerstone of faith: faith in the Lord, as it is presented in the Hebrew Scriptures (Isaiah 8:14); faith in Christ according to the New Testament's revelation (1 Peter 2:4f). The only way to approach God is in submission, and what he gives has to be received as a gift through faith, not an award resulting from works.

Paul prays for Israel's salvation because of his deep personal concern for them (Romans 10:1). The very fact that he prays shows both his hope and his conviction that many amongst them would be free to come to faith in Christ if they chose. He did not accept, as much of the Church appears to, that Israel's exile and rejection were final. His concern was also driven by the belief that the salvation of Israel will bring untold blessings to all the people of the world. For the same reason the Church ought to have that deep concern and do all that it can through prayer, encouragement and witness to Christ, so that Israel comes to welcome Jesus as Messiah.

Unbelieving Israel is deeply devoted to the true and living God. Even today, Orthodox Jews can shame professing Christians with their sincerity and seriousness. Paul too commends the Jews, but makes it clear that 'their zeal is not based on knowledge' (Romans 10:2). Jews and Christians have much in common: they worship the same God; they both accept the witness of the Hebrew Scriptures. Yet according to Paul, the Jews have misinterpreted the Law and the Prophets. 'Christ is the end [*telos*] of the law' (Romans 10:4): that is to say, Jesus is the goal of the law, its reason for being. He is the authority and the sum of all that the law demands, and so, in this way specifically, he is its fulfilment.[4] God, in entering into a covenant relationship with his

---

4   With this view, Calvin, Barth and Cranfield concur. Sanday and Headlam and C H Dodd seem to express the view that 'Christ has brought the law

people, gave the law in order to give his people knowledge of himself and to help them practically to believe in him. Only through faith in God, in Jesus Christ, can the law be rightly understood, observed and kept. That is why Paul, quoting Moses, said, 'Whoever obeys the commands of the law will live' (Romans 10:5).[5] The emphasis on keeping the law should always rest on faith in God's word and not on the outward fulfilment of duties. The word of God, which was the inner substance of the law, became flesh in Jesus Christ, and as such the law points to him. Without faith in God, it is easy to turn from the substance of the law (which is Christ) to the externals of the law and this results in perverting it and misunderstanding its purpose. It results in depending on what we do, rather than on the mercy of God, to obtain the promised blessing. According to the Bible, this is exactly where unbelieving Israel went wrong.

Moses understood that Israel was prone to turning away from God and his mercy. Hence he warned that they must not strive by their own efforts, in the outward keeping of the law, to climb up to heaven or to probe the mystery of the depths below, as if they could discover for themselves what is God's mind concerning righteousness (Romans 10:6-8). It is only by faith in the word which they have heard and received, which is within them, and to which the law points, that the law can be kept and a right relationship with God enjoyed. That word, to which the prophets bore witness, is the same as the Gospel to which Paul and the apostles testify (Romans 10:8-9).

Faith means confessing that 'Jesus is Lord' (Romans 10:9). This was the earliest Christian confession: it was that heartfelt acknowledgement that, in Cranfield's words 'Jesus shares the name and the nature, the holiness, the authority, power, majesty and eternity of the one and only true God'.[6] It involves complete submission to him. Faith also means believing 'that God raised him from the dead' (Romans 10:9). The resurrection of Jesus Christ is at the heart of authentic faith. By his resurrection Jesus conquered sin, death, the powers of darkness and of hell, and by his resurrection he imparts to us his new risen human life. Faith is both what is believed with the heart and what is confessed with the lips. For the Early Church it was inconceivable that once a person believed in Christ he or she should not confess the faith openly. Confession confirmed the person's own faith and helped others to believe as well.

---

to an end' (Good News Version). See Barth, *Church Dogmatics*, Vol.2:2, page 245.

5   Good News Version.

6   C.E.B. Cranfield, *op. cit.* page 529.

Israel might try to excuse and justify their unbelief (Romans 10:14-15). How can they call to God for help if they have not believed on him (or known him)? How can they believe if they have never heard him? How can they hear him speak unless someone actually proclaims his message to them? How can someone proclaim his message to them, unless God has commissioned that person to proclaim his message? These may well have been questions which Paul had encountered in his preaching, and he answered them by way of quotations from the Hebrew Scriptures. These make it abundantly clear that God has commissioned his servants; they had proclaimed his message; Israel has heard God's message and had every opportunity to believe and be saved. They are therefore without excuse.

In the passage running from verses 14 to 21 in Romans 10, Paul does not actually mention the gospel of Christ, nor yet his ministry or that of his fellow apostles. Yet the gospel is present in the Old Testament passages which he quotes. All along, the law was on the lips and in the heart of Israel pointing to Christ. All along, Jesus was the inner meaning and substance of the law; hence unbelieving Israel had heard the message. In Romans 10:21 Paul quotes from Isaiah 65:2 – 'All day long I have held out my hands to a disobedient and obstinate people' – as if to stress the fact that despite Israel's disobedience, God continues to be merciful and patient.

3 Romans 11:1–10 Israel's scattering is not forever

In chapter 11, Paul maintains that Israel's rejection is not terminal. Israel's temporary rejection will, in the end, lead to her salvation. He begins by asking the anti-Semitic question: 'Did God reject his people?' (Romans 11:1). By 'his people', Paul refers to all Israel, as he did in Romans 9:1-5, including the inner elect who believe in Jesus and the unbelieving majority. Because Israel heard the good news, and in their freedom refused to believe, some in Paul's day must have been tempted to ask whether God had rejected the people whom in the beginning he chose, but his answer to them is emphatic: 'By no means!' (Romans 11:1). For Paul, God's rejection of Israel is utterly impossible. Even in their unbelief and disobedience, God has not rejected them. His mercy embraces them in the same way that it continues to embrace the unbelieving Gentile world.

Paul himself was a Jew. He was once vehemently opposed to the gospel of Jesus Christ, but he became a disciple of Jesus and God's specially chosen messenger to the Gentile world. If God had really cast off his people, he would not have chosen Paul as an apostle to the

Gentiles, because that would fulfil Israel's missionary vocation to the world.

> 'I the Lord ... will make you to be a covenant for the people and a light for the Gentiles, to open eyes that are blind, to free captives from prison and to release from the dungeon those who sit in darkness'.[7]

These words of commission were fulfilled in Jesus Christ, and furthermore were being fulfilled in him through his servant Paul. If God had severed links with the Jewish people, then he would not be choosing Paul to fulfil his covenant with the Jewish people.

Paul and the Jewish apostles were a remnant in the same way as the seven thousand who did not bow the knee to Baal were a remnant in Elijah's day (Romans 11:4). Those who believe are few in number compared to the majority who do not. Yet their faith and election by grace is a pledge and proof that God has not rejected his people. They are a sign and pledge of God's continuing love and concern for his elect people as a whole.

4 Romans 11:11-24   Israel's hardening and the world's salvation

In verses 11-24, Paul develops his theme to explain the way in which God's hardening of the unbelieving majority in Israel belongs to his purpose of redemption for Jews and Gentiles alike. In Romans 11:11, he again raises a Gentile anti-Semitic question: 'Did they stumble so as to fall beyond recovery?' Paul answers with an emphatic, 'Not at all!' Israel's unbelief and their rejection by God is not for ever. Paul anticipates the day when the majority in Israel will turn to the Lord in repentance and faith. More than that, Paul says that, '*because* of their transgression, salvation has come to the Gentiles'.

If Israel had not sinned, then much of what is written in the Scriptures would never have been written, and the greatness and the glory, the mercy and salvation of God would not be understood in the way they are today. Even more importantly, the consummation of Israel's sin was used by God to put Christ to death. As our representatives and acting on our sinful behalf, God's over-ruling grace used Israel's sin to act as the instrument of the divine work of atonement that was completed in Christ's crucifixion. Israel's sin became the means under God of bringing salvation to the world. Within God's same purpose, the inner elect, the minority chosen by

---

7   Isaiah 42:6,7.

grace, understood what God was doing in Christ and launched his gospel of salvation into the world. The world owes an immense debt both to the inner elect who believed and to the elect majority who did not believe.

Israel's rejection of Jesus resulted in judgement: the physical destruction of the temple and the city of Jerusalem in AD 70; the break-up of the nation and the subsequent expulsion from the Promised Land. Israel's collapse was important for the spreading of the gospel throughout the world. It confirmed that Christ's kingdom was a spiritual kingdom and a kingdom for all nations. The scattering of Israel, however, was not a final sentence. Paul looks forward to the day when a great multitude from within Israel will come to believe in Christ. The vision of that day fills him with joy because of the blessings that will follow for the Gentile world and for Israel as well: 'If their transgression means riches for the world, and their loss means riches for the Gentiles, how much greater riches will their fullness bring!' (Romans 11:12). 'If their rejection is the reconciliation of the world, what will their acceptance be but life from the dead' (Romans 11:15).

Most commentators agree that Israel's rejection was spiritual and yet had a material dimension in that it involved the break-up of the nation and their expulsion from the Land. Strangely, most of these same commentators suggest that Israel's restoration to faith in Jesus as Messiah, that is, their 'fullness' (Romans 11:12) or 'acceptance' (Romans 11:15) is only spiritual. This is poor exegesis. It makes no sense to interpret the last part of a particular passage of Scripture using different standards to those used in interpreting the first part. If Israel's rejection was both spiritual and physical then their acceptance must also be both spiritual and physical. It has to involve a restoration to faith and a restoration to the Land of Promise, with all that involves in the rebuilding of a nation.

According to Ezekiel, faith follows restoration to the Land. God would restore Israel to their land in unbelief, and once they were back in the Land, the people would be restored to faith. God said, 'It is not for your sake, O house of Israel, that I am going to do these things, but for the sake of my holy name, which you have profaned among the nations where you have gone' (Ezekiel 36:22). 'I will gather you from all the countries and bring you back into your own land. I will sprinkle clean water on you and you will be clean' (Ezekiel 36:25).

A large proportion of Jews has now been restored to the Land. After nineteen hundred years the nation of Israel has been reborn. The majority of its people still do not believe in Jesus. The creation of the State of Israel, however, has touched the heart of Jews throughout the world. Following its creation more have turned to faith in Christ in

Israel, in the USA, in the former USSR and elsewhere, than since the days of the Early Church. This would seem to be the beginning of the great multitude that Paul anticipated would come to faith. God continues to use the hardening of the Jews for the salvation of the Gentiles. Far from casting the Jews away, he has made them even more his concern so that, provoked by jealousy over the blessings that have come to the Gentiles, they too will turn and be saved.

Israel's witness in unbelief to God's power and glory, is different from, and complementary to, the witness of the Church. Abraham, the Patriarchs and spiritual Israel are the first fruits, which, in the making of bread, sanctify the whole batch of dough; they are the root, which sanctifies the tree. The Gentiles who have come to saving faith in Christ should remember in humility that they have been introduced as strangers into the people of God. They are branches from a wild olive tree which have been grafted into Israel. Their faith does not sustain the people of God. It is the people of God that sustains them.[8] Some of the natural branches of the olive tree, because of unbelief, have been cut off, but with faith they could easily be grafted back in. Gentile believers who do not continue in faith, could just as easily be cut out. They can only live and bear fruit as they share in the spiritual life and heritage of the Jews. It is a humbling thought that the Gentile branch of the Church has no independent life or glory of its own, apart from Israel.

5 Romans 11:25-36 The wisdom and knowledge of God

Here Paul wants to share his insight into the mystery of God's merciful purpose for both Jews and Gentiles. He recognises that God's plan has three stages. The first stage is temporary: 'Israel has experienced a hardening in part' in order that salvation may come to the Gentiles (Romans 11:12,15). The second stage is the completion of the coming to God of the Gentiles (Romans 11:25). The third stage is the salvation of all Israel (Romans 11:26).

Commentators are divided on when the second and third stages will be reached. Considerable controversy has centred on the meaning of the words, 'And so all Israel will be saved' (Romans 11:26). Some, like Calvin, interpret these words to mean all the elect, both Jews and Gentiles. With this interpretation, however, we have to take 'Israel' in verse 26 in a difference sense to the 'Israel' of verse 25, and this does not seem feasible. Paul, as has already been noted, anticipates a day

---

[8] Anders Nygren, *op. cit.* page 399.

when a large number of unbelieving Jews will turn in faith to Jesus as the Messiah. With that in mind, Cranfield suggests that these words mean 'the nation of Israel as a whole, but not necessarily including every single member'.[9]

When 'all Israel will be saved', it is impossible to say. In the light of Jesus' teaching in Matthew 10:23 – 'You will not finish going through the cities of Israel before the Son of Man comes' – it could be that the conversion of Israel will not be accomplished until the Second Coming. At present, 'as far as the gospel is concerned', Israel resists God for the sake of the Gentiles; 'as far as election is concerned', Israel is loved on account of their covenantal heritage, 'for God's gifts and his call are irrevocable' (Romans 11:28-29). Because of Israel's disobedience the Gentiles have received mercy. As a result of God's mercy to the Gentiles, Israel too will receive mercy, 'for God has bound all people over to disobedience so that he may have mercy on them all' (Romans 11:32).

Far from being ground down by the complexity and the paradoxes of his insights and observations, Paul sets an example as to how to respond to God's plans and purposes as we see them unfold in history. He concludes with an outburst of praise: 'Oh, the depth of the riches of the wisdom and knowledge of God . . .' (Romans 11:33ff).

---

[9]   C.E.B. Cranfield, *op. cit.* page 576–577.

Chapter Twelve

TO THE JEW FIRST

1 The priority of Jewish mission

In Romans 1:16, Paul says, 'I am not ashamed of the gospel, because it is the power of God for the salvation of everyone: both to Jew first and to Greek'. Most translations read, 'first for the Jew, then for the Greek'. That is to say, most translations miss out the word 'both' (*te*), presumably because it does not read especially well in English. However, as C.E.B. Cranfield points out in his commentary,[1] the word 'both' serves to stress that the salvation of Christ is for everyone. As far as God is concerned, there is no difference between Jew and Gentile, when it comes to their need for salvation. Jesus loves both Jew and Gentile in equal measure. He died for Jew and Gentile alike, and is determined that both share in the benefits of his salvation. Nonetheless, Paul inserts the word 'first' (*proton*) to indicate that there is more to God's purposes than equality. Cranfield explains that 'within the framework of this basic equality there is a certain undeniable priority of the Jew'.[2] The meaning and the implications of this priority are unwrapped by Paul in Romans 9 – 11 and have much to do with the ordering and organisation of salvation history, as God steers it. The word 'first' is not simply to be understood chronologically, but also theologically.

Chronologically speaking, the apostles and first evangelists did in fact take the gospel to the Jew first. Paul, although called particularly to be an apostle to the Gentiles, frequently went first to the local synagogue where Jews assembled, together with believing Gentile adherents, during the course of his missionary travels. It was a pattern followed by other early apostles and evangelists too. It was a matter of missionary strategy: the apostles found in the synagogues a ready-made audience of people who believed in the living God. They were

---

[1]   C.E.B. Cranfield, *The International Critical Commentary, Romans*, page 91.
[2]   *Ibid.*

also acting in obedience to Jesus' command to preach the gospel 'among all nations, beginning at Jerusalem'.[3]

In theological terms, prioritising the Jews struck a chord with Jesus' own ministry. He made it clear that he came first 'to the lost sheep of the house of Israel'. Paul was following in Jesus' footsteps then, in his approach. In each city that he visited on his missionary journeys, he went first to the Jews and then subsequently to the Gentiles, although his calling, his objective, was to reach the Gentile world. This suggests that only by giving the Jewish community the attention it was due, could Paul be effective in taking the gospel to the nations and in doing so fulfil his special commission. The Church would do well today to consider the reasons behind this evangelistic template.

> This is not to imply that Jewish evangelism is more important in the sight of God, or that those involved in Jewish evangelism have a higher calling . . . We do not suggest that there should be a radical application of 'to the Jew first' in calling on all the evangelists, missionaries, and Christians to seek out the Jews within their sphere of witness before speaking to non-Jews! Yet we do call the church to restore ministry among the covenanted people of God to its biblical place in its strategy of world evangelisation.[4]

The Jews continue to be God's covenant people. God's covenant with them is an everlasting covenant. He made it, not because Israel was more loved than any other nation, but in order that through them he might redeem the entire world. During the course of hundreds of years he taught and trained Israel so that they could act as a guiding light for other nations. He spoke to the world through Israel. From within the fold of Israel, God sent his only Son to become the Saviour of the world, the Saviour of both Jews and Gentiles. The coming of Jesus Christ did not cancel but rather confirmed God's role for the Jewish people as a light to the world, and they remain at the heart of God's strategy for saving the world. Jesus said, 'salvation is from the Jews'.[5] Because of what God has revealed here of his strategy for world evangelisation, the Church today must have at the heart of its efforts to evangelise the world the calling of the Jews to faith in Jesus Christ. If it does not, it is out of step with God!

Without faith in Jesus Christ, the Jews cannot fulfil God's calling in the way that he wants. In John 14:6 and Acts 4:12, it is clear that for

---

[3] Luke 24:47.
[4] Lausanne Occasional Papers. No 7 *Christian Witness to the Jewish People*, page 5.
[5] John 4:23.

both Jew and Gentile, Jesus Christ is the only way to the Father. But
God certainly uses the Jewish people as a witness to himself whether
they accept or reject him. Simply by being present in the world, calling
attention to their sacred history, enduring despite repeated attempts
to remove them, Israel is an affront to the pride of the nations. Their
reinstatement in the Promised Land has also refocused world attention
and once again has placed them at the pivot of political history. Just
by being there, Israel has aroused Islam from centuries of sleep, and
has shaken and challenged its followers in a way that they never before
have been – certainly not by the Church. But we return to the fact that
only by coming to faith in Jesus Christ will the Jewish people present
the witness to the world that God intends, and this is the prime reason
for the Church to take the gospel to them as a matter of urgent priority.

The Church's attitude to the Jewish people can be seen as a
touchstone of its attitude to God. Likewise its attitude to Jewish
mission provides a measure of the Church's keenness to accomplish
God's salvation project according to God's design. In so far as the
Western churches are confronted with the State of Israel and with
Jews living throughout the Western world and in Russia, if they are
not sufficiently interested in taking the gospel of forgiveness to the
Jew, then they are unlikely to be engaged with the task of taking the
gospel to the other nations. In recent years, all the mainstream churches
in the West have witnessed a marked decline in support for world
mission. There is of course a general decline in concern for the conversion
of all nations to Christ. But at the heart of that indifference is the almost
complete failure of the Church to take the gospel of Christ to the Jews.

God promised Abraham that he would bless him and his
descendants after him, and that through them he would bless the
whole world. God has kept that promise in many ways. He also
continues to be true to his guarantee, and it is the whole thrust of
Scripture that he will yet bless the world through Israel in ways that
surpass anything that has gone before. As we have seen, it is Paul's
argument in Romans 9 – 11, that when the Jews come to faith in Christ,
they will be a source of world-wide blessing far surpassing previous
blessings: 'Because of their transgressions, salvation has come to the
Gentiles . . . how much greater riches will their fullness bring!'
(Romans 11:11-12).[6] In its commitment to world mission, the Church
ought to be deeply committed to taking the gospel to the Jew as an
integral part of that outreach, because the Bible is clear that their
conversion to Christ will advance the cause of world redemption.

---

6   See above, Chapter 11.

Over the years, the Islamic world has been hard to win for Jesus Christ. The Church has made little headway. According to the Biblical pattern, it is almost certain that a significant advance will come only through the conversion of the Jews to Christ. As the late Dr Zwemer,[7] perhaps the greatest authority on the ministry of the gospel to the Islamic world, said, 'the converted Jews make the best missionary to the Arab. Their conversion to Christ should be the abiding passion and concern of the church'. God loves the people of Islam as much as he loves the people of Israel, and as much as he loves any people. As such, he longs for them to share in the salvation of Christ. The very presence of the State of Israel, and all that has happened in recent years, has shaken the Islamic world. God is challenging Islam through Israel, and confronting the Islamic peoples with himself. At the same time, the witness of believing Jews in the Middle East, their quiet, powerful testimony, is being blessed by God. It is a matter of great thanksgiving that our generation is almost certainly seeing more Muslims come to faith in Christ than any previous generation.

At the present time there is considerable tension between Israel and the Palestinians and neighbouring Arab states. Many injustices have been perpetrated by all involved. The injustices perpetrated on the Palestinians by the Israelis hinders the witness of the gospel and hinders the witness of the Jewish people to God. Many Christians struggle now to see beyond the accounts of oppression and the abuse of power, to the real purpose of God for the Jews and for their place in world mission. This again underlines the urgent need for the Church to call the Jews to faith in Jesus Christ. In him alone is the answer to the intractable problems of the Middle East and the problems of the world.

2 The nature of the Church's mission to the Jews

The priority of reaching Jewish people with the gospel is seen in Paul's deep longing for their salvation. The Church needs to have this same prayerful and passionate concern for Israel. Mission to the Jews, however, inevitably takes a different form to that which is extended to other peoples. Israel, after all, continues to be the covenant people of God:

---

[7] Samuel M. Zwemer (1867-1952). Commencing 1890 he preached the Gospel to Muslims, in many of the bastions of Islam, Beirut, the Balkans, India, China, Africa, the Middle East, including Arabia and Yemen. In 1929 he was appointed Professor of Missions and Professor of the History of Religions in Princeton Theological Seminary, USA. He authored or co-authored at least 48 books chiefly concerning the Gospel and Muslims.

Theirs is the adoption of sons; theirs the divine glory, the covenants, the receiving of the law, the temple worship and the promises. Theirs are the patriarchs, and from them is traced the human ancestry of Christ, who is God over all, forever praised! Amen.[8]

On that account the Church needs to think carefully about its approach. We cannot rightly seek to evangelise them in the same way as others. The Orthodox Jew believes in the same God, the same divine person, as the Christian does. The gospel was born out of Judaism. Paul says, 'I can assure you that they are deeply devoted to God; only their devotion is not based on true knowledge' (Romans 10:2). The Church should approach Israel as an elder brother who belongs to the same family, Israel by birth and the Church by adoption. Necessarily the Church speaks differently to a brother than to a stranger.

The reality of Christian anti-Semitism will also influence the way the Church presents itself to Israel. The long history of persecution and prejudice, which the Church largely spearheaded, means that its approach to the Jewish people can only be one of deep, sincere repentance and humility. Far too often in history the symbol of the cross has been the symbol of bitter persecution for Jews. The Church also needs to meditate upon and confront the terrible significance of the Holocaust. In Jewish terms, the memorial for the Holocaust is now regarded as the third most significant event in the calendar. If the Church is to reach Jews today, it needs to begin to grasp the impact that the Holocaust has on the Jewish people. What it must not do, however, is make the Holocaust a reason for not taking the gospel of Christ to the Jew.

Finally, in approaching the Jewish people, the Church should go as those who have a lot to learn. It needs to be ready to be taught as well as to teach. Paul said unashamedly, 'I am debtor to Greeks and non-Greeks, both to the wise and to the foolish' (Romans 1:14). Clearly the Church needs to bear witness to the gospel of Christ, yet not simply, and perhaps not primarily, in words, but in a way of life characterised by understanding, love, repentance, humility, acceptance and compassion. The Jews long to be loved and accepted. We all do. The Church should above all pray for the Jewish people, so that Jesus might make himself known to his own beloved people, so that they might be saved both for their own sake and for the sake of the world.

---

[8]   Romans 9:4-5.

3   Jewish Christian believers

The Western Gentile Church's response to Israel, and the way in which it presents the gospel to them, can be transformed by the witness and collaboration of Messianic believers. Whilst accurate figures are hard to come by (see Appendix 6), Hebrew Christians integrated into churches and Messianic Jews meeting in independent fellowships are in a strategic position.

In principle there is no difference between Hebrew Christians and Messianic Jews, although the latter term is used to convey the fact that many Jewish believers are keenly aware of their Jewish identity and heritage, and are reluctant to be absorbed into a Gentile Christian culture. After conversion to Christ, Jews often find it difficult to integrate into Gentile churches. They may find them lacking in joy and warmth, and often find it hard to come to terms with the apparent neglect of the Hebrew tradition in the way that most Gentiles worship today. Michelle Guinness[9] in her books makes all of this very clear. There is also an understandable aversion to Gentile liberal theology. As a result, particularly in the last thirty years, when Jews have come to faith in Christ they have formed Messianic congregations. In these fellowships they welcome Gentile believers but seek to worship and serve in what they feel is a more Jewish way. These assemblies have proved to be very fruitful in attracting other Jews. Most Jews who turn to Christ today come because of friendship with believing Jews or through their independent reading of the Bible. According to an Israeli pastor the congregations that are growing most in Israel have little or no contact with Gentile churches.

The growth in number of Jewish believers in America has been considerable during the last thirty years. Today there are reckoned to be over 100,000 Jewish believers out of a Jewish population of almost 6 million. In the UK the Jewish population is about 350,000 and is in decline. The number of Jewish believers is probably between 3,000 and 5,000. In Russia and in the states which formerly belonged to the Soviet Republic, tens of thousands of Jews (or hundreds of thousands according to some sources) have come to faith in the Lord in the last ten years. In Israel today there are over 100 indigenous congregations or fellowships. Those worshipping each week may vary in size from 10 or 20 to 300 or more members. Around one hundred of these assemblies are Messianic. Most are Arab/Jewish. Others are Russian and Ethiopian.

---

9   Michele Guinness, *Child of the Covenant,* 1985, and *Promised Land,* 1987, published by Hodder.

Appendix 6 gives accurate figures for the number of Messianic groups, dating from a survey done in 1999, and it is known that the number of fellowships has grown since then. Appendix 7 gives an overview of para-church bodies working with Messianic believers and Palestinian Christians.

The Bible affirms that whether Jew or Gentile, all are of equal value before the Lord. All are equally loved: 'There is neither Jew nor Greek, there is neither slave nor free man, there is neither male nor female; for you are all one in Christ Jesus' (Galatians 3:28). Even so, just as men and women are different and have distinctive contributions to make in life, so Jews and Gentiles are different. In the calling and purposes of God they have particular roles within the Church and complementary parts to play in the outworking of redemption of the world. Therefore, the news of so many Jews coming to faith in Jesus their Messiah in recent years should be a cause for great thanksgiving to God and should be a great encouragement toward world mission.

The Church needs to be aware of how little mainstream Christianity is contributing towards taking the gospel to the Jew, or encouraging Messianic believers. When churches think of the indigenous fellowships in the Middle East and seek to confer with them, almost always they think only of the Arab churches. Far too often they take no account of the growing number of Messianic congregations. That is contrary to the teaching of Scripture, where we are commanded to take the Gospel 'to the Jew first' and it is out of step with God's strategy for world mission. The Gentile Church needs to make it a matter of regular and persistent prayer to ask for guidance as to what it can do.

Clearly churches cannot engage in open evangelism in Israel. It would be counter-productive. They can however pray and work hard to build up Messianic believers who have a great love for the Lord and a great concern for evangelistic outreach among fellow Jews and among Arabs. Whilst their congregations are growing in number, they are facing difficult times.

The growth in number of Jewish believers has aroused considerable opposition, particularly among the Orthodox. Israel's parliament has several times debated a bill (sponsored by a member of the Torah Judaism Party) banning the printing and distribution of evangelistic literature. If such a bill should ever become law it would be an offence 'to hold, print, distribute or hand out' literature of any kind which seeks to persuade others to change their religion. The penalty proposed for violation has been one year's imprisonment. Jewish believers need the prayers and all the support and encouragement that their Gentile brothers and sisters can muster. Perhaps things may be starting to change (see Appendix 6).

Jewish believers in Israel find it very difficult to find large enough places in which to worship and teach their young people. Some of necessity worship in the open air. They are desperate to build churches of their own, but their applications to buy ground and to begin construction are regularly and consistently frustrated by the ultra-Orthodox. Grace and Truth Christian Assembly in Rehovot is the first assembly to receive official approval, but it is still facing severe opposition from the ultra-Orthodox community. When considering how best the Gentile churches can help, it is worth remembering that the Church of Scotland, for example, has considerable property and grounds in Tiberias and also in Jerusalem and Tabeetha.

Messianic Jews have a theological college in Israel with about 100 students. Are there areas here where churches could help and give encouragement? Messianic Jews have a natural and rightful desire for freedom. They do not want to be dictated to or told what to do by others. They want to be treated as equal partners with older churches in the sharing of the gospel to the world. Yet they want the help of the Gentile churches, materially, spiritually and theologically. Equally, the Gentile churches also need the spiritual and theological support of the Messianic assemblies.

The Church could benefit enormously from the help of believing Jews with whom to enter more deeply into the Scriptures, to understand more fully the word of God. Without the partnership of Jewish believers, the Church is spiritually impoverished and is hamstrung in its mission to the world. The political and social issues of the Middle East, and the desperate need for justice and peace for Jews and Palestinians can easily blur our vision of God's purpose for Israel. It is easy to lose sight of his commission to evangelise and to forget the need to call all in the Middle East to faith in Jesus. The reconciliation of all people in Jesus Christ is the only answer to the problems in Israel, the Middle East and the world at large. These are desperate times and there is an urgent need for the Church to pray for a new spiritual vision of Christ's work of redemption among the Jewish people.

In Christ, the hope of the Jewish people and the hope of the world belong together.

Appendix One

THE REFUGEE QUESTION

In 1948 when the State of Israel was founded, as a result of conflict, 'somewhere between 430,000 and 650,000' Arabs fled, most of them becoming refugees. According to UNRA[1] a refugee was defined as someone who had lived in Palestine for a minimum of two years preceding the 1948 conflict. Arabs contest the number of refugees. They claim that many more Arabs were displaced. The exact number has never been accurately determined, 'because the Arabs refused to allow official censuses to be completed among the refugees'.[2] In exile, the number of refugees has increased. Arab families are generally large. Again, that number, and for the same reason, cannot be accurately determined. Arabs claim that it has risen to three, or even six, million.

Many or most of those Arabs who were displaced, and this is an issue which Arabs contest, cannot trace their ancestral roots more than three generations as living in what is now Israel and the West Bank. This fact harmonises with the figure of Arab population in 1918 as recorded by Martin Gilbert and by the survey carried out by the Anglo-American Committee of Enquiry, quoted in chapter 1. However these Arabs and their descendants have rights which should be recognised. This being the case, it is extremely hard politically, and on the human level, to determine what is just when two peoples claim the same piece of land.

The situation of the Arabs who were displaced by the founding of the State of Israel, or who fled through one of the many wars, is further complicated. As Joan Peters has pointed out, these Arab refugees remain virtually unique in this world in that they have never been really absorbed by, or integrated into, the surrounding Arab nations to which they fled, despite speaking the same language and sharing the same religion.

Commenting on the uniqueness of the Palestinian refugee problem, BIPAC[3] said, 'The history of the twentieth century is full of examples of people being resettled after conflicts that devastated entire nations.' After World War II there were at least 40 million refugees in the world. In

---

[1] Special report of the Director, UNRA, 1954-55, UN document A/2717. Cited by Joan Peters, *op.cit.* pages 18 and 447.

[2] *Ibid.* page 17 and Appendix 41, page 446.

[3] British Israel Information Committee, Briefing, 1986.

every case the answer to their problems lay in resettlement rather than in repatriation. For example, nearly 10 million displaced persons were absorbed by West Germany. France absorbed a million and a half people from Indo-China and emerging states in North Africa formerly under its rule. And in the most famous example, more than 15 million people were exchanged after partition between India and Pakistan. In the Middle East there were actually two refugee problems stemming from 1948. First about 600,000 Arabs of the total 750,000 then living in the area of Israel fled, some at the request of Arab leaders who asked them to step aside during the war. About 20 per cent of these were resettled in Arab countries, many thousands returned to their homes in Israel after the hostilities ceased, but the remainder found themselves in territory seized by Jordan. With them were many thousands of Palestinians who had never lived in Israel, the UN relief agencies found it easier to lump them all together and give them aid, at a time when many lives had been disrupted by the conflict. Arab governments have not chosen to absorb these refugees into their populations.

Accordingly, Kuwait during the Gulf war in 1980 expelled 100,000 Palestinians, because the Palestinian Authority under Yasser Arafat supported Iraq. These Palestinians had lived for many years in Kuwait, but were never fully integrated or regarded as Kuwaiti citizens.

The second refugee problem stemming from 1948 concerns about 700,000 Jewish refugees.[4] Many of them came from communities who had been settled in their host countries like Iraq for over 2,000 years. They lost everything. They were deprived of their properties and financial assets and expelled. About them the world has generally been strangely silent. They were absorbed into the state of Israel.

When we ask why Palestinian refugees have been different from other refugees in the world, the answer lies in part because of their own strong desire, and the desire of the Arab nation, that they preserve their Palestinian identity. There is also another reason.

As a matter of policy, other Arab states have wanted to keep as many of them as possible in refugee camps. Colonel Gamal Abdel Nasser, late President of Egypt dreamed of a pan-Arab, or even pan-Islamic, empire led by Egypt.

> When my mind travels to the eighty million Muslims of Indonesia, the fifty million in China, and the several other millions in Malaya, Siam and Burma, and the hundred million in Pakistan, the three or more in the middle East and the forty million in Russia, as well as the other millions in the distant parts of the world, when I visualize these millions

---

[4]   Martin Gilbert, *The Arab-Israeli Conflict – its History in Maps*, page 50.

united in one faith, I have a great consciousness of the tremendous potentialities that co-operation among them achieve.[5]

Determined to try and make this vision a reality, he began by making overtures to Syria, seeking an alliance.

Nasser recognised the many divisions in the Arab world and the hostility that existed between different Islamic countries. He recognised the hurdles that must be overcome in order to create a pan-Arab empire, and ultimately an all-Islamic empire. In his many speeches, therefore, he said two things, which have had far reaching significance.

First, that which unites the Arab nations is hostility to Israel. Second, Palestinian refugees should be kept in refugee camps in order to continue their hatred of Israel and in order to encourage them and the other nations in their hostility to Israel.

Other Arab and Islamic nations concurred. It has been a policy, which has been extraordinarily successful, as far as they are concerned. As a result of it the Palestinian refugees have suffered inordinately. In part their suffering was their own responsibility because of their continued refusal to accept the state of Israel. A major part of their suffering and poverty has arisen because of the refusal of the other Arab states to recognise and accept the state of Israel, and because of the attitude of these other states in failing to help the Palestinians or to welcome and integrate them into their societies. In short, by keeping them in refugee camps, the Palestinians have, to a great extent, suffered as pawns in the wider political struggle between Israel and her Arab neighbours.

Israel also has contributed toward the increase of the number of refugees and to their suffering and poverty, in part because of Israel's unjust treatment of them and, more particularly, by the way that Israel has acted out of concern for her own safety and security. According to Gary M.Burge[6] between the years 1987 and 2002, Israel destroyed 'as a punitive measure and out of concern for her own security' 2,911 Palestinian homes in East Jerusalem and the West Bank. Her desperate desire for security has always prevented Israel from addressing the needs of Palestinians. This is particularly true during the present *intifada*, when the Palestinians, sadly, have grown even poorer and their suffering has increased. They deserve our understanding and sympathy.

---

5   Nasser in *The Philosophy of the Revolution,* 1995. Quoted by John Laffin in *The Dagger of Islam*, page 3.
6   Gary M. Bruge, *Whose Land? Whose Promise? – What Christians are not Being Told about Israel and the Palestinians*, Paternoster Press, page 148.

Appendix Two

The *INTIFADA*, the PLO and HAMAS

The Palestine Liberation Organisation (PLO) was founded at the first meeting of The Palestinian National Council, which lasted from May 28th to June 2nd, 1964, in East Jerusalem

Ahmed Shukeiry, a Palestinian lawyer and former Saudi Arabian ambassador to the United Nations was appointed chairman. The assembled delegates drew up the Palestinian Covenant, or National Charter. In it were declared the principles and goals of the PLO, until it was rewritten at the fourth meeting of the PNC held in Cairo, 1 to 17 July 1968 under the chairmanship of Yasser Arafat.

In the 33 clauses of the new Charter[1], the aims of the PLO are clearly stated. Several of the articles echo the earlier thinking of Col Nasser.

Article 1: Palestine is the homeland of the Palestinian Arab people; it is an indivisible part of the Arab homeland, and the Palestinian people are an integral part of the Arab nation.

Article 2: Palestine, with the boundaries it had during the British mandate, is an indivisible unity.

Article 9: Armed struggle is the only way to liberate Palestine. Thus it is the overall strategy, not merely a tactical phase. The Palestinian Arab people assert their absolute determination and firm resolution to continue their armed struggle and to work for an armed popular revolution for the liberation of their country and their return to it. They also assert their right to normal life in Palestine and to exercise their right to self-determination and sovereignty over it.

Article 11: The Palestinians will have three mottoes: national unity, national mobilisation and liberation.

Article 12: The Palestinian people believe in Arab unity. In order to contribute their share towards the attainment of that objective, however, they must, at the present stage of their struggle, safeguard their Palestinian identity and develop their consciousness of their identity, and oppose any plan that may dissolve or impair it.

---

[1]   Joan Peters, *op. cit.* Appendix III, The Palestine National Charter, page 417.

Article 13: Arab unity and the liberation of Palestine are two complementary objectives, the attainment of either of which facilitates the attainment of the other. Thus, Arab unity leads to the liberation of Palestine; the liberation of Palestine leads to Arab unity; and work towards the realisation of one objective proceeds side by side with work towards the realisation of the other.

Article 15: The liberation of Palestine, from an Arab viewpoint, is a national duty and it attempts to repel the Zionist and imperialist aggression against the Arab homeland, and aims at the elimination of Zionism in Palestine. Absolute responsibility for this falls upon the Arab nation – peoples and governments – with the Arab people of Palestine in the vanguard. Accordingly the Arab nation must mobilise its military, human, moral and spiritual capabilities to participate actively with the Palestinian people in the liberation of Palestine...

Article 20: The Balfour Declaration, the mandate for Palestine and everything that has been based upon them are deemed null and void...

Article 21: The Palestinian Arab people, expressing themselves by the armed Palestinian revolution, reject all solutions which are substitutes for the total liberation of Palestine and reject all proposals aiming at the liquidation of the Palestinian problem, or its internationalisation.

Article 22: Zionism is a political movement organically associated with international imperialism and antagonistic to all action for liberation and to progressive movements in the world. It is racist and fanatic in its nature, aggressive, expansionist and colonial in its aims, and fascist in its methods. Israel is the instrument of the Zionist movement, and a geographical base for world imperialism placed strategically in the midst of the Arab homeland to combat the hopes of the Arab nation for liberation, unity and progress. Israel is a constant source of threat *vis-à-vis* peace in the Middle East and the whole world...

Article 33: This Charter shall not be amended save by (vote of) a majority of two-thirds of the total membership of the National Congress of the Palestinian Liberation Organisation (taken) at a special session convened for that purpose.

Certain points are worthy of note. In declaring that the boundaries of the Palestine which must be liberated, are 'the boundaries it had during the British mandate' (article 2), the Palestinians were not only seeking to liquidate Israel but were, by implication, seeking the liquidation of the Hashemite kingdom of Jordan. What is more, the drafters of the charter placed the Palestinian question in a larger geopolitical context, calling Israel 'the instrument of the Zionist movement and a geographical base for world imperialism placed strategically in the midst of the Arab homeland to combat the hopes of the Arab nation for liberation, unity and progress' (article 22). That is to say, they 'were declaring, in effect, war not only on Israel but also on the United States and the other nations of the West, which they blamed for imposing Israel on the Arab regimes in their midst'.[2]

The Charter helps us to understand the tension that has existed between the PLO and Jordan, the attempts at assassination of King Hussein and the war between the Jordanian army and the PLO, which took place between 1970 and 1971, following which the PLO were expelled from Jordan and retreated to Lebanon. It also helps to explain the many terrorist attacks carried out by the PLO against USA military and civil personnel and other citizens of Western countries.

During the 1970's the PLO established ties with the Soviet Union, Europe, the Third World, and the world's terrorists organisations. PLO members have carried out many hundreds of attacks – hijackings, bombings, kidnappings, massacres and individual murders. They deny few of these crimes. The PLO became during the 1970s, the pivot of international terrorism in training, finance and inspiration and involved itself in terrorism in most countries.[3]

Many covert terrorist attacks were made against both Israel and the West. In its terrorist camps in Lebanon, until 1983 when the PLO were forced to leave Lebanon, many terrorist groups came to train. Among them were The German Red Army Faction (Baader-Meinhof), the Japanese Red Army, the Irish Republican Army (IRA), the Turkish liberation army, the Armenian secret army for the Liberation of Armenia (ASALA), France's Direct Action and many Latin American terrorists.[4]

Remarkably, during this period the PLO gained international recognition and credibility and became a legitimate political organisation, recognised to be the official representatives of the Palestinian people.[5] In that capacity Yasser Arafat was invited to address the United Nations Organisation in 1974.

Yasser Arafat, as a shrewd politician and as a matter of policy, began to present to the world a moderate, accommodating political face,

[2]   Neil C. Livingstone and David Halevy, *Inside the PLO*, Quill/William Morrow, New York, page 70.
[3]   John Laffin, *The PLO Connections*, Corgi Books, page 17.
[4]   Neil C. Livingstone and David Haley, *op. cit.* page 82.
[5]   *Ibid.* page 94.

while at the same time continuing to encourage covert, armed struggle against Israel and the West. When speaking in English for Western politicians and the Western public media to hear, he encouraged moderation and peace, while at the same time when speaking in Arabic to the Arab masses, he actively encouraged confrontation and struggle.[6] His success in presenting to the West a face of moderation was such that the judges awarded him in 1993, following the Oslo Peace Accord, a Nobel Peace Prize. It was not long however before his reputation in the West as a man of peace became considerably diminished.

The PLO is an umbrella organisation bringing together as many as 22 revolutionary movements. Since its inception the PLO acquired through its assets and many investments, a multi-million dollar empire, and became one of the richest, if not the richest, revolutionary movement that this world has ever known.[7] Its annual revenues have exceeded the gross national products of some Third World countries. Some of its leaders and members of the PLO cabinet, soon became millionaires while the ordinary Palestinian people remained desperately poor, and through the *intifadas* have become poorer. Millions (although, today, primarily by Hamas) are still spent on acquiring military weapons, a fact, which can only indicate a preparation for war. Yasser Arafat had a secret fund of several millions of dollars, although the exact amount was known only to himself. As one unnamed Jordanian official once said in *The Wall Street Journal, July,* 'They have to keep him alive because if he goes, no one will know where the money is'.[8] Certainly, he became one of the richest people in the world and his widow is a millionaire many times over.

In 1974 the PLO abandoned its aim of destroying Israel in a single blow because of its inability to do this, and replaced it by a phased programme in which the whole of Palestine would be taken stage by stage. Thus, instead of deciding to liberate all of Palestine at once, the PLO planned to initially take control of the West Bank and Gaza Strip, afterwards to force Israel back to the lines of the 1947 Partition Plan, and finally to eliminate Israel altogether.[9] However, the PLO did not cease its covert terrorist attacks against Israel and the West.

At the Palestinian National Council (PNC) meeting in Algiers on 15 November 1988, the PLO spoke for the first time of the possibility

6   *Ibid.* pages 85,86.
7   *Ibid.* pages 162-198.
8   *Ibid.* pages 185, 313.
9   Christian friends of Israel, *Has the PLO Changed?* 1989.

of a Palestinian state existing alongside Israel and of their acknowledging Israel's existence. Yasser Arafat in his speech to the UN in Geneva was ambiguous but at a press conference the following day he spoke for the first time of Israel's right to exist and of an independent Palestinian state existing alongside Israel. This was widely welcomed; the hope in the West being that the PLO had changed.

Israel remained distrustful and their distrust has been confirmed by what many Palestinian and Arab leaders have since said, namely that the acceptance of an independent Palestinian state alongside Israel was an interim measure. Their ultimate intention was still to liberate the whole of Palestine. Dr George Habbash, Leader of the Popular Front for the Liberation of Palestine (PFLP), in an interview with Al-Qabas (Kuwait) on July 8th, 1988, could not have been clearer. He said, 'The Phased Programme speaks of the right of return . . . Everyone must realise that a Palestinian state in the West Bank and Gaza strip solves the problem of but a third of the Palestinian public. I come from the city of Lydda (Lod), and it is unimaginable that I will cease my struggle until I return to the city of Lydda'.[10]

Continuing terrorist attacks against Israel have helped to confirm their original intention as outlined in the Palestinian Charter of 1968. A condition laid down in the signing of the Oslo Agreement of 1993, to negotiate for peace, was the removal of those clauses in the Palestinian Charter which called for 'the liberation of Palestine', that is, the destruction of Israel. Despite repeated calls by Israel for the removal of these clauses, they still to this day remain in the Charter. Neither the PLO nor its Executive under Yasser Arafat ever had a two-third majority wishing to remove them and to recognise Israel. No special session of the National Congress of the PLO, as required by Clause 33 of the Charter, has ever been convened for the purpose, not even after Arafat's death.

Furthermore, the Oslo Peace Agreement laid down strict controls concerning the amount of arms that may be possessed by the Palestinian Authority (PA) police. Throughout the years that have followed, these agreements have been continually broken and are now a dead letter. The PLO and organisations such as Islamic Jihad, PLFP and Hamas have acquired considerable stockpiles of military weapons, as already mentioned in chapter 1.

Ehud Barak as Prime Minister of Israel agreed to 98 per cent of the requests in the Oslo agreement. He agreed that Israel should hand

---

10   Cited by CFI, *op. cit.*

over the whole of the West Bank and Gaza, that there should be an independent Palestinian State with East Jerusalem as its capital and the PA should have control of the Temple Mount. The PA rejected the offer. The fact the PA rejected the offer and the fact that preparations for the present *intifada* began three months before the end of the Camp David Peace talks and were put into operation immediately following the cessation of the talks, plus the acquiring of military hardware contrary to the Oslo agreement all indicate that the PLO still actively endorses those clauses that call for the destruction of Israel.

A conference of Islamic clerics in Beirut in January 2002, reported in the Public Press, called for the elimination of the whole of Israel.

Today, Hamas has become the most prominent and influential voice of Palestinians, especially since winning a landslide majority in the general election held in Gaza in 2005. Its leaders have shown themselves to have greater integrity than the leaders of the PLO and to be far less corrupt. They have devoted considerable energy and finance to the establishment of schools, hospitals and general social welfare, which accounts very largely for their popular support. They are totally committed in a fundamentalist way to Islam, more so than the PLO, and are much more aggressive toward Israel. They do not recognise Israel's right to exist as a state, in what they feel is Islamic territory and have refused to negotiate with Israel. They differ from the PLO as their charter makes clear, in that their struggle against Israel is a religious one and Israel must be liquidated not by stages through negotiation, as the PLO advocate, but by armed struggle from the beginning.[11] They have strongly supported the *intifada*, are responsible for many of the suicide attacks and continue to fire rockets into Israeli settlements, despite the peace agreement of November 2006. Although Sunni they have close links with Shiite Iran. They receive military support and equipment from Iran and many of their number have been and are being trained by the Iranian Revolutionary Guard. According to Israeli military intelligence, the global Al Qaida movement, operating from its notorious Iraqi branch, has succeeded in organising terror cells in Gaza, as they have in Judea and Samaria and also in southern Lebanon.[12] Because Hamas refuses to recognise the state of Israel, is committed to violence and terror, and because of their links with the Al Qaeda movement, Europe and the USA have drastically cut their aid to the Palestinians, thus reducing them to greater poverty.

---

[11]   See chapter 2, pages 33ff.
[12]   David Dolan, Israel News Report, February 2007.

Appendix Three

A JEWISH VIEW OF THE LAND

By Dr Henry I. Tankel[1]

Introduction

Little political progress will be made to-day by trading arguments about the precise meaning of biblical verses. Nevertheless people are influenced by their understanding and their perception of ancient covenants and promises, based on longstanding tradition. We must also remember that biblical prophesies and covenants are not detailed blueprints from which we can map out precise boundaries and dates. The writings are by their very nature and antiquity obscure. They serve a religious purpose not a legal one. Yet biblical promises were re-affirmed on several occasions over a long period and have been accepted by Jewish people as promise and prophesy for the future. They are among the reasons why there are still Jews to-day when one would have expected them to have disappeared. It is why I represent an unbroken line of thought, argument and tradition almost four thousand years old – a daunting task. Nevertheless, perhaps I should start by going over some old ground.

---

[1]   Dr Henry I. Tankel OBE, MD,FRCS, is a retired consultant surgeon. He is a former chairman of the Scottish Joint Consultants Committee of surgeons and physicians, a former president of the Glasgow Jewish Representative Council and for about 10 years was joint chairman of the Christian/Jewish Dialogue between the Church of Scotland and the Jewish Community in Glasgow.

This paper was presented to a Church of Scotland Group chaired by Professor Robert Davidson looking at the 'theology of land' a group, which aimed to report to the General Assembly of 2003. It was amended and updated in April 2007.

We thank Dr Tankel for his willingness to allow it to be reprinted here.

Covenant and Land: Promise, Prayer and Actuality

Jewish self-perception about the Land of Israel is that the promise to Abraham in the Abrahamic covenant was without conditions and for all time. *'For I give all the land that you see to you and your offspring forever'* (Genesis 13:15) and *'In that day the Lord made a covenant with Abram, saying: "To your descendants have I given this land from the river of Egypt to the great river, the river Euphrates"'* (Genesis 15:18). This was a covenant without the imposition of obligations with reference to an area of land which was never, in its entirety, a part of a Jewish state at any time in its history.

A little later it is repeated in slightly different terms – *'And I will establish My covenant between Me and you and your descendants after you throughout their generations for an everlasting covenant, to be a God to you and to your descendants after you'* (Genesis 17:7); *'And I will give to you, and to your descendants after you, the land of your sojournings, all the land of Canaan, for an everlasting possession; and I will be their God'* (Genesis 17:8).

This covenant was reaffirmed in the desert by Moses and accepted by the people. *'And he took the book of the covenant, and read in the hearing of the people; and they said: "All that the Lord hath spoken we will do, and we will listen"'* (Exodus 24:7).

And although later the agreement came with both a blessing and a curse there was always the promise of final redemption and return to the land of our fathers. Even the most terrifying curse in the Bible ends with the verse, *'Yet in spite of all this, when they are in the land of their enemies, I will not reject or abhor them so as to destroy them completely, breaking my covenant with them'* (Leviticus 26:44). *'Then the Lord your God will restore your fortunes, and have compassion upon you, and will return and gather you from all the peoples, where the Lord your God has scattered you'* (Deuteronomy 30:3). *'And the Lord your God will bring you into the land which your fathers possessed, and you will possess it'* (Deuteronomy 30:5). This was to be a physical return with sovereignty, and not merely a spiritual return.

Our prayers over the last 2000 years bear witness to this unshakeable belief.

> May it be Your will . . . that you be compassionate and . . . draw our scattered ones near, from among the nations, and bring our dispersed from the ends of the earth . . . Bring us . . . to Jerusalem, home of your sanctuary. (*Musaph service of the pilgrim festivals*)

> Gather us together from the four corners of the earth. (*Daily Amidah*)

But we are your people, the children of your covenant *(Daily morning service)*.

And bring us in peace from the four corners of the earth, and lead us . . . to our land.

And may you return in compassion to Jerusalem your city and build it speedily in our days as an eternal structure *(Daily Amidah)*.

Even the prayer for rain and dew which we say three times every day in the *amidah* refers to rain and dew in the land of Israel.

These and many other similar references make it clear that our prayers and our hopes were for this return to be to a real land, with real sovereignty.

For the traditional Jew, the people Israel and the Land of Israel are inextricably bound together. Judaism as a religion cannot be completely fulfilled except in the land of Israel. Israel was the place of the pilgrim festivals and the length of these festivals is different in Israel and outside Israel to this day. Jerusalem and the temple were the focus of organised religion. The laws of *Shemitah* (the Sabbatical year) and of *Yovel* (Jubilee) which apply to the land can only be observed when there is a sovereign state and indeed they have been re-introduced in present day Israel. Also the laws of *Trumah* and *Maaser* (various tithes on produce) can only be observed in Israel and are once again being observed.

The duty to live in Israel was elevated to that of a positive command, not in the recent past but in the Talmud and by Maimonides (1135-1204). *'One should always live in the land of Israel . . . for whoever lives in the Land of Israel may be considered to have a God but whoever lives outside the land may be regarded as one who has no God.'* (T.B.Ket.110b) *'Whoever is domiciled in the land of Israel lives without sin'*, and *'it is forbidden to leave the Land of Israel'*. (T.B.Ket.111a) These statements are not to be taken literally. But they are an example of the depth of feeling and belief and of the drive to travel to Israel to live there or, at the very least, to die there.

Even the secular Zionists recognised a mystical and historical connection with the land of Israel. It was for this reason that the offer of Uganda (1903) was a non-starter and the state of Azerbaijan in the twenties a failure.

There is no argument among religious Jews about the meaning of covenant or the significance of the land. The argument of the ultra-orthodox is not on whether it is a duty to live in Israel nor about the eventual outcome of a sovereign state, but merely on the manner of its eventual coming to pass. The differences are on whether a return to the land will come about gradually as the result of ordinary political process or whether it can only be by an obvious miracle heralded by a visible messiah. Some ultra-orthodox groups believe that only the latter can be valid, but they are in the minority and consist mainly of the Neturai Karta and a few members of Chassidic groups. In an extreme viewpoint, the late Rabbi Joel Teitlebaum of the Satmar Chassidim considered the Holocaust to be a punishment for Zionism. The Jewish people had broken their oath to remain patiently in exile and had tried to force the course of Jewish history. On the other hand the Israeli thinker, Menachem Hartom, had reached the opposite conclusion, that the Holocaust was a punishment for Jewish people ceasing to be real Zionists and imagining that their comfortable exile was their real home.

Rabbi Joel Teitlebaum's views were based on three conditions mentioned in the Talmud (T.B.Ket. 111a). The first two are that Israel shall not go up as if like a wall (meaning all together), and this they have not done, and that they should not rebel against the nations of the world (and as Israel was the result of the Balfour Declaration and a UN resolution there was no rebellion), but the third one was that the nations of the world should not oppress Israel too much (and 2000 years of anti-Semitism culminating in the Holocaust are reckoned to be too much). These conditions have never acquired the status of universally accepted *halachah* (religious law). They are not mentioned in the *Shulchan Aruch* or by Maimonides (the two major authorities on *halachah*) and so have never entered the canon of accepted law, though some of the ultra-orthodox have given them credence. In this connection it is important to remember that the Talmud is not a collection of settled laws but rather a summary of the arguments which took place as these laws were evolving. But in any case, these conditions are considered by mainstream orthodoxy to be a package and as the third has been broken the others are no longer binding. So those who argue that Zionism has brushed aside Biblical and Talmudic laws are in error.

For observant Jews, the maxim that one must not rely on miracles holds good. All the events of this world take place in a human framework. All of the history of Israel has a political and historical background. The will of God can only be deduced, and the logic of the deduction is always open to argument. For many, the events of 1967 were miracle enough though they can be explained in purely human terms. So, some people truly believe that present events are the birth pangs of the Messiah and that the return to the land is indeed that which was prophesied.

Consequences

The strength of the belief in a future redemption and a return to a sovereign land of Israel throughout the last 2000 years has had certain results. First, there was always immigration to the land of Israel whenever it was possible to do so. For those who could not go there to live, there was at least an attempt to go on pilgrimage. Many tried to go toward the end of their lives in order to die there. Safed has been a spiritual centre of the land and of Judaism since the 16th century. There was large immigration to Tiberias in 1740. There has been a Jewish majority in Jerusalem since the middle of the 19th century, a period of at least 150 years, with a population large enough to support the installation of a printing press in 1841 and the foundation of a Jewish hospital in 1854. Moses Montifiore bought an orange grove in 1856 and an agricultural school was founded in Mikveh Yisrael in 1870. Rosh Pinah was founded in 1878, not by immigrant Jews but by Jews from Safed who went back to the Middle Ages. All this before there was a Zionist movement.

There is in fact a record of continuous habitation since Roman times. Jews came and bought land when and where they could and continued to buy it right up to 1948 and after. The immigration which markedly increased after the Balfour Declaration in 1917 continued to be into land purchased from a willing seller. The population statistics show that the Arab population also markedly increased after the Balfour Declaration particularly in those areas close to Jewish development and because of it. There was at least as much, and almost certainly a great deal more, Arab immigration, much of it illegal, to Palestine between 1918 and 1948 as there was Jewish immigration. It is important to remember that a significant proportion of the Palestinian population of 1948 was no older than the Jewish one.

Supercessionism

I do not wish to enter into a discussion of Christian theology. This is a matter for Christians. However, there are those who believe that following the rejection of Jesus by the Jewish people the promises to the Jewish people were abrogated and the Christian church, as the new Israel, became the true inheritor of covenant and land, much of which was to be treated in a symbolic fashion.

It is true that in our pilgrim festival prayers we say *'But because of our sins we have been exiled from our land and sent far from our soil'*. But we remember the verses quoted above in Deuteronomy, *'Then the Lord your God will restore your fortunes, and have compassion upon you, and will return and gather you from all the peoples, where the Lord your God has scattered you... And the Lord your God will bring you into the land which your fathers possessed, and you will possess it.'*

In our theology, removal from the land is not tantamount to banishment from the presence of God. Judaism has never accepted that idea. The Jewish view was that the *Shechinah*, the Divine Presence, went into exile with His people (*Mekilta Pisha* 14). We have never felt far from God. While our prayers have recognised that from time to time we have forfeited goodwill, we believed this would never be permanent. We have always prayed for and expected redemption.

If it is argued that any return is predicated on repentance and a return to observance then it is interesting to note that there are probably more observant Jews today and more *yeshivot*, (places of Jewish education) that at any time in the last 2000 years despite the obvious advance of secularism in all societies, Christian and Jewish.

Land and People Together

There is also a belief that the Land of Israel can only flourish when the people of Israel inhabit it. People and Land prosper or suffer together, and so it lay waste for centuries. Only when the Jewish people returned did the land become 'green again' and prosper. *'The Lord your God will make you abundantly prosperous in all the work of your hand, in the fruit of your body, and in the fruit of your cattle, and in the fruit of your ground, for the Lord your God will again take delight in prospering you . . .'* (Deuteronomy 30:9). *'The wilderness and the dry land shall be glad for them; and the desert shall rejoice and shall blossom as the rose . . .'* (Isaiah 35:1) *'Instead of the thorn shall come up the fir tree, and instead of the briar shall come up the myrtle'* (Isaiah 55:13).

I am well aware that this is considered to be an insulting statement which is vociferously denied by Palestinians but it is interesting to read the reports of travellers through the ages like Benjamin of Tudela in the 12th Century, the naturalist T. Shaw in 1722, and the French traveller C. F. de Volnay in 1783-85. H. B. Tristam noted in 1865 that *' . . . land is going out of cultivation and whole villages are disappearing from the face of the earth'.* Mark Twain wrote in 1881 *'Of all the lands there are for dismal scenery, I think Palestine must be the prince. The hills are barren – the valleys unsightly deserts'.*

The British High Commissioner reported in 1925, *'When I first saw it (the Jezreel valley) in 1920 it was a desolation. Four or five small and squalid Arab villages, long distances apart from each other . . . For the rest, the country was uninhabited, there was not a house, not a tree . . .'* The Palestine Royal Commission Report of 1937 stated that '*in 1914 the condition of the country was an outstanding example of the lethargy and maladministration of the pre-war Ottoman regime. The population . . . eked out a precarious existence . . . most of the maritime belt was only sparsely populated and only thinly cultivated. Esdraelon for the most part was marshy and malarious'*.

These people reported without any political axe to grind, certainly no pro-Israeli one. While the desolation of the land of Israel in the 18th and 19th centuries and before is really only of historical interest, the report of the British High Commissioner and the Palestine Royal Commission report are important because they demonstrate clearly the condition of large tracts of land from which there was no indigenous population to be displaced, despite Palestinian propaganda to the contrary. We have to beware of the rewriting of history to suit a political standpoint.

The flowering of the land of Israel is one more item in the list of confirmations to the observant Jew that the Jewish people have not been superseded and that promise is being fulfilled.

Suffering and God's Will

There is an argument that as God is on the side of the poor and the oppressed, the present suffering of the Palestinians means, *ipso facto*, that what is going on cannot be the fulfilment of a divine covenant and that God can have no part in it.

There is no such thing as perfect justice in human affairs. All human events are associated with pain from childbirth onwards. Innocent people have suffered throughout history in war and through natural disasters. There is an enormous catalogue of disaster in the 20th century. Millions have died: in the Great War, in the influenza epidemic that followed it, in the Second World War, in the division of India, in Cambodia, in Rwanda and now in Darfur. On whose side was God in all these catastrophes? The presence of pain and suffering does not prove the absence of God nor that what has passed is against His will. We would be on very shaky ground if we were unable to affirm that God was at work in Israel's return solely because it has been accompanied by violence and suffering, and not all on one side.

The *Kabbalah* (Jewish mysticism) also has difficulty with the concept of the co-existence of God and evil and tries to explain such events as the Holocaust and the other disasters I have mentioned as being due to *Tzimtzum* (a temporary withdrawal of the Divine presence). But such a withdrawal would, of course, be another example of God's will.

And what part does the question of responsibility play in the assessment of the moral and theological equation?. Would there have been Israeli tanks in Jenin if there had been no *intifada* and no suicide murderers? Would Israel have been in the West Bank and Gaza at all if Egypt had not removed the UN presence from Sinai so as to enable an attack on Israel along with Syria and later Jordan in June 1967. Does the response of the Arab League at Khartoum in September, 1967 of 'No negotiations, no recognition, no peace' when Israel was expecting to give up the West Bank and Gaza in return for peace carry any responsibility for the continuation of the occupation? What responsibility do the Arab nations have for going to war in 1948 against the UN resolution and to destroy the new Israel? But for that there could have been a Palestinian state in 1948 alongside Israel.

Would the misery of the last 6 years have taken place if Arafat had continued negotiating with Barak instead of unleashing an *intifada*? After all, at Oslo he agreed to negotiations instead of violence and signed to that principle. Do any of these facts affect the moral equation? There have been many examples of the Jewish people trying to reach an accommodation with their Arab and Palestinian neighbours, all of which were rebuffed. Is that important in assessing the moral balance? Is God playing a part in this either by His presence or by His absence? If God is on the side of the poor, then the Jewish people were certainly the poor 60 years ago.

But it is not who to blame that matters now but how to get out of the mess.

Israel as a Purely Secular Act

From the Jewish theological point of view, Land and People are inextricably intertwined and this relationship has been maintained throughout the centuries in our hopes and in our prayers. At no time has this claim and this hope been given up, nurtured as it has been by divine promise.

For the Jew, there has never been any question that a return of the Jewish people to the Land of Promise is meant literally and physically and not just spiritually. It has always meant sovereignty and the possibility of accepting once again the obligations (*mitzvoth*) pertaining thereto. Just as there was theological significance in our exile at the hand of Rome two thousand years ago, so there may be theological significance in our return. The involvement of the USA to-day is little different from that of Rome 2000 years ago. God works with the instruments that are to hand. There is no land which has not been peopled by conquest at some time in the past.

I can understand why Arab Christians reject any theological endorsement of the State of Israel. It is easier than coping with the theological endorsement of a situation which they find politically unacceptable. But they do have to explain how a promise made so long ago seems to have come about against all the odds. It is unique in world history that a nation has returned to its soil after two dispersions and two millennia. The Jewish people are in the land they prayed for during all that time, and after maintaining their faith, belief and hope that such would eventually come about. The situation is no longer one of theoretical promise but of actual fact of which we have to take account.

However, if you ask me if I believe that what is happening are the birth pangs of the Messiah or the early stages of divine redemption, the answer is – I do not know. I look at the evidence of the last 100 years and I find it remarkable that a Jewish state exists at all against all the odds – but I do not know. Only time can tell and even then we may be in doubt. One thing is certain. It could not have happened now in this secular unbelieving world.

For the only time in 2000 years a window of opportunity in 1917 allowed for the Balfour Declaration to create a Jewish National Home. That was certainly influenced by Christian belief in the sort of biblical reading that I have outlined, though it was also influenced by the fact that Chaim Weizman, who was an industrial chemist and who later became the first President of Israel, was the man who found a way to make acetone which had a significant effect on the Allied war effort in the first World War. To that extent it was a payment for services rendered, cutting out of the Turkish empire a tiny National Home the size of Wales at the same time as the other Arab states were created in the region in payment for their war effort against Turkey. The pressures created by European anti-Semitism and in particular Hitler and the Second World War then forced the United Nations to turn this home into a state called Israel and give it legal status. Those are the secular facts, the man-made events, which created Israel. Do they have theological significance? It is a matter of opinion. I don't know – but I wonder.

I have spent a lot of time on theological material but between Christianity and Judaism the problem is no longer theological but political and moral. However, in the last four or five years it has been complicated by the Muslim assertion that former Muslim lands cannot be permitted to remain under non Muslim control.

Attitudes

I have already referred to the small minority of ultra orthodox people who deny validity to the state of Israel because they are still waiting for the Messiah to come to fulfil the prophecies. They live in a world of their own. What goes on outside is of little concern to them. They live their lives as they have always done and for them what will be will be. They will not influence it.

Then there are the observant Jews who believe in the imminent arrival of the Messiah and who see in the events of the present time the birth pangs of the Messiah. They believe so fervently in the imminent apocalypse that they feel they have the right and the duty to inhabit the whole of the land of Israel regardless of the present inhabitants. Some of these would like to see a greater Israel . . . Some also believe that it is forbidden to leave the land of Israel in which they live. Many settlers belong to this camp and are a vocal and well armed group. They constitute a major problem by looking at very difficult and complex problems in a simplistic and unrealistic fashion. However, they are very influential and they have important support within the Israeli government. They have the power to be dangerously disruptive.

The modern orthodox are also very fully observant but take a more pragmatic attitude to the world about them. They fully believe in the interpretation of covenant which I have given you but they accept the practical politics. Many are perfectly prepared to give up settlements and the West Bank in the same way as they accepted the evacuation of Gaza almost two years ago. The late Lord Jakobovits, the previous Chief Rabbi, was quite prepared to give up the West Bank on the grounds of *Pikuach Nefesh*, the duty to save life. He was much criticised in Israel over his remarks but there were also many people who were in agreement.

Many orthodox people would even be prepared to give up sovereignty over the temple mount because observant Jews do not go there in any case lest in a state of uncleanness they accidentally pass over the site of the Holy of Holies of the Temple. I once asked a very observant Jew if he would be prepared to give up the jurisdiction over the Temple Mount for the sake of peace if that were the only outstanding issue in an otherwise agreed negotiation. The answer was an unequivocal 'yes'.

There have been many opinion polls to show that a majority of Israeli citizens is prepared to give land for peace and to give up settlements. However, they do not believe that this option is open at the present time as they do not believe that there would be peace after a return to the 1967 borders. Those borders were not safe before 1967 and while the Israeli public over time has been prepared to make concessions, there has been no sign of any attempt to prepare the Palestinian population for compromise. Hardly any Palestinians even know what was offered at Camp David in 2000 and at Taba in 2001. There was never any attempt to inform the Palestinian people that Israel was prepared to offer anything.

The secular community is also ready to compromise but there are also hardliners there who are against any concessions, partly on the grounds that terrorism should have no reward, partly on the grounds that terrorism would not stop if a Palestinian state was created. Terrorism did not start in 1967. It has been a continuous process, before there were settlements, before Israel was in the West Bank and Gaza, indeed before there was a state at all. Israelis, and not only Israelis, view the indoctrination of children and the incitement of the Arab press with alarm since it is producing the very attitudes that would make a Palestinian state a very undesirable and dangerous neighbour.

Unfortunately, what happened in Gaza following the evacuation does not give any encouragement to continue the process. Had there been any attempt to create a small but effective model state it would have been different. But the creation of an area of chaos and violence and its use as a platform for the daily delivery of missiles into Israel without any sign of governmental control, indeed with the approval of Hamas, does not give any promise that giving up the West Bank would be practical or safe.

Epilogue

If we turn from theology to politics then we turn to the art of the possible. Whatever the rights or wrongs of the 20th century may be, the pressure of events and their effect on population movements have created new facts on the ground. There is now in Israel a Jewish population the majority of whom have been born there. They have no other homeland and no other passport and so have no right to be admitted to any other country. While the parents of these people came from all over the world, they also include approximately 700,000 refugees from Arab lands, and an appreciable number whose parents and grandparents were part of the indigenous population of the Palestine of Turkey and of the Mandate.

On the other hand there are Arabs who live in their own homes within Israel as well as in the West Bank and the Gaza strip. There are also Arab refugees who have lived in camps throughout the Middle

East for the last 60 years because no Arab state would accept them as citizens nor provide the funds to rehabilitate them despite a common language and, for the vast majority, a common religion. They are the only group of refugees in the world to have been so treated by people of their own culture in the 20th century.

There is no way that these people can now return to their former homes and open doors that no longer exist with the keys that hang on their walls. There is also no way in which the population of Israel could be expected to up sticks and depart.

With the best will in the world Israel, having withdrawn from Gaza, cannot just withdraw from the West Bank and leave a vacuum. No matter what difficulties the *intifada* may produce, Israel cannot withdraw without agreements and security guarantees. Such agreements would also have to take into account the settlement of refugees outwith Israel and the West Bank as well as a settlement of the state of war with the surrounding Arab states. To ignore this is to ignore the very genuine security needs of Israel and the very genuine concerns that Israel has over the aims of a Palestinian leadership committed to the destruction of Israel.

Israel's paranoia, if indeed it is paranoia, is based on a reading of history. Israel remembers only too well the threats of destruction and of a second holocaust that preceded the Six Day War in 1967, as well as the deafening silence of the world. Israel also noted the silence or inability of the Christian world to ameliorate the plight of the Christian community in the Lebanon during the civil war (1975-90) and wonders even more if anyone would come to the help of a Jewish community in such circumstances. She therefore feels that she must rely, in the end, on her own strength and will not make any move which it believes could be a threat to its survival whatever the consequences in unpopularity. They would rather be unpopular than dead. 'Never again' is a watchword whose implications must be clearly understood by all.

On the other hand the Palestinian people in the West Bank and Gaza have been under occupation for almost 60 years, first under Jordan and Egypt and since 1967, under Israel. They wish political freedom and independence – self determination – and they are undergoing considerable privation and suffering to achieve this.

Any attempt to create a situation which could lead to the dismantling of the State of Israel, or anything which supports the idea of a return of all, or even most, of the refugees, to the land on the Israeli side of the Green Line, is not an aid to the peace process. Anything which encourages false hope can only lead to further alienation and conflict and may even sow the seeds of yet another war.

The call for the two sides to talk to each other is necessary. The path to peace will take many years because it has to be built on a basis of mutual confidence which can only develop in an atmosphere of quiet, and with mutual understanding for the genuine difficulties of both sides. There is no sign of this happening – quite the opposite. It is very important that all comment and encouragement should be seen to be fair and even-handed by both parties or it will be ignored. Every comment needs to be weighed in order to be sure that it will indeed be helpful. It will be a long slow process. But then, so it was in Northern Ireland.

Appendix Four

ANCIENT ISRAEL'S CONQUEST OF CANAAN

Shout! For the Lord has given you the city! The city and all that is in it are to be devoted to the Lord. Only Rahab the prostitute and all who are with her in the house shall be spared . . . They devoted the city to the Lord and destroyed with the sword every living thing in it - men and women, young and old, cattle, sheep and donkeys. . . . But Joshua spared Rahab the prostitute, with her family, and all who belonged to her. (Joshua 6:16-17, 21,22)

Then the Lord said to Joshua . . . I have delivered unto your hands the king of Ai, his people, his city and his land. You shall do to Ai and its king as you did to Jericho and its king, except that you may carry off their plunder and livestock for yourselves. (Joshua 8:1-2)

Ministers often avoid reading these and similar passages in church. Many today find them difficult. How should we interpret them? Do they have anything to say, or shed any light, in regard to Israel's present return to, and occupation, of the land?

Colin Chapman in his book, *Whose Promised Land?* raises the difficulty that these and similar passages, relating to Israel's conquest of the land, present to modern Christians.

He wants to take these stories of the conquest of the land seriously and to regard both the Old and New Testament as inspired. In seeking to do so, he re-interprets them in the light of what he believes should be our understanding of Christ and the New Testament. He judges and re-assesses them, in accord with the ethical teaching which he believes is given to us through God's revelation in Christ. His views represent many Christians today and require consideration.

And what can any reader in the twenty-first century make of the biblical account, which says that God not only condoned the conquest and all that went with it, but actually *commanded* it? Is it conceivable that a God of love could actually have *ordered* the Israelites to engage in what we today would call 'ethnic cleansing'? For many Christians, these are some of the hardest questions in the whole Bible.[1]

---

[1]   Colin Chapman, *Whose Promised Land?* page 127.

Chapman seeks to resolve the problem through the perspective of progressive revelation:

> According to this understanding of revelation, we would have to say that God was obliged, as it were, to limit himself in the process of revelation. The truth that he wanted to reveal had to be adapted and accommodated to what people could understand at any given time in history . . . The full Christian understanding of the love of God as it has been expressed in the life, death and resurrection of Jesus could never have been understood at the time of Abraham, Moses, Joshua or David. It took many centuries to prepare the Children of Israel for the fuller revelation that was to come in the person of Jesus.

> Anyone, therefore, who sees Christ as the fullest possible revelation of what God is like and the kind of moral standards that God sets for human beings, will see many of the actions of Joshua as very wrong and abhorrent.[2]

> So those who see Jesus as the climax of God's revelation to the human race can never imagine him acting in the way that Joshua did. . . . The life of Jesus becomes a kind of filter through which they interpret everything in the Old Testament.[3]

Chapman resists the temptation to describe these early accounts of Israel's conquest of Canaan as 'purely human and distorted interpretations of history, and not in any sense as inspired Scripture'. As an evangelical he wants 'to take seriously *everything* that the Bible (both Testaments) says about the conquest'. Hence, in his understanding of 'progressive revelation', he is led to say that 'the conquest of the land becomes one stage in the unfolding of God's plan for history – a shameful but vital stage, one that was not to be repeated, and need never be repeated'.[4]

Israel and the land find their fulfilment in Christ, but for Chapman they are spiritualised. They lose, as it were, the physical dimension, which they had in the Old Testament. The nation of Israel and the land cease to have any theological significance. Israel represents the Church (of Jew and Gentile) and the conquest of the land represents the work of seeking to win the peoples of the world for Christ.

In reply to Chapman, consider the following observations.

Chapman is right to say that revelation in the Bible is progressive. Through the course of Israel's history God gradually revealed more

---

[2]   *Ibid.* page 132-133.
[3]   *Ibid.* page 133.
[4]   *Ibid.* pages 133-134.

and more of himself until his revelation of himself climaxed in Jesus Christ. God did accommodate himself to 'what people could understand at any given time in history'. His greatest accommodation of himself to our understanding of him is in the Man Christ Jesus.

Chapman, however, is wrong to suggest that in accommodating himself to what people could understand at any given time in history, God not only condoned but commanded people to do what, at a later stage, was seen to be morally wrong and repugnant! God is holy and forever faithful to himself. While he did accommodate himself to the needs and understanding of the people at the time, God never would, or could, command what was morally wrong. Chapman's view undermines our understanding and worship of God as holy and righteous.

Chapman's position opens the door to the argument (although Chapman may not wish to go this far) that all the teaching of the New Testament is culturally conditioned and time limited. It is on this ground, for example, that those of a liberal persuasion argue that the biblical condemnation of homosexuality was culturally conditioned but time limited. It was right for an earlier generation – but today in the light of our understanding of Christ's love we should see that homosexual unions are legitimate and of God!

With reference to the indiscriminate slaughter, in Jericho and Ai, of men, women and children, if this had been done simply as a human decision, then it would have been utterly wrong and worthy of all condemnation. In so far as God commanded it (and with Chapman I believe that God did command it), then it was right. As John Calvin said, 'The indiscriminate and promiscuous slaughter, making no distinction of age or sex, but including alike women and children, the aged and decrepit, might seem an inhuman massacre, had it not been executed by the command of God. But as he, in whose hands are life and death, had justly doomed these nations to destruction, this puts an end to all discussion'.[5]

In so far as God, and not a human, commanded this slaughter, we can never attempt to repeat this action. It cannot be held up as a precedent to be repeated by Israel or by any nation today - unless God so commanded, which he has never done.[6] It is not a precedent or guide for Israel's repossession of the land today no matter how much we may affirm that Israel's return to the land today is God's doing.

5   Calvin, *Commentary on Joshua*, page 97.
6   The vision in which Joshua (5:13-15) met an archangel underlines this point – God does not take sides in a human way in battle.

The indiscriminate slaughter of the inhabitants of Jericho and Ai does not differ morally from the wiping out of the inhabitants of the earth in the time of Noah or the destruction of Sodom and Gomorrah. All three forms of destruction were acts of God. The only difference is that in the case of Jericho and Ai and the destruction of others in the conquest of the land, God used the human agency of Israel.

The Bible records that in the time of Noah, people had become altogether wicked. 'Every inclination of the thoughts of his heart was only evil all the time. God was grieved that he had made man on the earth, and his heart was full of pain . . . The earth was corrupt in God's sight and full of violence'.[7] In order to prevent the whole world rushing to destruction, God removed humankind and spared Noah and his family in order to create a people who would worship and obey him. Sodom and Gomorrah had become so corrupt that God destroyed them. Had there been ten righteous people God in his mercy would have spared those cities. Only Lot and his daughters were ultimately rescued.

Likewise in the days of Joshua the peoples of Canaan had become fearfully corrupt and wicked. God, however, takes no pleasure in the death of the wicked but wants all to turn to him in repentance and live.[8] Although he promised the land of Canaan to Abraham and his descendants, it was more than 430 years before that promise was fulfilled and Israel took possession of the land, because, as God said, the sin of the Amorites had not yet 'reached its full measure'.[9] God in his mercy held back his judgement. He waited until the Amorites in their sin had passed beyond repentance and they were unable to turn to God. Only Rahab and her house were saved. A testimony to the wisdom and mercy of God!

The sins of the Amorites as listed in the Bible were many and varied. They had utterly abandoned obedience to and worship of the Living and True God. They worshipped idols, evil spirits and demons. Of those who worshipped idols, Scripture says, 'Those who make them will be like them, and so will all who trust in them'.[10] Morally they became utterly depraved. Sexual perversion was common and so was child sacrifice. Sexual perversion generally involved shrine prostitution. It could also take the form of homosexuality and gang rape of people of the same sex[11] or sexual relations with animals.

---

7   Genesis 6:5,6,11.
8   Ezekiel 18:23; 33:11.
9   Genesis 15:16.
10   Psalm 115:8. See also Psalm 138:18.
11   Genesis 19:4f; see also Judges 19:22f.

Do not give any of your children to be sacrificed to Molech, for you must not profane the name of your God. Do not lie with a man as one lies with a woman; that is detestable. Do not have sexual relations with an animal and defile yourself with it. A woman must not present herself to an animal to have sexual relations with it; that is a perversion. Do not defile yourself in any of these ways, because this is how the nations that I am going to drive out before you became defiled. Even the land was defiled; so I punished it for its sin, and the land vomited out its inhabitants.[12]

They engaged in child sacrifice, offering their children's blood to their idols. Archaeological studies have shown that this practice of child sacrifice was almost universal in ancient paganism and has reached into more modern times.

In Palestine, numerous bodies of children discovered in the foundations of buildings leave no room for doubt that offerings of this character were of common occurrence among the Canaanites to strengthen the walls of houses and cities.[13]

Child sacrifice . . . was practised by the Irish Celts, the Gauls, the Scandinavians, the Egyptians, the Phoenicians, the Moabites, the Ammonites, and in certain periods by the Israelites. Thousands of bones of sacrificed children have been dug up by archaeologists, often with inscriptions identifying the victims and first-born sons of noble families, reaching in time all the way back to Jericho of BC 7000. Sealing children in walls, foundations of buildings and bridges to strengthen the structure was also common from the building of the wall of Jericho to as late as 1843 in Germany.[14]

A modern form of child sacrifice is teaching children to love and engage in suicide bombing, as we have seen in the Middle East. It was and is a sin abhorrent to God and seems particularly to incur his anger. God warned Israel against it, with the direst penalties for such transgression.[15] 'Do not defile yourselves in any of these ways, because this is how the nations that I am going to drive out before you became defiled. Even the land was defiled: so I punished it for its sin, and the land vomited out its inhabitants'.[16] Despite God's commands and

---

[12] Leviticus 18:21-25.
[13] *Sacrifice and Sacrament* by E.O. James (Barnes and Noble, NY) page 95. Dr James is professor emeritus of the History of Religion at London University.
[14] The History of Childhood edited by Lloyd De Mause (The PsychoHistory Press 1974) page 27 with a foreword by William Langer, emeritus professor of History at Harvard.
[15] Leviticus 18:21; 20:2-5; Deuteronomy 18:10.
[16] Leviticus 18:24-25.

warnings Israel and her kings in later years followed 'the detestable ways of the nations that the Lord had driven out before the Israelites'[17] and suffered banishment from his presence.[18]

It is worth citing just a few out of many references in full:

They sacrificed their sons and daughters in the fire. They practised divination and sorcery and sold themselves to do evil in the eyes of the LORD, provoking him to anger. So the LORD was very angry with Israel and removed them from his presence. Only the tribe of Judah was left. (2 Kings 17:17-18, NIV)

They sacrificed their sons and their daughters to demons. They shed innocent blood, the blood of their sons and daughters, whom they sacrificed to the idols of Canaan, and the land was desecrated by their blood. (Psalm 106:37-38, NIV)

You burn with lust among the oaks and under every spreading tree; you sacrifice your children in the ravines and under the overhanging crags. (Isaiah 57:5, NIV)

They have built the high places of Topheth in the Valley of Ben Hinnom to burn their sons and daughters in the fire - something I did not command, nor did it enter my mind. (Jeremiah 7:31, NIV)

It should be said in fairness that, in the war between Iran and Iraq, children were encouraged with promises of paradise, to give up their lives, either in fighting or as being used as human minesweepers. Likewise, it is with promises of paradise, that Palestinian children and teenagers are encouraged to be martyrs – at the same time, many of the suicide bombers are people who find their lives of so little worth that they prefer to give them up against an enemy they have come to hate. It is this combination of religious and political motivation, which is so intractable. The circumstances of many Palestinians, young or old, are such that they conclude, 'I have nothing to lose and paradise to gain'. This explains why the efforts of the Israeli Government to increase security have often relatively little success.

In their abandonment of God and in their utterly depraved morality, the Amorites and the people whom God commanded Israel to drive out, engaged in all kinds of bestial sins, having sexual relationships with animals. This was especially listed as one of the many sins, which they committed and one, which was utterly abhorrent to God.

---

[17]   2 Chronicles 28:3.

[18]   2 Kings 17:17-18, Psalm 106:37-38, Isaiah 57:5 and Jeremiah 7:31 are cited in the text. A full set of references would also include 2 Kings 3:26-27; 16:3; 21:6; 23:10; 2 Chronicles 28:3; 33:6; Jeremiah 19:4-7; 32:35; Ezekiel 16:20-21; 20:26,31; 23:37; 23:39; Micah 6:7.

God's redemption and God's holiness always belong together. His love and holiness are inseparable. When he redeemed Israel out of Egypt he revealed to them his holiness and utter abhorrence of all sin. Only as Israel walked in obedience to God and in holy fellowship with God would Israel enjoy the salvation of God. This was a hard lesson for them to learn. For Israel, as for these other nations, sin meant the judgement of God and suffering.

The destruction of humankind in the days of Noah, the destruction of Sodom and Gomorrah and the command to destroy the Amorites because of their sin and because of their continued attempts to turn Israel away from God, helped Israel to learn the reality and horror of sin. It taught them that God is holy.

God's mercy and compassion to sinful Israel and to the sinful peoples of the world are continually manifest throughout the Old Testament. There are many references to aliens, such as Rahab and her household, Ruth the Moabitess, Uriah the Hittite, Ittai and the six hundred Gittites, being welcomed into the house of Israel. The book of Jonah witnesses to the marvellous compassion of God and his readiness to forgive and to save a wicked and violent people who will manifest the first signs of repentance.

Israel was frequently commanded not to oppress an alien in the land.[19] Aliens who settled in the land and worshipped the God of Israel were to be regarded as belonging to the house of Jacob.[20] They were to receive an inheritance and be regarded as 'native born Israelites'.[21] This was a foretaste of the day when in Christ the barrier between Jew and Gentile would be broken down and in Christ they would become one.[22] (We today, humbly and lovingly, need, as Gary Bruge says[23], to remind Israel about God's teachings of righteousness and justice for all people).

The holiness of God and his abhorrence of sin, which we gain from the Old Testament, are all-important for our understanding of Jesus Christ. They are important for our understanding of who the Lamb of God is, why he came into this world, why, when he had no sin of his own, he clothed himself with our sin, why he bore all the judgement

---

19   Exodus 22:1; 23:9; Leviticus 19:33; Deuteronomy 1:16; 10:18; 23:7; 24:14; Malachi 3:5.
20   Isaiah 14:1.
21   Ezekiel 47:22.
22   Ephesians 2:11-22.
23   Gary M. Burge, *Whose Land? Whose Promise?* – Paternoster Press, pages 98f.

of God on our sin and died physically. At the cross we see the depths of sin and how sin can have no claim on God. We see how sin means utter separation from God. We see the holiness of God and his judgement on sin. At the same time, we see the incredible love and mercy of God. We see how it took all that God had to remove our sin in the flesh. We see how Christ rose bodily in the triumph of his resurrection and lifts us up to a new and holy life in fellowship with God.

In Jesus Christ we have the fullness of God's self-revelation. Through Jesus Christ and his atonement we are enabled through grace rightly to understand God, his holiness, his love and saving power. We are enabled to understand his loving purpose for mankind and all creation and his desire that everyone, whoever they are, should turn unto him and be saved.

Both the Old and New Testaments witness, in their physical and spiritual dimension, to Jesus Christ. Together they constitute the Word of God. We cannot just spiritualise the happenings and teachings of the Old Testament, as Chapman and others do, and rightly understand the holiness and judgement of God on sin, nor understand the wonder and depths of his salvation in Christ, together with his purpose of redemption of the world.

There is much that will always remain a mystery and be beyond our understanding. We must however hold firmly to the tools given to us by the Old Testament. These include the stories of Noah and the flood, the destruction of Sodom and Gomorrah, Joshua and the conquest of Canaan, in their physical as well as spiritual dimension.

Appendix Five

JIHAD AND SUICIDE BOMBERS

There are four kinds of *jihad*, which means literally 'striving' or 'struggle':

The *jihad* of the heart, to achieve peace in ourselves.

The *jihad* of the tongue, preaching.

The *jihad* of the hand, good works including education and healing.

The *jihad* of the sword, to defend faith, family or community.

A commonly cited *hadith* is, 'We have returned from the lesser war (*al jihad al-asghar*) to the greater war (*al jihad al-akbar*)'. On being asked, 'What is the greater war?' Mohammed replied, 'It is the struggle against one's self'.[1]

Jihad is thus described as essentially an inner fight for purity – but although often quoted, this saying is not from any of the most authoritative traditions. It may come from an early Sufi manual of encouragement and instruction, where it occurs without any *isnad* (the list of people who have handed it down and given the saying authenticity). The central text is of course the Qur'an, and there *jihad* does not necessarily have military connotations – indeed Sura 8:39 instructing Muslims to fight unbelievers uses a different verb altogether. The Qur'an does not give a clear overall picture. And while Mohammed himself killed the Jews of Medina, ignoring their pleas for mercy or exile, in the period of Muslim expansion Jews and Christians were often regarded as second class citizens rather than as material for slaughter.

This appears to have been the position until comparatively recent times. And most Muslims would still hold this nuanced view of *jihad*. Sadly, Islamists now seem more and more to focus on the *jihad* of the sword, especially since the events of September 11th.

The frequent calls for *jihad* (Holy War) against the State of Israel together with the repeated calls for suicide bombers and their endorsement by the majority of Palestinians in the Gaza Strip and in the West Bank, confirm that the present crisis in the Middle East is

---

[1] Taken from a Rutherford House paper on the subject.

primarily religious. And it appears that for fundamentalist Muslims, Jews are now regarded as unbelievers or infidels.

Islam is the only religion in the world that has sanctified war. The purpose of this extreme form of *jihad* is to destroy the infidel and promote the cause of Islam. *Jihad* aimed at Israel is to destroy Israel in the name of Allah.

Suicide bombers are hailed as martyrs in the religious war that honours Allah. Muslims are desperately afraid of hell. Allah hates sinners, those who do not submit and obey the laws of Islam, which are the declared will of Allah. While Allah is merciful, there is no clear assurance of forgiveness in Islam, and the only certainty for a Muslim to enter heaven is to die in *jihad*. Hence, despite the fact that Palestinian leaders have repeatedly said that bombings inside Israel are detrimental to the life and well being of Palestinians, suicide bombings continue, and it is estimated that two thirds of Palestinians in Gaza support their continuance. That is to say, suicide bombings cannot be understood solely or primarily on political grounds. It is their essential religious dimension which gives them approval and guarantees their support.

Suicide itself is forbidden in Islam, so Islamic radical groups do not speak about 'suicide bombers' but instead refer to '*shahids*' (martyrs). In training such people, they would try to weed out any with a history of mental instability so that the motives of the *shahids* are kept pure. The idea of suicide bombing has received support not only from radicals but from the prestigious Al-Azhar University in Cairo, seen as the foremost institution of Sunni Islam, whose Imam, Sheikh Muhammad Sayyid Tantawi changed his previous position in April 2002 to permit the killing of civilians by Palestinian suicide bombers. He said:

> Every martyrdom operation against any Israeli, including children, women and teenagers, is a legitimate act according to [Islamic] religious law, and an Islamic commandment, until the people of Palestine regain their land . . . [2]

In encouraging their children to die as suicide bombers, parents are not primarily motivated by the $15,000 reward promised by Iraq and Saudi Arabia. Material considerations cannot be primary, especially when their homes are liable to be demolished by the Israelis. Their

---

[2]   Spoken at a reception given for Israeli Arab Democratic Party leader, Abd Al-Wahhab Al-Darawsheh. Posted on www.lailatalqadr.com (a website associated with Al-Azhar) and also reported in MEMRI No. 363 (7 April 2002). Information courtesy of Dr Patrick Sookhdeo.

death, which is a modern form of human sacrifice,[3] guarantees not only their, but also their families', entry into heaven. This is clear proof of the religious dimension of the present crisis.

Sabeel Ecumenical Liberation Theology Center published an interesting paper on *Suicide Bombers* in Summer 2002.[4] In the paper, Naim Ateek points out that Samson is an early example of the suicide bomber, the one who prays before his death, '*Lord God, remember me and strengthen me only this once, O God, so that with this one act of revenge I may pay back the Philistines for my two eyes.*' The paper goes on to condemn suicide bombing in principle because it is a crime against God, the author of life, because it inflicts suffering and death on civilians, and because the Christian way to resist perceived evil is different. The greatest form of bravery is to bear suffering rather than to inflict it.

---

[3] See also Appendix 4.
[4] Their website is given in the Bibliography.

Appendix Six

MESSIANIC CONGREGATIONS IN ISRAEL TODAY[1]

By Kai Kjær-Hansen[2], translated from Danish by Birger Petterson

It is a fact that there are Jesus-believing Jews in Israel. It is possible to talk about a messianic movement. But their number is smaller than expected by many of those who are favourably disposed to the movement. The movement is a heterogeneous entity whose common denominator is the believer's faith in Jesus as Messiah and Saviour.

This outline is based on a survey, conducted by Bodil F. Skjøtt and the present writer and published in 1999 under the title 'Facts & Myths About the Messianic Congregations in Israel 1998-1999' (Mishkan 30-

---

[1]   This article was based on a survey of Messianic Congregations/Fellowships conducted in 1999. No further survey has been carried out so that it is impossible to be certain how many there are today. Clearly however there has been considerable increase. An official broadcast on Israeli Television gave the numbers as between 10/15,000, indicating how the Holy Spirit is working in Israel. Today there may be over 100 Congregations/ Fellowships.

The Caspari Centre Media Spotlight in Jerusalem has recently produced a video, with English subtitles, entitled 'Yeshua Superstar' (http:// caspari.com/yeshuaSuperstar.wmv). Their advert about the film reads, 'In this video translated by Caspari Centre, witness one of the most surprising secular media presentations on the Messianic Movement in Israel to date. In February 2007 Israel's Channel Two news, watched by millions of Israelis, presented a thoughtful documentary portraying the Messianic community in worship and family life. Often the Messianic community is portrayed in the media with stereotypes, misperceptions, and hype. Here Channel Two listens carefully to articulate representatives of the Messianic community, notes their contributions to Israeli culture, and even casts a negative picture of their Ultra-Orthodox critics. This can only be an indication that the Messianic community is breaking into mainstream Israeli consciousness at a time when the country desperately needs to hear the message of peace, hope, and forgiveness through Messiah Yeshua. (Copyright 2007,(http://www.caspari.com) Caspari Center.')

[2]   International Co-ordinator of the Lausanne Consultation on Jewish Evangelisation.

31/1999, Caspari Centre, Jerusalem). It was based on the fundamental view that the messianic movement in Israel has nothing to hide, that openness is the best way to counter the formation of myths about the movement and that the anti-mission organisations are fully aware of its existence. In the messianic movement there are leaders who do not share our view that openness about the movement is really in its own best interest.

Our interpretations in *Facts & Myths* are obviously open to debate. But the statistical material presented here gives a clear answer as to the size of the movement. In this sketch the exact figures found by the survey are presented, and they show a clear tendency. In most cases the figures for the congregations were supplied by the respective leaders.[3]

Realistic figures

The *Facts & Myths* survey covers 69 congregations and 12 house-groups, a total of 81 units. A house-group refers, in our terms, to an independent group or fellowship, which does not define itself as a congregation – even if the borderline between congregation and house-group can be difficult to draw. In some cases a congregation gave its 'core group' as the total of its membership. The total number of 'members' of both groups reached 4957 – distributed with 3560 adults and 1397 children under 18 years.

Since the members of these messianic groups consist of Jews as well as non-Jews, it was our job to find out how many of the 3560 adults were Jews. A rather broad definition was used. This means that the number of Jesus-believing Jews would have been smaller if a more exclusive – orthodox Jewish – definition had been chosen as the criterion.

Four categories were listed. Here are the figures concerning membership/core groups in the 81 congregations and house groups.

1. *Jewish*	*2178*
2. *Non-Jewish but married to a Jew*	*649*
3. *Non-Jewish with Israeli citizenship* *(of whom 21 are Arabs/Palestinians)*	*212*
4. *Non-Jews and without Israeli citizenship*	*521*

---

[3]   There are also several hundred, if not several thousand, Ethiopian Jewish believers, but these keep a low profile and their number is not known.

These findings would be disappointing to some. In our opinion, however, it is a sad thing if one's joy is founded on numerical myths. It is equally sad if one cannot rejoice in realistic figures – however small they might be. The messianic movement is a small but growing movement. This last point can hardly said to be true about the majority of churches in e.g. Western Europe.

Our next challenge was to find out how many of the 2178 Jewish members had come from the former Soviet Union. Russians – whether in Russian-speaking or in Hebrew-speaking congregations – proved to constitute 1495 of the 2178 Jewish adults. The number of Jewish believers in the Messianic congregations born in Israel is about 650 – the full article shows how the calculations are made.

In other words, without the Jewish believers in Jesus who have come from the former USSR in the 1990s, the numerical increase of the Messianic movement in Israel would have been significantly smaller. In one way or another, nearly all congregations, including the Hebrew-speaking congregations, have been influenced by the Russian influx.

The Russian 'invasion'

The denominational background from which the majority of the Russian believers come is primarily Baptist or Pentecostal. Those who have not been influenced by a Western form of the charismatic movement are often described as 'the quiet Russians'. Those under charismatic influence are described as 'the noisy Russians'. The difference is perceptible not least by their style of worship: 'quiet' or 'noisy'.

The leadership structures are generally speaking loose. Few of the leaders have any long experience of leadership. And few have a theological education proper. But the level of boldness and activity is high. They don't have much faith in 'high profile' evangelism. Not because they are afraid of the consequences as such, but because their focus is on non-believing Russian immigrants whose confidence has been won through care and friendship.

The question of theology and identity that shaped most pre-1990 congregations (see below) has not in any significant way influenced the Russian congregations. For the pre-1990 congregations it has been important not only to be Jewish but for some also to be different from the Gentile church. For example: 'No Christmas!' Some Jewish Russian believers have, however, turned this upside down. Many of them find it natural to celebrate Christmas and have a Christmas tree. And only limited emphasis is given to Jewish tradition and Jewish holidays.

Church as well as Jewish holidays are primarily an occasion to come together and to include new people in the fellowship. If you will: bring others to faith in Jesus! Jewishness or not!

The marks of an indigenous Israeli Jewish congregation in the 1980s

The development in Israel in the 1990s has turned upside down issues which many believed were solved at the end of the 1980s or which were at least in the process of being solved. With optimism and direction people were then committed to the establishment of local indigenous Israeli Jewish congregations which should be different from the expatriate churches controlled by Gentiles. The attitude was expressed in almost programmatic form: 'The age of "Ecclesiastical Colonialism" and the rule of expatriate missions over the local Christians are basically over.'

In a number of areas, the situation around 2000 is comparable to the situation prior to the indigenization process. Perhaps it is more like the situation of the 1950s, 1960s and early 1970s than the situation of the 1980s. The main difference is that whereas expatriates prior to the 1970s to a large extent were made accountable for, and by some even were found guilty of, a lack of will to indigenize, this has now become an Israeli issue. It is Jewish believers who now are not very concerned with this process and thereby slow down the indigenization process of the 1980s.

When local believers in the 1970s and 1980s described the process of indigenization, the following points were important ingredients: Hebrew language, less translation to foreign languages during the worship, and a development of Hebrew liturgy and forms of worship compared to what was found in expatriate churches. But new circumstances and factors,which were unknown at the time have now influenced the process significantly. The Russians have come!

It is interesting to note how Hebrew-speaking congregations have responded to this influx of Russians. As already mentioned, all Hebrew-speaking congregations are, with a few exceptions, affected by it. A few are affected to such a degree that old members have left their congregation for this reason. These congregations have got earphones, and they offer translation during their worship so that what used to be a mark of expatriate churches is now common in local indigenous congregations. Consideration for actual needs is seemingly (and to my mind: fortunately) weightier than consideration for the process of indigenization, which as a result of this may now progress more slowly than intended. We could also say that it is an indication of a high level of maturity that consideration for the Gospel is more important than for the Hebrew language.

Torah-oriented Messianic congregations in Israel

We are now going to take a brief glance at those congregations in Israel, which may be termed Torah-oriented. It is true that this term is open to misunderstanding – it might give the impression that Jesus is not at the centre of their faith, which all emphasize that he is. But it will also not do to call them 'Messianic Israelis': for some of the congregations this might indicate a closer attachment to North American style Messianic Judaism than they wish. What they do have in common is that they do not think that a 'Jewish flavour' in the congregations is enough. They see the question of Jewish identity as an important part of their faith. The emphasis differs, but all agree that it is important for Jewish believers to keep the Torah, whether they define themselves as Torah-positive or emphasize that the Torah is important because it was important for the first believers. In general there is no wish to interpret the Torah through Jewish tradition but rather through Jesus. For a majority it is important to practise Jewish traditions as long as they do not contradict the Gospel. The importance of an identifiable Jewish life-style as a testimony to the Jewish people is a central point. They recognize the unity of Jews and Gentiles in the body of Messiah.

Of the 81 groups surveyed in *Facts & Myths* nine fall into this category, in our opinion. Two of these nine congregations have a long history in Israel, namely Ramat Gan Congregation (1957) and Roeh Yisrael (1972/refounded 1993) in Jerusalem. After a split of the Ramat Gan Congregation in 1996, Yad Hashmona House Group was set up. Three of the nine congregations were formed in the 1990s and led by Eli Levi, and probably formed under the inspiration of Joseph Shulam, who is the leader of Roeh Yisrael. In one way or another, these six congregations are a product of – if you will – *Eretz Israel*.

The remaining three congregations were formed by American Jews who prior to their immigration were involved with the North American Messianic Movement, namely Ohalei Rachamim in Kiryat Yam north of Haifa (1995), Kehilat Neveh Tzion in northern Jerusalem (1995) and Yeruel in Arad in Negev (1998.). The leader of this last congregation, Milton Maiman, died in May 1999, and I have not been updated on its subsequent development.

On the basis of the figures mentioned in *Facts & Myths* it is possible to assess how much space they take up in the overall Messianic landscape in Israel.

The total number of Jewish adult members in the 81 congregations/ house groups is 2178. 223 of these are members of, or belong to, the core group in these nine congregations. You could say that they form a minority in 'the Messianic movement in Israel' in terms of congregations and adult membership.

The total number of members in the nine congregations is 300. In accordance with the criteria we set up in Facts & Myths, these 300 adult members may be split up in the following categories:

1. *Jewish* 223

2. *Non-Jewish but married to a Jew* 38

3. *Non-Jewish with Israeli citizenship* 14

4. *Non-Jewish without Israeli citizenship* 25

Out of the total number of 300 adult members in these nine congregations, immigrants who have come throughout the 1990s (mainly from North America, the former Soviet Union and Bulgaria) make up about 50 percent. The number of non-Jews is about 25 per cent.

If we look at external features which characterize the Messianic Congregational Movement in North America, it would seem that these have had little impact in these nine congregations in Israel, for example the use of kippa and prayer shawls in the worship. Only two congregations use a Torah scroll in their worship – and in one of them it is only on every other Sabbath. None use the word synagogue about their congregation, and the leaders do not call themselves rabbis (apart from the late Milton Maiman).

If you bear in mind that these congregations have a common point of departure, you cannot help being surprised at the diversity. I just mention a few examples.

Ohalei Rachamim defines itself as 'charismatic', Roeh Yisrael and the three congregations under the leadership of Eli Levi, as well as Ramat Gan Congregation and Yad Hashmona House Group, define themselves as 'non-charismatic'. Roeh Yisrael does not have music at their worship, which all the others have. All celebrate Jewish holidays and emphasize the importance of this. That also goes for Ramat Gan Congregation, which however sees no problem in celebrating the birth of the Messiah at Christmas. But then Ramat Gan Congregation finds it difficult to formulate a creed or a statement of faith because they are convinced that by doing so they would stand in danger of minimizing the biblical faith. Ohalei Rachamim and Neveh Tzion have a statement of faith. Milton Maiman had plans to write one. Joseph Shulam has written a personal statement of faith but Roeh Yisrael, whose leader he is, has no such statement. All underscore the importance of Jewish expression in their worship, but only Ramat Gan use the Lord's Prayer, which is a Jewish prayer if anything, even given by the Jew Jesus. That others refuse to adopt this Jewish prayer may very well be because it is part of the liturgy of some Christian churches – though I cannot help wondering that this in itself should be enough to avoid using it. But the biggest surprise is perhaps that only two of these nine Torah-oriented congregations define their worship as liturgical, namely Roeh Yisrael and Neveh Tzion. Practically all read from the weekly synagogue portions, Parashat Hashavua, but none seem to take the time to read them in their entirety. And strangely enough, there is no reading from the New Testament on the basis of a similar cycle. Many other things could be mentioned.

In other words: the North American Messianic Movement has only had a modest impact on the Messianic congregations in Israel. The attitudes which characterize the Torah-oriented congregations with a long history in Israel have only to a small extent influenced other congregations. And again: the greatest obstacle to the propagation of 'the cause' up through the 1990s has been other local Israeli Jewish believers, not the Christian mission.

Granted that these observations are subjective, they are not intended as a value judgment of attitudes in these congregations.

We shall now deal with the congregations which, though not Torah-oriented , yet want an Israeli Jewish flavour in their worship.

Congregations which want to give the Gospel an Israeli cultural relevance

This is the case with a great number of Hebrew-speaking Israeli Jewish congregations, whether they are pre-1990 or later, and whether or not they have a denominational background. Even those old congregations with a long history in Israel, which some might still call denominational, have a considerable element of Jewish flavour in their worship. There are still differences in terms of worship and differences between liturgical and non-liturgical, charismatic or non-charismatic, etc.

Quite a few of those congregations which identify themselves as non-liturgical have, nonetheless, adopted elements from the Jewish worship in their own worship, such as the *Sh'ma*, other liturgical elements and the weekly synagogue portion (*Parashat Hashavua*).

Practically all celebrate the Jewish holidays in one way or another. The flavour has become more Israeli but not necessarily more Jewish. The desire is to retain an Israeli and culturally relevant identity. But they are not in the same way as the above-mentioned congregations oriented around the Torah. No strong emphasis is placed on being Messianic in the sense that adherence to the Torah or the Jewish traditions is observed. Celebration of the Jewish holidays is also seen as a tool for evangelism. Their concern is to make the Gospel culturally relevant in an Israeli Jewish society, which may also rub off on the form of worship. Generally speaking there is a vision of the 'one new man' of Ephesians 2, constituted by Jews and Gentiles. It would be wrong to say that the question of Jewish identity is irrelevant in these congregations, but it does not have the same weight as in the above-mentioned congregations. And generally speaking, they do not feel the same need to dissociate themselves from the Christian church as some of the Torah-oriented leaders do.

Of course I am aware that there are individuals in these congregations who share the vision of those above who were termed Torah-oriented.

Allow me to give one more example of how an Israeli Jewish congregation which wants to be culturally sensitive has nevertheless found a liturgical form in their worship. I choose Beit Asaf Congregation in Netanya (founded in 1978/re-founded in 1983) and with David Loden and Evan Thomas as keypersons today. The service in Beit Asaf is described in this way in *Facts & Myths*.

The service follows a set order made up for the congregation:

1. Song.

2. Reading from the weekly *Torah* portion in Hebrew, English and Russian.

3. Worship (20 minutes).

4. Responsive reading of either the *Amidah* or the creed written for the congregation.

5. Intercessory prayer for (a) the nation of Israel; (b) the world; (c) new groups.

6. Communion.

7. The *Sh'ma* said in Hebrew.

8. The sermon (30 minutes).

9. The *havdala* service (if the service is in the afternoon).

10. Announcements.

11. Aaronic blessing.

One comment on this: Even if Beit Asaf in its theology is not Torah-oriented, it nevertheless wants to be culturally relevant and to express an Israeli Jewish identity. For this congregation it has led to a liturgical form of worship. And for this reason a service in Beit Asaf may by some be experienced as more 'Jewish' than what may be experienced in some non-liturgical Torah-oriented congregations.

So, compared to the situation of the 1960s quite a lot has been accomplished in the process of indigenization in the Hebrew-speaking local Israeli Jewish congregations – and more than appears from this sketch. The process may have been different from what some people predicted in the late 1980s, and maybe it has also been slower and more difficult than foreseen. Perhaps it has not got as far as many people had expected and has not led to the unity which many hoped it would.

But the process is in motion. I am convinced that it will continue.

And who says – or demands – that the process should be quick? And be easy? And just follow one track? And who says – and demands – that Jewish believers in Israel should be more of one mind than Christians are in other places in the world?

By way of conclusion I would like to reflect on this.

'Are we really so few Jewish believers?'

In the light of the statistical material and the comments on it, presented in *Facts & Myths*, it is understandable that heart-searching painful questions present themselves for those who through a long life have fought for an indigenous Israeli Jewish body and now face the reality:

'Are we really so few Jewish believers?'

'Are we really so different?'

'Have we really not come further than this in the formation of an indigenous Israeli Jewish body?'

'Have we really had so many internal splits which we ourselves are responsible for?'

'Are we really no better than non-Jewish believers?'

'Have we, when all is said and done, been as ineffective as non-Jewish believers?'

Now I would like to turn things upside down by asking some counter-questions:

Where do the Scriptures say that Jewish believers in Jesus should be better than non-Jewish believers? Or should be able to do things better? If they have been pressurized to this attitude by well-meaning

Christians, they should settle this with those Christians. If this is a pressure they have imposed on themselves, they should settle this with themselves. If, consciously or unconsciously, they believe that Israeli Jewish believers would be able to handle things better than the Gentiles and also better than the first Jewish believers, I don't think there is any basis in Scripture for this view, is there?

The conviction of living in the end times – and not only that, the conviction of being in the focal point of the end times and part of the eschatological drama – has possibly put an unreasonable pressure on parts of the movement and given some people the mistaken expectation that they should represent a golden age with progress, agreement and – Jewishness. Reality contradicts this. So far.

It is not difficult to find examples of Jewish believers who have argued that living in *Eretz Israel* and being part of the national restoration gives them a unique opportunity to develop a genuine expression of Jewish Messianic faith. But the question is whether they have really faced the fact that holy ground under your feet does not guarantee anything at all.

In this respect we all need each other – whether we are Jewish or non-Jewish believers in Jesus. And we all need to practise being each other's humble servants. As the servant of the Lord, Jesus has given us an example to follow.

Appendix Seven

PARA-CHURCH ORGANISATIONS WORKING WITH MESSIANIC BELIEVERS AND PALESTINIAN CHRISTIANS[1]

By Bodil F. Skjøtt[2]

Bet Il Liqa – Beit Jala. Founded in 1996, Beit al Liqa ('house of meeting') is a Christian Cultural Centre. Its purpose is evangelism and outreach to the community through children's clubs and youth programs, a kindergarten and day care. www.liqa.net

Bethlehem Bible College – The Bethlehem Bible College is an interdenominational Christian Bible college, located in Bethlehem, Palestine; with extensions in Gaza and the Galilee. Founded in 1979 by local Palestinian leaders, it has an average enrolment of 135 students.

Bethlehem Bible College seeks to train and prepare Christian servant-leaders for the churches and society within an Arab context. They are people who model Christ-centredness, Godly humility, Biblical wholeness, creative mercy and justice in their jobs and ministries as life-long learners.

Bethlehem Bible College also seeks to minister to the local community, through the Al Aman Counseling Center, Shepherd's Society, and Bethlehem's first Public Library which opened recently on the BBC campus, www.bethlehembiblecollege.edu

Fellowship of Christian Students in Israel – a network of Evangelical Christian Arab and Israeli student groups at universities in Israel. The network is part of the International Fellowship of Evangelical Students.

---

[1] This material was researched in 1999 and while it has been updated some facts may no longer be current. However all the websites listed were in live use at the time of publication.

2 Mrs Skjøtt formerly worked in Israel at the Caspari Centre in Jerusalem, in the fields of Danish mission history, education and theological research relating to Jewish evangelism.

House of Light – Shfaram. This ministry in the Galilee runs various evangelistic and service programs for the community. Their programs include:
- King's Kids: Up to 50 young people participate in their King's Kids weekly meetings, which include a program or worship, dance, drama and Bible study. The youth also travel inside the country and abroad for outreach and camps.
- Assistance and refuge to unwed mothers and recovering addicts.
- Prison ministries. They visit prisoners and assist the families of prisoners.
- Meetings and Conferences between Palestinian Christians and Messianic Jews.

Lech Lcha – A biblical outreach among young men and women, Jewish and Arab, organising courses and camps, lasting several weeks at a time, to provide biblical teaching and equipment for the Christian life.

Life Agape – Israel and PA areas. An evangelistic outreach among university and school age students. They partner with the Bible Society to distribute printed material and run evangelistic outreach programs.

Middle East Council of Churches – (www.mecchurches.org) This is a fellowship of churches relating itself to the main stream of the modern ecumenical movement, the same which gave birth to the World Council and other regional ecumenical councils throughout the world.

The MECC is also a meeting-place for the indigenous churches of the region, a facilitator of their common response to common needs. It encourages and supports relationships between its member churches in an ecclesiastically sensitive manner, adhering to the historical confessions of the united Church, the Apostles' and Nicene Creeds, to which all its members subscribe. Its family structure emphasizes consensus and participation in community. Programs include:
- Studies and research
- Human rights, justice and peace
- Inter-religious dialogue
- Department of Service to Palestinian Refugees
- Emergency Relief, Rehabilitation and Reconstruction in Lebanon
- Ecumenical Relief Services in Response to the Gulf War
- Al-Muntada Magazine: Arabic language reports on church and Council activities

- New Report Magazine: English language quarterly
- *Courrier OecumUnique du Moyen Orient*: French journal on Middle East churches.

Among the member bodies within Israel and the Palestinian territories are the Oriental Orthodox Churches, the Orthodox Church and the Catholic Church. Also the two evangelical churches, the Episcopalian Church and the Lutheran Church are members.

Musalaha – Jerusalem. Musalaha is a ministry that seeks to promote reconciliation between Palestinian Arabs and Israelis according to scriptural principles. The central theme is Christ's atonement on the cross and His resurrection as the only hope through which this can be accomplished. They seek to be a model, an encouragement and a facilitator of reconciliation first to our own Palestinian Arab Christians and Messianic Israeli Jewish communities, then beyond, to the nations. Founded in 1990, Musalaha implements this vision through desert encounters, theological conferences, reconciliation seminars, leadership training, women's and youth activities, and publishing. www.musalaha.org

Palestinian Bible Society – Established locally in 1993, they distribute Bibles and Christian literature in Gaza, West Bank and Jerusalem. They also conduct the following projects:
- Children's gifts and outreach to Bedouin village in Gaza strip
- Donating Christian literature to 6 public libraries
- Living Stones Student Centre in Bir Zeit: a haven for Christian and Muslims students from Bir Zeit University
- Nablus Teachers' Bookshop
- Comfort Bethlehem: food, toy and Scripture distribution
- Schools ministry team: visits 25 schools with a Bible program for young Christian and Muslim children
- Old City Fountain Bookshop in Jerusalem: video library and internet Bible outreach center
www.biblesociety.org/bs-wbk.htm

Palestinian Christian Youth Movement – A group of Palestinian Christians from many denominations who connect with youth from communities of faith across the land, cultivating discipleship and faithful citizenship. They seek to nurture in young people a sense of self-worth and to feed the truth that they belong – belong to Christ, belong to our land, and belong to one another. They strive to raise and train leaders for our church, our society, and our future, such that today's young people may be the builders of tomorrow. They hope to instil compassion and fellowship among ourselves and build bridges of understanding and partnership across geographic, social, and religious divides.

Palestinian Christian communities are engaged in a variety of programs and activities, primarily at the local level. Most groups have weekly meetings. For younger children there is a "Friday School" and for older youth there are discussion groups. They incorporate cultural activities, such as dance troupes, and sporting events and camps.

Sabeel – Jerusalem. www.sabeel.org - An ecumenical center for Palestinian Liberation Theology which seeks to make the Gospel contextually relevant. In Arabic, Sabeel means 'The Way' and also a 'Spring of Water'. Sabeel strives to develop a spirituality based on justice, peace, nonviolence, liberation and reconciliation for the different national and faith communities. Sabeel also works to promote a more accurate international awareness regarding the identity, presence, and witness of Palestinian Christians.

Their programs include:
- Women's programs: ecumenical meetings, pilgrimage trips, group discussions
- Youth programs: leadership programs, exchange visits, Youth Action Plan for human rights, justice and peace
- Clergy programs: works with 13 indigenous denominations in Jerusalem through monthly meetings, conferences, retreats and personal visits
- Publishes *Cornerstone*: quarterly newsletter in English

Shepherd Society – Bethlehem. A Christian not-for-profit relief organization aiding Palestinian families in times of crises. They distribute food and clothing, and provide financial assistance to people in need.

Shevet Achim (Light to the Nations) – Jerusalem. A mercy ministry working the Gaza Strip bringing children in need of heart surgery and other life-threatening conditions into Israel for medical treatment. Hundreds of Palestinian children are born each year with congenital heart defects and are unable to obtain open-heart surgery. Shevet Achim finds the children in need, transports them to Israel, and provides financial support as needed. Israeli doctors and hospitals perform the surgeries, often bearing a majority of the expense themselves.

Caspari Centre for Biblical and Jewish Studies in Jerusalem is an educational institute for academic study and training where Messianic Jews and Gentile Christians work in co-operation. The Caspari Centre desires to contribute to the recognition and acceptance of the legitimate place of Jesus-believing Jews in history and in the Church today. The Israeli focus is providing local believers with theological training and education, teaching about the Jewish Roots of Christianity and the ongoing history of the Jewish Jesus believers.

The Centre was established in 1982 to fill the need in the Messianic community. There was no organized Bible training available in Hebrew when the centre opened. Today vast changes have occurred in the Messianic community in Israel.

Caspari contributes academically to Jewish and Christian studies. One current project is advanced study and research on the history of Jesus-believing Jews up to today's Messianic Jewish movement. Caspari Centre also publishes the journal Mishkan, a bi-annual theological journal in English. It is a forum on the Gospel and the Jewish people with a special emphasis on Jewish evangelism and the Messianic movement. Other parts of its vision is implemented through lectures, seminars, study program, library and data-collections. www.caspari.com

Israel College of the Bible (ICB) is an Israeli Bible College founded in 1990 as King of Kings College. In 1998 the name was change to Israel College of the Bible. ICB offers a range of academic programs from a Certificate of Biblical Studies to a four year Bachelor of Theology. Studies are aimed to prepare students for ministry 'under the Lordship of Yeshua the Messiah'. Part of this preparation includes participation in congregational life to enable them to receive practical ministry experience useful to their development as leaders. At the same time it is the educational philosophy of ICB that local pastors should function as continuing mentors and overseers of the local students they have entrusted to ICN.

The school also offers a 'One year in Israel' program in English for foreign students. www.israelcollege.com

Israel Bible Society is located on Jaffa Road opposite the site bought already in 1923. Because of the war the site was abandoned and the society moved to Haifa until 1979 when it returned to Jerusalem. Altogether the Israeli Bible Society today operates from three locations in Israel: Jerusalem, Tel Aviv, and Nazareth.

The Bible Society in Israel serves churches and congregations of all denominations. Its goal is to supply the churches and congregations with their Scriptural needs. In addition to the many Jewish and Arab people the society also reaches out to the new immigrants, foreign workers, and visitors who come into this Land. And because Israel is an international crossroads and the Bible Society provides Scriptures for people of many nations, many Romanians, Thais, Chinese, and Filipinos are being reached with the Gospel for the first time with Scriptures in their own language.
www.biblesocietyinisrael.org

There are also many groups based outside Israel who relate to Messianic believers, such as (in the UK):

Christian Friends of Israel, www.cfi.org.uk and Box 1813, Jerusalem 91015

Christian Witness to Israel, 166 Main Rd, Sundridge, Sevenoaks TN14 6EL

Church's Ministry among Jewish People, 30c Clarence Rd, St Albans AL 1 4JJ

The Messianic Testimony, 93 Axe St, Barking IG11 7LZ

Selected Bibliography

General

Bailey and Bailey: *Who are the Christians in the Middle East?* (Eerdmans 2003)

Baron, David: *The Ancient Scriptures for the Modern Jew* (Hebrew Christian Testimony to Israel, 187 Whitechapel Rd, London E1)

Baron, David: *Israel in the Plan of God* (Kregel Publications, Grand Rapids, Michigan ISBN 0 8254 2241 8)

Barth K: *Church Dogmatics* Vol. 2, part 2, pages 3-506
Vol. 3, part 1, pages 42-329
Vol. 4, part 1, pages 3-78

Booker, Richard: *Christians and the State of Israel* (ISBN 0 9711313 1 7)

Brueggemann, Walter: *The Land* (SPCK, London)

Burnett, Ken: *Why pray for Israel?* (ISBN 0 551 01042 8)

Church of Scotland, General Assembly Reports 1985: *Christians and Jews Today*

Kjaer-Hansen, Kai: *Joseph Rabinowitz and the Messianic Movement* (Handsel Press, Edinburgh and Wm B. Eerdmans, Grand Rapids)

Lambert, Lance: *The Uniqueness of Israel* (Kingsway, Eastbourne)

Lambert, Lance: *Battle for Israel* (Kingsway)

Lambert, Lance: *Till the Day Dawns* (Kingsway)

Leviti, Zola: *Meshumed! Jews . . . Nazis . . . Terror . . . Dachau!* (Moody Press, Chicago)

Maoz, Baruch: *Mishkan*, issue no. 5, 1986, 'Israel-People, Land, State and Torah'

Moltman J: *On Human Dignity*

Moltman J: *The Church in the Power of the Spirit*

Riggans, Walter: *Israel and Zionism* (Handsel Press)

Riggans, Walter: *The Covenant with the Jews* (Monarch, Tunbridge)

Saphir, Aloph: *Christ and Israel* (Yanetz, Jerusalem)

Taylor, Howard: *World Hope in the Middle East* (Handsel Press)

Torrance D W (ed): *The Witness of the Jews to God* (Handsel Press, 1982)

Walker, J B: *Israel - Covenant and Land* (Handsel Press)

An Intercessors' Guide to the Jewish World (YWAM Jewish World Office, Box 7736 Richmond VA 23231 USA)

Williams, Rowan: *Lecture at 5th International Sabeel Conference, 14 April 2004* (Internet)

History

Davis, L J and Decter, Moshe: *Myths and Facts 1982* (Near East Report, Washington DC)

Dayan, Moshe: *The Story of my Life* (Sphere Books, London)

Gilbert, Martin: *Israel, a History* (Black Swan)

The Arab-Israel Conflict: its History in Maps (Steimatsky)

Hansard: *A Collection of Speeches in UK Parliament, from 1917 to 1945*

Kac, Arthur: *The Rebirth of the State of Israel*

Kollek, Teddy with his son Amos: *For Jerusalem* (Futura Publications)

Lambert, Lance: *Battle for Israel* (Kingsway, Eastbourne)

Meir, Golda: *My Life* (Futura Publications)

Peters, Joan: *From Time Immemorial: The Origins of the Arab-Jewish Conflict over Palestine* (Michael Joseph, London)

Prittie, Terence: *Whose Jerusalem?* (Frederick Muller Ltd London)

Sharon, Ariel (with David Chanoff): *Warrior* (Simon &Schuster, New York & London)

Schneider, Peter: *The Christian Debate on Israel* (Centre for the Study of Judaism and Jewish Christian Relations)

Commentaries

Baron, David: *Commentary on Zechariah* (Kregel Publications, Grand Rapids, USA)

Barth, K: *A Shorter Commentary on Romans* (SCM Press Ltd)

Barth, K: *Church Dogmatics* Vol 2 part 2 (pp.213-259 – on Romans 9-11)

Brunner, Emil: *The Letter to the Romans* (Lutterworth Press)

Calvin, John: *The Epistle of Paul to the Romans* (St Andrew Press, formerly by Oliver and Boyd)

Cranfield, C E B: *Romans* in the International Critical Commentary Series

Ellison, H L: *The Mystery of Israel* (The Paternoster Press)

Luthi, Walter: *The Letter to the Romans* (Oliver and Boyd 1961)

Nygren, Anders: *Commentary on Romans* (SCM Press Ltd)

Islam and Islamic Organisations

Dolan, David: *Holy war for the Promised Land* (Hodder & Stoughton)

Kemp, Jeff: *A Brief Introduction to Islam* (Rutherford House)

Kemp, Jeff: *Reflections on Jihad* (Rutherford House)

Kemp, Jeff: *Introduction to the Shari'ah* (Rutherford House)

Ibraham, Ishak: *Black Gold and Holy War* (Marshall)

Laffin, John: *The Dagger of Islam* (Sphere Books, London)

Laffin, John: *The PLO Connections* (Corgi Books)

Laffin, John: *Holy War. Islam Fights* (Grafton Books)

Laffin, John: *Israel – Always in the Wrong?* (The Anglo-Israel Association)

Lambert, Lance: *Islamic Fundamentalism: Is it a Threat to World Peace?* (Christian Friends of Israel)

Livingstone, Neil C and Halevy, David: *Inside the PLO* (Quill/William Morrow, New York)

Nettler, Ronald L: *Islam and the Minorities: Background to the Arab-Israel Conflict* (Israel Academic committee on the Middle East)

Qur'an: Translation by Abdullah Yusif Ali (Amana Publications, Beltsville, Maryland 1995)

Sookhdeo, Patrick: *A Christian's Guide to Islam* (Christian Focus Publications and Isaac Publishing)

Sookhdeo, Patrick: *Islamic Terrorism* (Isaac Publishing)

Sookhdeo, Patrick: *Islam, The Challenge to the Church* (Isaac Publishing)

Susser, Asher: *The PLO and the Palestinian Entity* (The Anglo-Israel Association)

Anti-Semitism and the Church

Brearley, Margaret: *A Christian Response to the Middle East and the Palestinian Question* (The Anglo-Israel Association)

British Council of Churches: *Towards Understanding the Arab-Israeli Conflict* (1982)

British Council of Churches: *Impressions of Intifada, 1989*

British Council of Churches: *Israel and the Churches - Where do we Stand?*

Church of Scotland General Assembly Reports 1985: *Anti-Semitism in the World Today*

Croner, Helga: *Stepping Stones to further Jewish-Christian Relations: An Unabridged Collection of Christian Documents* (Stimulus Books, London & New York 1977)

Eban, Abban: *The Holocaust* (Weiss Press)

Englander, David: *The Jewish Enigma* (Open University and Peter Halban Publishers, London, 1992)

Gilbert, Martin: *The Holocaust; Maps and Photographs* (Clifford-Thames Printing Company)

Gilbert, Martin: *The Jews of Russia: Their History in Maps and Photographs* (Burlington Press, Foxton, Cambridge)

Jocz, Jacob: *The Jewish people and Jesus Christ after Auschwitz* (Baker Book House, Grand Rapids)

Keith, Graham: *Hated Without a Cause? A History of Anti-Semitism* (Paternoster)

Schapiro, Leonard: *The Jews in Soviet Russisa since 1917* (Oxford University Press)

Solomon, Rabbi Norman: *Jewish Responses to the Holocaust* (Studies in Jewish/Christian Relations, Selly Oak Colleges, Birmingham)

Torrance, David and Lamont, Alastair: *Anti-Semitism and Christian Responsibility* (Handsel Press)

Wright, Fred: *Father Forgive Us. A Christian Response to the Church's Heritage of Jewish Persecution* (Olive Press – Monarch)

Mission

Broadie, Alexander: *The Mission of Israel* (Handsel Press)

Bonar, Andrew and R.M.McCheyne: *Mission of Discovery – The Beginnings of Modern Jewish Discovery* (Christian Focus)

Fieldsend, John: *Messianic Jews, Challenging Church and Synagogue* (Marc Olive Press)

Lausanne Occasional Papers: *Christian Witness to the Jewish People*

Oduor, Reginald: *To the Jew First* (Norwegian Mission to Israel)

McDougall, David: *In Search of Israel* (Thomas Nelson and Sons Ltd)

Torrance, D W: *The Mission of Christians and Jews* in *A Passion for Christ*, edited by Gerrit Dawson and Jock Stein (Handsel Press and PLC Publications)

Journals

Christian Jewish Relations (ISSN 0144 2902)

Mishkan (Box 47, Jerusalem 91000, Israel)

Note: While books listed above are generally supportive of the viewpoints expressed in this work, books below take in part at least a different viewpoint.

Ateek, Naim S: *Justice and only Justice: a Palestinian Theology of Liberation* (Orbis, 1990, with foreword by Rosemary Ruether)

Ateek, Naim S: *Suicide Bombers, a Palestinian Christian perspective* (Sabeel, 2002)

Burge, Gary M: *Whose Land? Whose Promise? – What Christians are not Being Told about Israel and the Palestinians* (Paternoster Press)

Chacour, Elias: *Blood Brothers* (Baker Book House, Grand Rapids 1984)

Chapman, Colin: *Whose Promised Land?* (Lion, revised 2002)

Hendriksen, William: *Israel in Prophecy* (Baker Book House, Grand Rapids)

Hosain, Samuel: *Israel Reassessed* (Handsel Press)

Loden, Lisa, Walker, Peter and Wood, Michael (edited):   *The Bible and the Land: An Encounter* (Musalaha, Box 52110, Jerusalem 91521)

Qutb, Sayyid: *Milestones* (translation of *Ma'alim fi al-Tariq*, giving an Islamic theological basis for terrorism)

Prior, Michael: *Speaking the Truth about Zionism and Israel* (Melisende 2004)

Riah Abuel El-Assal, Bishop of Jerusalem: *Caught Between* (SPCK)

Said, Edward: *After the Last Sky* (Faber and Faber 1986)

Sizer, Stephen: *Christian Zionism: Road-map to Armageddon?* (IVP 2004)

Walker, Peter: *Jesus and the Holy City: New Testament Perspectives on Jerusalem*

Useful websites, with different viewpoints:

www.mfa.gov.il	Israeli Govt English website
www.fateh.net	Fatah organisation
www.israelunitycoalition.com	American National Unity Coalition for Israel
www.palestinefacts.org	Another American website
www.jewsforjesus.org	Jews for Jesus
www.haaretz.com	Israeli National Daily Paper (English edition)
www.gush.shalom.org	Israeli Human Rights Organisation
www.btselem.org	Another Human Rights Organisation
www.sabeel.org	Ecumenical Centre with a focus on liberation theology
www.caspari.org	Centre for research on Israel and messianic theology
www.memri.org	Middle East Media Research Institute – with up to date translations of Arabic press articles
www.debka.com	Jewish American website
www.eauk.org	Evangelical Alliance – contains papers from a theological consultation on the 2003 'Road Map'

See also Appendix 7

Index

O

Oslo accord 16, 32, 171, 172, 181

P

Palestine 9, 32, 171
   population of 9, 165
Palestinian covenant (1968) 76, 168
Palestinians 2, 44, 165
   hardship of 160, 166, 180
   injustice to 1, 37, 48, 167, 185
Panentheism 101
Pantheism 101
Peters, Joan 165, 215
PLO 15, 25, 168, 171
Prayer 3, 29, 41, 43, 110, 175

Q

Qur'an 25, 43, 78, 104, 106, 108, 195, 216
Qutb, Sayyid 29, 218

R

Rabinowitz 23, 214
Refugees 13, 27, 114, 165ff., 184
Replacement Theology 45, 59, 86, 127, 130ff., 146, 188
Rockets 18
   from Gaza 17
   from Lebanon 15, 21
Roman Catholic Church 40, 95, 97

S

Scotland 7, 95
Sookhdeo, Patrick 30, 216
Skjøtt, Bodil 198, 208
Syria 9, 14, 20, 167

T

Talmud 176
Tankel, Henry 174
Tertullian 91
Trinity, doctrine of 102